THE ORIGINS OF JUDAISM

The Origins of Judaism provides a clear, straightforward account of the development of ancient Judaism in both the Judean homeland and the Diaspora. Beginning with the Bible and ending with the rise of Islam, the text depicts the emergence of a religion that would be recognized today as Judaism out of customs and conceptions that were quite different from any that now exist: special attention is given to the early rabbis' contribution to this historical process. Together with the main narrative, the book provides substantial quotations from primary texts (biblical, rabbinic, and other) along with extended side treatments of important themes, a glossary, short biographies of leading early rabbis, a chronology of important dates, and suggestions for further reading.

Robert Goldenberg is Professor of History and Judaic Studies at Stony Brook University (SUNY). He has published in numerous journals, including the *Journal of Jewish Studies; Journal of the American Academy of Religion; Judaism; Harvard Theological Review; Journal for the Study of Judaism in the Persian, Hellenistic, and Roman Periods*; and *Jewish Studies Quarterly.* His most recent book is *The Nations That Know Thee Not: Ancient Jewish Attitudes toward Other Religions* (1998).

For my children,

Alex, Shifra, and Jacob

The Origins of Judaism

FROM CANAAN TO
THE RISE OF ISLAM

ROBERT GOLDENBERG

Stony Brook University

CAMBRIDGE
UNIVERSITY PRESS

CAMBRIDGE UNIVERSITY PRESS
Cambridge, New York, Melbourne, Madrid, Cape Town, Singapore, São Paulo, Delhi

Cambridge University Press
32 Avenue of the Americas, New York, NY 10013-2473, USA

www.cambridge.org
Information on this title: www.cambridge.org/9780521844536

First published 2007

Printed in the United States of America

A catalog record for this publication is available from the British Library.

Library of Congress Cataloging in Publication Data

Goldenberg, Robert.
The origins of Judaism : from Canaan to the Rise of Islam / Robert Goldenberg.
    p.   cm.
Includes bibliographical references and index.
ISBN-13: 978-0-521-84453-6 (hardback)
ISBN-13: 978-0-521-60628-8 (pbk.)
1. Judaism – History.   I. Title.
BM155.3G65   2006
296.09′01–dc22   2006036066

ISBN   978-0-521-84453-6 hardback
ISBN   978-0-521-60628-8 paperback

Contents

Illustrations

Acknowledgments

My editor at Cambridge University Press, Mr. Andrew Beck, and his associate, Ms. Faith Black, have been models of encouragement and professional assistance. I must begin by recognizing their contribution to this project. I also wish to acknowledge the editorial assistance of Helen Wheeler and Helen Greenberg and to thank Kate Mertes for her preparation of the index.

My colleagues in the History Department at Stony Brook University provided me with two semesters free of teaching obligation to work on this book. In addition to their support and friendship day by day, that was a gift without which I could not have finished the task.

Finally, this project would have been impossible without the constant encouragement and practical assistance of my wife, Nina. The final product stands as a token of my indebtedness to her.

Abbreviations and References

All translations of biblical and rabbinic texts are the author's own except where otherwise indicated. Translations from Greek normally follow the *Loeb Classical Library* edition, though occasionally with modifications, again except where otherwise indicated. Biblical texts are cited by chapter and verse according to the Hebrew text; it should be noted that Christian translations follow the ancient Greek and Latin versions and sometimes display different chapter divisions. Rabbinic texts are cited as follows:

Mishnah (sometimes abbreviated M.) and Tosefta by tractate, chapter, and paragraph.

Jerusalem Talmud (sometimes abbreviated J. or JT) by tractate, chapter, and paragraph, also by page and column in the first Venice edition.

Babylonian Talmud (sometimes abbreviated B. or BT) by tractate and page (nearly all editions since the sixteenth century have used a standard pagination). It should be noted that a page number designates both sides of the leaf; these are distinguished by the letters *a* and *b*.

Midrash Rabba by section and paragraph.

Sifre by book (1 for Numbers, 2 for Deuteronomy) and section.

NOTE: Transliterations of personal names, literary titles, and the like are often phonetic rather than technical. In particular, letters with diacritical marks such as *š* often omit those marks.

A Note of Introduction

THIS BOOK TELLS THE STORY OF THE EMERGENCE OF JUDAISM out of its biblical roots, a story that took well over a thousand years to run its course. When this book begins there is no "Judaism" and there is no "Jewish people." By the end, the Jews and Judaism are everywhere in the Roman Empire and beyond, more or less adjusted to the rise of Christianity and ready to absorb the sudden appearance of yet another new religion called Islam.

It may be useful to provide a few words of introduction about the name *Judaism* itself. This book will begin with the religious beliefs and practices of a set of ancient tribes that eventually combined to form a nation called the *Children of Israel*. Each tribe lived in a territory that was called by its tribal name: the land of Benjamin, the land of Judah, and so on. According to the biblical narrative, these tribes organized and maintained a unified kingdom for most of the tenth century BCE, but then the single tribe of Judah was separated from the others in a kingdom of its own, called the *Kingdom of Judah* (in Hebrew *yehudah*) to distinguish it from the larger *Kingdom of Israel* to its north. Thus the name *Israel* was essentially a national or ethnic designation, while the name *Judah* simultaneously meant a smaller ethnic entity, included within the larger one, and the land where that group dwelt for hundreds of years. In ancient times, the single word *Israel* was never used to designate a territory; for that purpose the phrase *Land of Israel* (*Eretz Yisra'el*) was always employed.

To complicate matters further, there was another self-designation, *Hebrews*, that was used by Israelites only when they were speaking to outsiders or by outsiders when referring to the people of Israel. That term eventually gave its name to the language in which most of the

Jewish Bible is written, the language still spoken in the modern state of Israel today.

The last king of Israel was overthrown, and the kingdom was destroyed, in 722 BCE during an Assyrian invasion. Most of the population were carried off by the conquerors, but some escaped down into the surviving Kingdom of Judah, where they were welcomed (with some hesitation) as fellow Israelites. Over the next century, as Assyrian power faded, the Kingdom of Judah expanded and brought much of the former Israelite territory under its control. Now, for the first time, it was possible to use *Judah* and *Israel* as synonyms.

From around this time (the late eighth and early seventh centuries BCE), various words that later meant *Jew* or *Jewish* begin to appear in our biblical sources. In a narrative from the time of King Hezekiah[1] the language of the Kingdom of Judah, which moderns would call *Hebrew*, is called *yehudit*, or Judahite, as distinct from *aramit* or Aramean (later Aramaic), a more widespread language spoken throughout much of the Near East.[2] In addition, the people of Judah are more and more often called *yehudim*:[3] in modern English this word is often translated as "Jews," and that is its meaning in modern Hebrew as well. But within the Bible the term never lost its specific connection to the tribe or the kingdom or the territory of Judah.

In 586 BCE the southern Kingdom of Judah was destroyed in its turn, this time by the Babylonians under King Nebuchadnezzar, and the leadership of the realm was carried off to exile in Babylon. In 539 BCE, Babylon in turn was vanquished by the growing Persian Empire, and the exiles from Judah were allowed to return home. (Many declined the offer and voluntarily remained in exile.) Under the Persians, the territory was called *Yehud*, and then, as one conquest followed another, *Ioudaia* in Greek and *Iudaea* in Latin. In rabbinic writings of the second and third centuries CE, the term *yehuda* still designates the particular territory of ancient Judaea. In rabbinic parlance the larger Jewish homeland, embracing Galilee to the north and other territories as well, was always called the Land of Israel, *Eretz Yisra'el*.

As *yehudim* (Greek *ioudaioi*, Latin *iudaei*) spread out into the Mediterranean world, they preserved their ancestral identity and thus maintained a strong link with their ancestral homeland. In Hebrew they called themselves *yisra'el*, but in Greek or Latin they were "people from Judaea." In Greek or Latin the language of the Bible was called *Hebrew*, and by extension the Jews themselves were sometimes called *Hebrews*. It is not clear whether *ioudaioi* and *hebraioi* suggested different connotations in Greek or were used interchangeably.

* * *

Ancient Jews, the people this book has set out to discuss, rarely used the term *Judaism*, or its equivalent in any ancient language, to identify their way of life; it was only in modern times that Jews adopted that word. In Greek, the word *Ioudaismos* roughly means "the way Jews live," and it was normally used by outsiders when speaking of Jewish customs.[4] More particularly, early Christian writers began to use the term to designate the way of life against which their own new religion was struggling to define itself.[5] "The emergence of Judaism" thus means the historical development of a way of life that came to be associated with a people called *Judaeans* or *Jews*.

This book will trace that emergence, beginning with the beliefs and practices of a set of Near Eastern tribes living in their native land. Conquered by successive foreign armies, surviving remnants of those tribes had to adapt their ancestral laws and customs to the wishes of foreign empires. Increasingly dispersed throughout the Mediterranean world and beyond, they had to adapt a way of life that began as the native culture of people living in their own land to the pressures of living in other countries. As their nation lost its political freedom, the religious dimensions of their shared heritage grew in importance, until finally most onlookers saw them as a widely scattered religious community that once had enjoyed political significance but did so no longer. Defined by their religious customs (some of which would strike modern observers as cultural patterns and not strictly religious at all), the Jews preserved the hope of national restoration but could do nothing to bring that hope to reality. Their God would have to do that for them in the fullness of time.

The focus of this book, however, will remain on religious phenomena: texts, customs, beliefs, modes of leadership. Judaism is an ethnic religion, a religious heritage tied to a specific ethnic or national identity, so it will be impossible to trace the history of the religion without also keeping track of the history of the nation. However, the rise and fall of kingdoms and empires, the names and dates of battles and of kings, will receive only as much attention as is needed to present the circumstances under which religious developments took place. Some coverage of these other matters will be necessary, but it should never distract the reader from a more central concern with the Jews themselves and their way of life.[6]

* * *

This book was designed for two distinct audiences: undergraduate students in university courses and nonacademic lay readers. Academic specialists may find it useful in their teaching, but this book is not primarily intended for them. For that reason, presentation of evidence is suggestive rather than comprehensive, though readers can consult the Suggestions for Further Reading at the end of the volume to learn more about key issues: those Suggestions indicate both primary sources – where the ancient evidence can be located – and secondary sources – places where modern scholars have considered that evidence and figured out ways to interpret it.

The Jewish religion has seen much contention in its long history. Jews have disputed among themselves and do so still. Others have disputed with the Jews and do so still. Some of the ancient disputes have subsided; others remain bitter and passionate. Some of the modern disputes continue ancient battles; others revolve around new concerns. Some of the disputes involving Jews have turned violent or even murderous; others have remained "wars of words." This book will aim to remain neutral in its treatment of all such quarrels, though, of course, the author's own opinions and preferences will unavoidably be visible from time to time.

Readers of this volume will note that certain key primary texts, and consideration of certain key issues and themes, have been removed from the main text and printed by themselves in boxes. This allows the main text to flow more smoothly and provides isolated materials for focused classroom discussion, writing assignments, and the like. It is hoped that instructors will find this useful and that private readers will not be disturbed in their enjoyment of the narrative.

1

The Prehistory of Judaism

THE JEWISH RELIGION (JUDAISM) EMERGED OUT OF THE writings of the Hebrew Bible, but it is not actually to be found in those writings. Judaism is a religion that worships God[1] through *words* – prayer, sermons, the reading of scripture, and the like – in buildings called *synagogues* under the leadership of learned *rabbis*. The Bible knows something of prayer but nothing of the rest: the Bible portrays a religion centered on a single building commonly called the *Temple* and led by hereditary *priests* who worship through *actions* – elaborate sacrificial rites and other ceremonies of purification and atonement. The transition from that earlier religion to one that modern people would recognize is the story line of this book.

Almost all our information about the early parts of this story comes from the pages of the *Bible*[2] (see "What Is in the Bible?"). The Bible is actually not a single book; it is an anthology of materials that were written over a span of many centuries – perhaps as much as 1,000 years – in two different languages and in at least two different countries. Not surprisingly, its writings show a variety of styles and a variety of outlooks on many important questions (see Chapter 2). This diversity of content allowed later readers to find many different messages in its pages and to apply those messages to the great variety of situations that they faced. This flexibility is the key to the Bible's remarkably long success at sustaining individuals and communities of faith over more than two millennia.

However, from the historian's point of view, the Bible presents a very difficult problem. Many, perhaps most, of its narratives were written long after the occurrences they describe (the story begins with the creation of the world!), and almost nothing in the Bible can be

WHAT IS IN THE BIBLE?

Jewish tradition divided the Bible into three sections containing a total of twenty-four books.

I. The Torah

1. Genesis. Background for the emergence of the people of Israel, from the creation of the world through the lives of the patriarchs (Abraham, Isaac, Jacob) and matriarchs (Sarah, Rebecca, Leah, Rachel) up to the death of Joseph in Egypt.

2. Exodus. Slavery in Egypt, then liberation. Covenant at Sinai, revelation of God's commandments, construction of the Tabernacle for formal worship. Story of the Golden Calf: Israel's first lapse into idolatry.

3. Leviticus. Rules for maintenance of ritual purity and proper conduct of sacrifice; also for creation of a holy community. First description of dietary laws and the festivals of the year.

4. Numbers. Census in the desert prior to the march toward the Promised Land. Incidents in the course of that march, further legislation.

5. Deuteronomy. Moses' farewell address: review of his career, summary of God's commandments, warning of the consequences of disobedience. Moses dies at the edge of the Promised Land.

II. The Prophets

a. The Early Prophets. Despite its traditional name, this section actually contains very little prophecy. Instead, it mainly continues the narrative beyond the death of Moses.

6. Joshua. Israel's conquest and initial settlement of the Promised Land.

7. Judges. The next several generations. Disloyalty to God brings foreign oppressors; repentance brings liberation.

8. 1 and 2 Samuel. The last of the judges and the first of the kings of Israel up to David's death.

9. 1 and 2 Kings. The history of the kingdoms through their destruction.

Note: The books now cited as numbered pairs were originally single works. They were divided by copyists in the Middle Ages on account of their great size. This is not the case with the numbered books of the New Testament, which are separate documents.

b. The Later Prophets. These are the great orators and writers of the Bible.

10. Isaiah. The historical Isaiah lived around 700 BCE, but much in this book seems to date from a later time, during the Babylonian Exile and perhaps even later.

11. Jeremiah. Lived around the time of the Exile; the book contains significant biographical narrative along with Jeremiah's orations.

12. Ezekiel. Contemporary with Jeremiah, but lived and prophesied among the exiles in Babylon.

13. The Twelve. Twelve much smaller books of prophecy, attributed to writers who lived over a span of several centuries. Only Jonah contains significant narrative.

Hosea	Obadiah	Nahum	Haggai
Joel	Jonah	Habakkuk	Zephaniah
Amos	Micah	Zechariah	Malachi

III. The Writings

14. Psalms. A collection of 150 religious poems, many attributed to King David.

15. Proverbs. A collection of wisdom teachings, largely attributed to King Solomon.

16. Job. A story of righteousness tested by suffering.

The *Five Scrolls,* so called because they are liturgically read on specified holidays (this grouping reflects later synagogue practice and is not a formally recognized section of the Bible).

17. Song of Songs. A love poem attributed to King Solomon. Read in synagogues on Passover.

18. Ruth. A brief narrative of loyalty and love set in the days of the judges; the origins of the dynasty of King David. Read on the Feast of Weeks.

19. Lamentations. Poems on the destruction of Jerusalem, attributed to Jeremiah. Read on the Ninth of Av, anniversary of the destruction of the Temple.

20. Ecclesiastes, or Qohelet. Philosophical musings, attributed to King Solomon. Read on the Feast of Booths.

WHAT IS IN THE BIBLE? (continued)

21. **Esther.** Intrigue at the royal court of Persia; the Jews narrowly defeat the evil designs of a powerful enemy. Read on Purim. This is the only book of the Bible in which God is never directly mentioned in the Hebrew text.

22. **Daniel.** Stories about loyal Jews in the royal courts of Babylon and Persia; also visions of the end of history.

23. **Ezra-Nehemiah.** Jewish leaders and their achievements in the period after the Babylonian Exile.

24. **1 and 2 Chronicles.** Retelling of Israel's history from the time of King David through the return from the Babylonian Exile. Largely a revision, but sometimes a straightforward repetition of the Books of Samuel and Kings.

In recent times the Hebrew acronym *Tanakh* (**T**orah, **N**evi'im [prophets], **K**etuvim [writings]) has been used to designate the entire twenty-four-book collection.

* * *

The Christian tradition, following the custom of ancient Greek-speaking Jews, arranged these books differently, in two sections (not formally separated) containing prose narrative and poetic compositions, respectively. The order was as follows:

Genesis	**1 and 2 Kings**	**Ecclesiastes**
Exodus	**1 and 2 Chronicles**	**Song of Songs**
Leviticus	**Ezra**	**Isaiah**
Numbers	**Nehemiah** (a separate book)	**Jeremiah**
Deuteronomy	**Esther**	**Lamentations**
Joshua	**Job**	**Ezekiel**
Judges	**Psalms**	**Daniel**
Ruth	**Proverbs**	**The Twelve**
1 and 2 Samuel		

confirmed from any other ancient source of information. As always with uncorroborated information, the modern observer is in no position to judge the Bible's historical reliability, in no position to measure the distance between description and event, in no position to read the Bible's stories and figure out what (if anything) really happened.[3] The

Bible can therefore not be read as a historical record: instead, it must be understood that biblical narrative is a distillation of national memory that has been designed to convey a religious message. The Bible's religious message is loud and clear, but we cannot always know how the described events would have appeared without the religious purpose that now shapes the narrative, or indeed how the authors of the Bible learned about those events in the first place.

Then can we modern readers not learn history from the Bible at all? Of course we can, just not in the way we can learn history from archives or other official documents. The key to learning history from the Bible is to focus attention *not on the content of the stories but on the stories themselves: Who told them? Why? How did the people who told these stories understand them? What truths did they find in them? What lessons did they seek to convey?* People have been reciting these narratives for well over 2,000 years; that by itself is a historical fact of enormous importance. After a brief summary of the narrative itself, it will be possible to think about those questions.

The Biblical Narrative

Early developments. The Bible begins with the creation of the world by Israel's God.[4] This is not a god who struggles or collaborates with other gods, as in the myths of other peoples; the God of Israel creates the world alone, without effort or difficulty, simply by commanding step by step that the cosmic order come into being. Into this world the Creator places all living species, including a human pair named *Adam* and *Eve*. Adam and Eve could have lived carefree under God's protection in the *Garden of Eden*, but they transgressed: there was a single tree in the garden, the "tree of knowing good and evil," whose fruit they were told to avoid, but they ate that fruit and as a result were expelled into the world of hard labor, the world of sex and birth and death. The very act of learning the difference between good and evil brought suffering into the world.

The early chapters of the Bible contain several other dramatic depictions of human beings' inability to live as they should. Adam and Eve had two sons named *Cain* and *Abel*, and one murdered the other. Sexual immorality and violence became widespread. Five generations after Cain, another murder occurred. By the tenth generation,

God was so disheartened that he destroyed the whole creation in a flood; only one righteous man (*Noah*) and his family were preserved in order to make a new beginning. But Noah too disappointed: on emerging from the ark in which he rode out the flood, he planted a vineyard, became drunk, and brought sexual humiliation on his family.[5] Noah's descendants again grew numerous, but then they built the famous *Tower of Babel* in rebellion against God's wishes. Forced as a result to speak different languages, they scattered around the world: the idyll had gone sour.

The modern reader can easily see that these narratives attempt to answer basic questions about the nature of human existence: Why don't we all speak the same language? Why do people have to work so hard for their food? Why do people die? Why is the sexual urge so powerful and childbirth so painful? Why are women subordinate to men? All ancient cultures told such stories, and modern scholars can compare the biblical versions with others that circulated in the ancient world, thus setting Israel more firmly in the cultural context of the ancient Near East.

But such comparisons do not explain why the Bible itself was preserved or how this particular version of those stories came to dominate our own civilization. Only the next stage in the narrative explains that.

God makes a choice. After twenty generations of human history, God suddenly instructed a man named *Abram*, from a family with roots in Mesopotamia, to travel to the distant land of Canaan and settle there. As it happened, Abram's father had set out for this very destination years earlier but had never reached his goal; now Abram could complete his father's journey and fulfill a divine mission at the same time. The Bible never quite accounts for God's choice of this man; we are told that he was righteous, but we are not told (as was said of Noah) that he was the only righteous man of his generation.

Whatever the reason for God's choice, the results were momentous. Abram settled in Canaan and received God's promise or *covenant* that his descendants would inherit that land and become there a great nation. The mark of this covenant would be the ancient rite of *circumcision*, performed on the body of every baby boy in the first week of his life. As a token of his new status Abram received a new name, *Abraham*; as a sign of God's special care for him, his son and heir *Isaac* was not born until Abraham was 100 years old. Isaac in time became the father of *Jacob*, who was also called *Israel*, and in the next generation Jacob's four wives bore him a total of twelve sons and one daughter.

A famine drove Jacob's family out of their destined homeland, and they settled in Egypt. One of Jacob's sons, *Joseph*, had after many adventures developed a plan to rescue Egypt from the effects of this same famine, and had therefore risen to great power in the land; under their famous brother's protection, the family multiplied and thrived in their new home. Eventually, however, a new king lost sight of his nation's debt of gratitude; suspicious of the Israelites' numbers, he reduced them to slavery.[6] They suffered greatly until finally God remembered their ancestral covenant and sent a new leader, *Moses*, to help them escape their bonds. God (and Moses) performed many wondrous acts, inflicting many "plagues" upon the stubborn Egyptians; finally, after the terrifying death of every firstborn son in Egypt, the people were allowed to leave. Even now, however, the king regretted letting them go and tried to pursue them: in a final miracle, the people crossed the sea on dry land but the pursuing Egyptians drowned while trying to follow them. Thus the descendants of Jacob became the free people of Israel, a nation of twelve tribes named after Jacob's twelve sons, a people nearly 2 million strong.[7]

The decisive covenant. Moses led the people into the desert of *Sinai*. There, from a mountaintop, God's own voice spoke to them and gave them the laws by which they were to live. God offered to renew his covenant with them as a people, and they enthusiastically agreed. Israel became God's own nation. They were now living under God's protection and subject to God's rule and God's judgment. The nation's fate would now depend on their loyalty to God and the covenant, on their obedience to God's commands.

Moses climbed the mountain and spent forty days and nights in God's own presence; when he returned, he brought with him the word of God written on stone tablets. He placed these in a special container, and to house this sacred chest he built a movable shrine where the people could encounter their God and worship him. However, almost at once, a soon-familiar pattern made its first appearance: time and again, the people forfeited their own hopes by betraying their obligations and violating the commands of God.[8] By the time of his death, Moses had become thoroughly disillusioned with his own people; in his farewell address, he warned them that continued disobedience would bring disaster in the end.

The people in their land. Out of loyalty to the covenant, God led the people through the desert for forty years and then brought them into the Promised Land. Again they continually betrayed the covenant by worshiping other gods. Without Divine protection they were repeatedly overrun and oppressed by foreign invaders. Each time, under pressure of suffering they would repent: God would rescue them from their enemies, but soon they would lapse once more.

After a few generations, the tribes combined their forces and built a kingdom under the heroic *David*. David was followed by *Solomon*, famous for his wisdom, who built the first permanent *Temple* to God in the new royal capital, *Jerusalem*. Through the *prophets* God gave assurance that David's family would sit on Israel's throne forever, but the old patterns of disloyalty kept returning; ten tribes out of twelve rebelled against the royal family, leaving only David's own tribe of *Judah* for his descendants to rule; in both kingdoms, the wealthy oppressed the poor and the worship of other gods persisted. The kingdom of Israel, embracing the ten rebellious tribes, was destroyed by Assyrian conquerors in 722 BCE. Then David's own kingdom of Judah was wiped out, Solomon's Temple was demolished, and the nation's leaders were carried off to exile in Babylon (the *Babylonian Exile)* in 586 BCE. It appeared that the holy covenant had collapsed.

But now the remnant of the people carried out a genuine reform of their ways. At last they abandoned their attraction to false deities; at last they accepted the authority of the one true God. A group of exiles returned to the land of their forebears and rebuilt the Temple. Under the leadership of *Ezra*, *Nehemiah*, and the last of the prophets, they dedicated themselves anew to building a holy community based on devotion to God's word and the teachings of Moses. Backsliding continued, of course, but no longer dominated the national life.

The troublesome people of Israel had become the holy nation of the Jews.[9]

* * *

It bears repeating that the preceding narrative cannot be verified as history. Most characters in the biblical saga do not appear in the historical writing of any other ancient nation; most incidents in this saga are not recounted in any other ancient document. The importance of the story lies not in the question of whether *the events took place,* which cannot be determined, but in the certainty that *the story was told* time and again, over countless generations: *this* fact, of the greatest importance, is beyond all question. The epic narrative just summarized has shaped the consciousness of Jewish men and women since the dawn of Jewish history.

The biblical narrative establishes certain conceptions that remained central to the emerging Jewish religion. The story identifies the God of the Jews as the creator and sole ruler of the universe. It asserts Israel's claim to a special relationship with this God and explains how this relationship came to be. The story depicts the Jewish way of life and the Jewish national homeland as gifts from God and gateways to holiness for those who abide by God's demands and teachings; on the other hand, it also contains a stark warning that those who depart from those teachings or who resist those demands unavoidably bring down disaster for themselves and those around them. These ideas form the context for understanding the formal structures of ancient Israelite religion.

The Religion of Ancient Israel

In their private lives, the people of early Israel seem to have been very like their neighbors. The economy was largely rural, based on agriculture and herding.[10] Biblical law presumes the existence of slavery, but scriptural narrative never mentions slaves outside the households of the very rich. Similarly, in theory, men could take multiple wives, but very few did so except for the exceedingly wealthy. Polygamy was expensive, and few could afford to maintain a large household; moreover, husbands and wives often developed ties of affection that left no room for parallel relationships. Biblical law takes for granted the existence of polygamy, but scripture actually reports very few cases of polygamous households.[11]

When women married, they came into their husbands' households. They might retain ties of affection to the families of their birth, but their legal identity was now determined by their marriage.[12] For this reason, biblical law took care to provide for widows: not only did such women often lack material support, they also had no secure legal identity in society.[13] Biblical law repeatedly outlaws marriage with foreign women; sometimes the reference seems limited to the non-Israelite native peoples of the Promised Land, but sometimes the prohibition seems absolute. Nevertheless, the law also recognizes that a soldier might fall in love with a woman captured in war (Deuteronomy 21:10–14), and scripture recounts several noteworthy cases of Israelite men marrying foreign women.[14] Since women took on their husbands' legal identity at marriage, Israelite women who married foreign men probably disappeared from Israelite society. To be sure, the Bible provides not a single instance of a woman who did this, but this may simply confirm that such women went off with their husbands and were gone.

Worship of a national god was typical of the Near East, but in other cases this was usually combined with reverence for the forces of nature, such as rain and storm or love and fertility, that seemed to rule people's lives; similarly, even in Israel, the idea that worship should be limited to one god met heavy resistance for generations. See Chapter 2 for further discussion.

Biblical narrative says almost nothing about the religious lives of private individuals. On special occasions people offered sacrifices to God, but it is hard to tell if the formal biblical rules of sacrifice applied to such private offerings. In addition to large-scale public altars, did private homes contain specific locations for domestic offerings? We cannot tell. We do not know whether marriage or the birth of a child was marked by religious ceremonies other than standard thank-offerings or the postpartum purification-offerings that are specified in Leviticus 12. We also cannot tell whether great festivals were marked by home rituals as well as the great ceremonies performed at public shrines.[15]

In any case, as with all ancient peoples, Israelites' public worship centered on *sacrifice*, the gift to God (usually by destruction) of some object of value. Biblical law provides detailed regulations for the proper offering of sacrifice: a suitable object of value (usually an animal, but sometimes grain or wine or olive oil), the correct occasion (sometimes required by the calendar or by an occurrence in one's own life such as the birth of a child, but also possibly the result of a spontaneous vow), the necessary procedures, the appropriate personnel.

As time went on, the right to offer sacrifice came to rest with hereditary priests (Heb. *kohanim*); national memory traced this priesthood back to Aaron, the brother of Moses, but this ancestry cannot be verified. Indeed, various biblical passages suggest that at an early time the priestly role could be assigned on a different basis; most importantly, the tradition suggests that before the inherited priesthood started, this role was filled by the firstborn son of every household. This tradition is clearly related to the narrative tradition that Israelite firstborns were spared when the firstborn of Egypt were all killed in the tenth and final plague.

For a while, there were local shrines and groups of local priests scattered across the country (Figure 1), but in the time of King Josiah (late seventh century BCE) all sacrificial worship was centralized at a single location (the Temple) in the capital city of Jerusalem. This shrine had been constructed under King Solomon about 300 years earlier, but scripture mentions renovations and other changes over the centuries. We cannot tell for sure what the Temple or its ceremonies were like in Solomon's own time (the descriptions may incorporate information from later on), but by its last years the shrine had become an important national institution, a focus of pride and veneration. Its loss in 586 BCE was considered a divine punishment and a national catastrophe.

From an early time, the Israelite religion had developed a calendar of festivals (see "The Biblical Calendar"). Of these, probably the earliest (and most famous) is Passover (Heb. *Pesach*), still in modern times an annual celebration of Israel's escape from Egyptian bondage. This spring holiday featured the annual offering of a new (*paschal*) lamb and the careful avoidance of all leavened food products for a week. Careful reading of the biblical materials (see especially Exodus 12–13) suggests that these observances may already have been ancient celebrations of the arrival of spring, but now a new level of meaning

1. A preexilic altar in Arad. This altar was found in a preexilic Israelite fortress at Arad near the Dead Sea. In construction – a square structure of uncut stone – it combines features of the instructions given in Exodus 20 and 27, but the pictured altar has no horns, as required in 27:2; it is possible that horns existed but were broken off, but this can no longer be determined. (Photo courtesy of Tim Bulkeley, University of Auckland, New Zealand)

was attached to these; in addition to acclaiming their god as lord of *nature*, the Israelites identified major events in their *history* as the work of his mighty arm. This pattern of reaching beyond the eternal, unchanging world of natural cycles to find religious meaning in the unique events of history was one of Israel's great contributions to Western thought. In a similar way, the fall harvest *Festival of Booths* or *Tabernacles* (Heb., *Sukkot*) receives a historical explanation through reference to events that actually are never recounted in the biblical narrative (see Leviticus 23:43).

Over the course of time, however, the most striking feature of the Israelite calendar turned out to be not an annual feast at all but the weekly Sabbath day when productive labor was forbidden. As far as we can tell, no other culture in the ancient Near East had a seven-day week.[16] Theories abound as to the origins of this idea, but we can simply note its prominence. God himself is said to have instituted

THE BIBLICAL CALENDAR

The earliest biblical evidence reflects a variety of calendar systems in ancient Israel; these are not fully compatible, so they must reflect either variation in local custom or (more likely) different stages in Israel's cultural development. Unfortunately, the evidence does not allow modern scholars to reconstruct these stages in any detail.

One calendar, apparently lunar, used names for the months, though only four such names have survived: most of these appear in the narrative of Solomon's construction of the Temple (1 Kings 6–8). A year of twelve lunar months lasts only 354 days, and several annual festivals (see the following description) had clear seasonal associations, yet there is no evidence explaining how the people who used this calendar kept those festivals from slipping out of season. (In later centuries the authorities occasionally added a thirteenth month in the spring to make sure that Passover did not fall too early.) For centuries, lunar months were declared based on actual observation of the new moon; the fourth-century rabbinic leader Hillel II is reported to have dispensed with this system and to have instituted mathematical formulas for determining lunation. See Chapter 8, especially "Early Rabbinic *Taqqanot* and *Gezerot.*"

Another calendar only numbers the months, starting with the month of the spring equinox, the month in which Passover falls. This may have been a solar calendar similar to those known from ancient Egypt and elsewhere, consisting of twelve thirty-day months and one extra day every quarter to complete exactly fifty-two weeks. Use of this calendar may explain why Genesis 1:14 indicates that the heavenly bodies serve to mark off days and years but says nothing about months.

The seven-day week is an entirely artificial unit; attempts to link this unit to the phases of the moon or to features of the Babylonian calendar have not been successful. Except for the Sabbath, the days of the week too are numbered, not named: the modern Hebrew language still has no names for the other days of the week.

From an early time, the Israelites celebrated annual festivals at certain key seasons of the year. In later years, three such festivals were marked by pilgrimage to the Temple in Jerusalem, and were apparently conceived from an early time as an annual cycle. Most famous of these was the spring *Passover* festival, connected to the *Festival of Unleavened Bread*. Combined, these festivals served to commemorate the Israelites' escape from

THE BIBLICAL CALENDAR (continued)

Egyptian slavery in the days of Moses. The observances may originally have been separate: the offering of a lamb on the fourteenth day of the first month, followed by a week-long abstention from leavened or fermented foods beginning on the fifteenth. From an early time, however, these two were combined into a single great celebration. A later report suggests that shortly before the Second Temple was destroyed, over 1 million pilgrims would gather in Jerusalem each year to celebrate this festival (see Josephus, *Jewish War*, 6.424).

Seven weeks later, the beginning of the harvest season was marked by a briefer festival; over time this observance too acquired a historical dimension as the anniversary of the revelation of the Torah at Mount Sinai.

Finally, the great autumn harvest festival was marked by the construction of booths in the fields where people would eat and sleep. These booths were probably utilitarian in origin: when every hour counted, farmers did not want to take time each day to travel between their villages and their fields. In time, however, the *Festival of Booths* or *Tabernacles* became another token of historical memory, recalling Israel's forty years of wandering in the desert before the liberated slaves reached the Promised Land (Leviticus 23:43).

An additional pair of holidays was celebrated every fall, though evidence of their actual observance only comes from the later biblical period. The fall new moon marked the beginning of the civil year, and the tenth day thereafter became an annual day of atonement marked by fasting and elaborate ceremonies. Initially this day seems to have focused on the Temple itself, and served once a year to purge the shrine of any accidental defilement of its holiness, but eventually the annual Day of Atonement (*Yom Kippur*) became the holiest day of the year, celebrated by Jews all over the world.

Later books of the Bible added several new holidays to the calendar. The Book of Esther instituted the early spring holiday of *Purim* to celebrate Persian Jews' escape from the evil designs of a hostile royal minister. The prophet Zechariah, toward the very end of the biblical period, hints at a series of fasts throughout the year that must have commemorated disastrous events from earlier times (Zechariah 8:19).

On the other hand, certain observances appear to have dropped out of practice. The offering of a sheaf of wheat every spring inaugurated the new year's grain crop (Leviticus 23:9–14), but this rite disappeared when the Temple was destroyed, giving only its name (*Omer*, the Hebrew word for "sheaf") to the seven-week period after Passover. The precise time for offering this sheaf became the topic of fierce controversy during the time of the Second Temple, and other partisan disputes among advocates of these different calendars seem to have arisen as well; see Chapter 5, "Calendar and Controversy."

The most detailed listings of biblical festivals can be found in Leviticus 23 and Numbers 28–29; see also Deuteronomy 16 and (more briefly) Exodus 23:14–19 and 34:22–26. Nehemiah 8 reports that at a later time the Judahites returning from the Babylonian Exile found the rules for these festivals in the Torah and were evidently unfamiliar with them. See Chapter 3, "King Josiah's Book," for a celebration of the Passover in the days of King Josiah, shortly before the first Temple was destroyed.

the Sabbath as soon as the world was created (Genesis 2:1–3). As a sign of its importance, the Torah threatens the death penalty for those who violate the Sabbath (Exodus 31:14 or 35:2), and Sabbath observance is the only ceremonial provision in the so-called *Ten Commandments* or *Decalogue* (Exodus 20:8–11; Deuteronomy 5:12–15), an early listing of basic religious principles. The Bible does not provide much detailed information about this important Israelite institution; we do not know what rituals were performed other than some special sacrifices (Numbers 28:9–10),[17] nor do we know what actions were deemed laborious and thus forbidden.[18]

The two versions of the Ten Commandments offer quite different explanations of the reason behind the weekly day of rest (see "'The Ten Commandments,' Two Versions"). The Book of Exodus describes the Sabbath as an acknowledgment of God as Creator of the world: God created the world in six days and then rested on the seventh, and those who worship him should do the same. In Deuteronomy, however, the focus shifts to the escape from slavery in Egypt: just as you were slaves but God gave you rest, so too you must rest and give rest to all who labor on your behalf. This is the only paragraph of the Decalogue in which the two versions significantly differ, and their combination once again presents a mixture of themes drawn from the contemplation of nature and from the study of the nation's history.

"THE TEN COMMANDMENTS," TWO VERSIONS

Note: Different religious traditions variously divide these instructions into the Ten Commandments. The following translations offer the traditional Jewish division.

I

I am YHWH your God who brought you out of the land of Egypt, out of the house of servants.

You shall have no other gods in my presence.

You shall not make for yourself a sculpture or a depiction [of anything] in the heavens above or that is on the earth beneath or that is in the waters beneath the earth. You shall not bow to them and you shall not serve them, for I, YHWH your God, a jealous God, visit the sin of fathers on sons until the third and fourth [generations] to those that hate me, while I perform mercy to thousands, to those that love me and observe my commandments.

Do not take the name of YHWH your God in vain, for YHWH will not hold guiltless the one who takes his name in vain.

Remember the Sabbath day to keep it holy. You shall work six days and perform all your labor, but the seventh day is Sabbath unto YHWH your God: do not perform any labor – you or your son or your daughter or your manservant or your maidservant or your cattle or your alien who is in your gates – for [in] six days YHWH made the heavens and the earth, the sea and all that is in them, and on the seventh day he rested. Therefore YHWH blessed the Sabbath day and made it holy.

Honor your father and your mother in order that your days may be long on the land that YHWH your God gives you.

You shall not murder.

You shall not commit adultery.

You shall not steal.

You shall not answer against your fellow [as a] false witness.

You shall not covet your fellow's house. You shall not covet your fellow's wife, or his manservant or his maidservant or his ox or his donkey, or anything that belongs to your fellow.

(Exodus 20:2–17)

II

I am YHWH your God who brought you out of the land of Egypt, out of the house of servants.

You shall have no other gods in my presence.

You shall not make for yourself a sculpture or a depiction [of anything] in the heavens above or that is on the earth beneath or that is in the waters beneath the earth. You shall not bow to them and you shall not serve them, for I, YHWH your God, a jealous God, visit the sin of fathers on sons until the third and fourth [generations] to those that hate me, while I perform mercy to thousands, to those that love me and observe my commandments.

Do not take the name of YHWH your God in vain, for YHWH will not hold guiltless the one who takes his name in vain.

Preserve the Sabbath day to keep it holy, as YHWH your God has commanded you. You shall work six days and perform all your labor, but the seventh day is Sabbath unto YHWH your God: do not perform any labor – you or your son or your daughter or your manservant or your maidservant or your ox or your donkey or any of your cattle or the alien who is in your gates – in order that your manservant and your maidservant rest as you do. And remember that you were a servant in the land of Egypt and [that] YHWH your God took you out of there with a strong hand and an outstretched arm; therefore YHWH your God has commanded you to keep the Sabbath day.

Honor your father and your mother as YHWH your God has commanded you, in order that your days may be long, and in order that it go well with you on the land that YHWH your God gives you.

You shall not murder,

And you shall not commit adultery,

And you shall not steal,

And you shall not answer against your fellow [as a] vain witness,

And you shall not covet your fellow's wife, and you shall not desire your fellow's house, his field, or his manservant or his maidservant, his ox or his donkey, or anything that belongs to your fellow.

(Deuteronomy 5:6–21)

The widespread appearance of such mixtures is a distinguishing characteristic of biblical literature.

Every ancient culture had its priests, but Israel had a second, very different kind of religious leader as well: the *prophets*. The Hebrew prophets (*nevi'im*) were not fortune-tellers but messengers, intermediaries between the people and their God; in this they differed from the fortune-tellers, astrologers, and oracles who could be found all over the ancient world. Moses is the prototype of the prophets (see Deuteronomy 18:15), and throughout the biblical period prophets served as vehicles by which God's word came to the people.

It can easily be seen that prophecy is inherently unsettling: a prophet can turn up at any time and announce that previous messages from God have been replaced by a new one. Naturally, those officials (priests, kings, etc.) responsible for maintaining the nation's stability often tangled with prophets; scripture is full of stories of prophets denouncing kings in the name of God, while priests at their holy shrines, dedicated to the regular performance of their ceremonial duties, sometimes tried to silence prophets or just to keep them away.[19] Such hostility might be avoided – a prophet who won the king's confidence could become an important royal advisor – but the tension between the priests' dedication to order and permanence and the prophets' unpredictable disruptions is one of the ongoing themes of the Bible.

Prophecy gave rise to another difficulty as well: how could you tell who the true prophets were? Anyone could appear and claim to bear a message from God: how could people distinguish false prophets – malicious or deluded individuals – from the real thing? Biblical law offers the simple but unhelpful solution that if the prophecy doesn't come true the prophet can't have been sent by God (Deuteronomy 18:22), but people couldn't always wait to see whether a prophecy would be fulfilled. And sometimes, as in the famous case of Jonah, prophecy achieved its purpose without coming true. Jonah predicted the downfall of a great city, but its people repented and were forgiven; this meant that, strictly speaking, the prophecy had not come true, but who could deny that it had achieved its true purpose? In addition to this intellectual puzzle, prophecy sometimes demanded action; when conflicting prophecies demanded incompatible actions, the prophets' audience was at a loss to know what God really wanted them to

THE TROUBLE WITH PROPHECY

As mentioned in the text, biblical law recognizes the importance of distinguishing genuine prophecy from false but sees that this can be difficult to accomplish. Scripture offers a very simple rule for sorting this out: genuine prophecy comes true, and false prophecy does not.

> If you should ask, "How will we know the word that YHWH has not spoken?," that which the prophet speaks in the name of YHWH and does not come about, YHWH did not speak that word. The prophet spoke thus defiantly, and you must not fear him.
>
> (Deuteronomy 18:21–22)

Biblical narrators, however, also seem aware that this rule is not always adequate. The famous story of Jonah, also mentioned in the text, contains a deep paradox. The prophet foretells the downfall of the great city Nineveh, but the people strive to change their sinful ways and God forgives them (Jonah 3). This angers the prophet greatly: now his prophecy has been falsified! The message of the book, however, is that *the prophecy succeeded by not coming true*. The destruction of the city, not its survival, would have been the real failure.

A less well-known incident, in Jeremiah 28, concerned a confrontation between two prophets: Jeremiah himself and another named Hananiah ben Azur. Jeremiah had consistently called for surrender to the Babylonians now besieging Jerusalem, but Hananiah disagreed and did so in the name of God: he foretold that within two years the besiegers would be gone. Jeremiah did not know what to do; he was deeply convinced that Hananiah was misleading the people and that his own advocacy of surrender was the true of word of God, but how could he prove this to the perplexed bystanders? When two prophets offer directly opposite proclamations of the word of God, how are people to know whom to follow? Jeremiah went home without responding, only to receive a new prophecy confirming his conviction, and then "Hananiah the prophet died that year, in the seventh month." God himself, so to speak, executed Jeremiah's rival on the charge of false prophecy, but could it really be that when two prophets disagree the nation must wait to see who dies first?

Another story (1 Kings 22:1–37) is more perplexing still. The two Israelite kings, Jehoshaphat of the south and Ahab of the north, met to consider making war on their common enemy the Arameans. Jehoshaphat, known

THE TROUBLE WITH PROPHECY (continued)

for his piety, was ready to agree but wanted to consult the prophets of God before deciding. Many prophets predicted victory, but finally one last prophet (his name was Micaiah ben Imlah, and Ahab disliked him because his prophecies were always hostile) offered a shocking vision: God had sent a spirit into all the other prophets in order to entice Ahab to war, *but the purpose of this message was to lure Ahab to his death*. Sure enough Ahab went to war, and sure enough he was killed. In need of prophetic guidance, Ahab had naturally followed the majority opinion, and this was fatal. The story of the prophet Micaiah raises the terrifying possibility that an authentic prophecy may come from God but with a hidden, deceitful purpose, so that those who follow the prophecy achieve no salvation but are led on to their own destruction. Once aware of this danger, who would ever follow a prophet again?

do (see "The Trouble with Prophecy"). These uncertainties combined to produce the worst dilemma of all: sometimes prophecies were designed to save their audience from disaster, as in the case of Jonah, but sometimes, as with King Ahab, they were intended to lead their audience to destruction. How could people tell which prophecies to follow? What were they to do when they could not tell? What might happen if they failed to consider all possibilities? What might happen if they guessed wrong?

Under the pressure of such uncertainty, later generations began to lose confidence in prophecy as a reliable method of learning God's will. The prophets of the past had been holy men and women, and their words were remembered and continually revisited, but no further messages from God were expected. Zechariah, one of the last biblical prophets, paradoxically foretells the end of prophecy: in the future, anyone who so much as claimed to bring a message from God would be put to death as a false prophet, so real prophets would have to lie about their identity to protect their own lives.[20] Throughout later centuries, prophet-like figures continued to appear, but they were greeted with resistance and skepticism. Later Jewish tradition claimed that prophecy disappeared around the time of Alexander the Great (reigned 336–323 BCE), and this memory is probably about right.[21]

The prophets were the second element of Israelite religious leadership to disappear from national life, the kings having been gone for centuries. That left the priests. After the Babylonian Exile, Israelite religion was increasingly dominated by priests, and the story of that domination – the rise and decline of priestly Judaism – will be told in the following chapters.

2

The Beginnings of Monotheism

THE GREAT RELIGIONS OF WESTERN CIVILIZATION, JUDAISM and those that followed, are all *monotheistic*: they claim that the God they worship is the only god there is. The Bible is an important source of this conception, but the scriptures of ancient Israel actually offer a more complicated picture.

That picture can begin with an intriguing diplomatic exchange said to have taken place around 1100 BCE. The people of Israel and the neighboring people of Ammon were locked in dispute over a certain border territory. This territory had previously belonged to neither group, but the Israelites had seized the land from the original Amorite inhabitants in the process of conquering the Promised Land. The Ammonites (a different people with a regrettably similar name!) wanted this land as well, on the ground that the Amorites had previously stolen it from them,[1] but the Israelite leader Jephthah rejected this claim:

> ...YHWH the god of Israel has granted possession of the Amorite [land] to his people Israel: will you now take possession from them? Do you not possess that which Kemosh your god grants to you? We will possess all that YHWH our god has granted to us. (Judges 11:23–24)

In this brief response Jephthah expresses a view that was widely held at his time. According to this view, every nation has its own guardian deity that watches over it in a land it has received as an inheritance. Under the protection of its god, every nation lives in secure prosperity unless it forfeits that god's protection, or unless some stronger god snatches away the land and gives it to some other people. This, of course, would have been an aggressive act, violation of the peace among the gods. Israel's god had fought and utterly defeated the gods of Egypt, but Jephthah had no reason to believe that his god and the Ammonites' were on bad terms: the Ammonites had received a gift from their god just as Israel had received the Promised Land from YHWH, and this should have been a stable arrangement under the gods' joint supervision.

This conception is not monotheism. This is a *polytheistic* view that expects each nation to have one special god with whom it is linked in some kind of special bond.[2] In this view, national alliances or rivalries could be seen as reflections of alliances or rivalries among the gods themselves. A nation's defeat was a defeat for its god; a nation's power reflected the power of its god. Throughout the story of the struggle between Moses and the Egyptian pharaoh, the Bible stresses that the downfall of the Egyptians would prove to the world that Israel's god was mightier than any other. The very purpose of the famous ten plagues was to convey this lesson (see Exodus 10:2), and Israel's triumph was remembered by later generations as YHWH's triumph over the gods of Egypt (Exodus 12:12, 15:11; Numbers 33:4). When Israel too was finally exiled, these same notions turned into bitterness. The Babylonian conquerors asked the people of Judah to sing some native songs, but the very request struck the captives as a mockery of their god (see Psalm 137:3–4).

The central biblical concept of covenant must be understood in these terms. The people of ancient Israel were firm in their belief that their nation and YHWH were intimately bound together; numerous biblical passages compare this bond to a marriage. But it was not clear what the terms of that relationship were going to be. Was YHWH going to be like a jealous spouse, unwilling to allow any friendship between Israel and its neighbors' gods, or was Israel obliged only to remember that after visiting the deities of other people it was always going to have to come home, so to speak, to its own? The prophets were fiercely committed to the notion that YHWH was jealous indeed,[3] and for centuries they insisted that national disloyalty to the national God would prompt him to withdraw his protection. Others, however, thought this was a foolish anxiety: why anger all the other gods out of excessive attachment to one? Could any god be so jealous as to require this? To many people the prophets' demand made no sense at all.

This issue remained unresolved for centuries. The prophets endlessly accused their listeners of defiant idolatry, but were the people really that wicked or that stupid? Did they really not understand that their God demanded exclusive loyalty and would punish them horribly if they failed to render such allegiance? On balance it seems more likely that the prophets' opponents simply had a different idea of what the covenant demanded; in their view, the prophets themselves were wildly unrealistic in their expectations and had to be resisted.

Only one passage in the entire Bible openly expresses this view, but that one passage makes the issue perfectly clear. When the Babylonians destroyed Jerusalem, they carried the royal family and many other leaders into exile, but they appointed Gedaliah ben Ahikam, a high-ranking aristocrat, to govern the province on their behalf. However, radical nationalists murdered Gedaliah and then escaped to Egypt before the enraged Babylonians could avenge his death. The prophet Jeremiah, for his part, had long advocated submission to Babylon, and the conquerors were prepared to bring him to Babylon and treat him generously; Jeremiah declined their offer, preferring to remain in his native land, but the fleeing assassins now compelled the prophet to travel with them. So Jeremiah found himself in exile, and his last recorded prophecy (Jeremiah 44) was delivered on foreign soil (see "A Debate on the Meaning of Disaster").

The prophet's own words are not especially remarkable. He reminds his hearers that they find themselves in exile "on account of their evil that they committed to anger [God], by going to offer incense and worship other gods which they (you and your ancestors) had not known" (44:3), and then he rebukes them for continuing those same practices in their new Egyptian exile: do they not realize that God's fury will pursue them even in a foreign land? Do they not realize the only possible outcome of their behavior? "They shall all meet their end in the land of Egypt: they shall fall by the sword and meet their end by hunger, small and great they shall die by the sword and by hunger, and they shall become an oath and a desolation, a curse and a shame. And [God will] visit those who dwell in the

A DEBATE ON THE MEANING OF DISASTER

As noted in the text, this chapter provides Jeremiah's last recorded prophecy. Delivered in Egypt to an audience of Judahite refugees, the chapter starkly lays out the problem of catastrophe: it is easy enough to say that the people have suffered at the hands of an angry deity, but which deity was it, and what had caused the anger? Any answer to that question had to come as an act of faith, and the stakes were very high.

The word which came to Jeremiah concerning all the Judahites living in the land of Egypt, in Migdol and in Tahpanhes and in Noph and in the land of Pathros, saying:

Thus says YHWH of Hosts, the God of Israel: "You have seen all the evil that I brought upon Jerusalem and all the cities of Judah; behold they are a ruin today, with no one living there. I sent all my servants the prophets to you, early and often, saying, 'Please do not commit this abominable thing that I hate,' but they did not listen or incline themselves to return from their evildoing, to refrain from offering incense to other gods. So my fury and my anger was poured out upon them, and it burned in the cities of Judah and the courtyards of Jerusalem, and these became a ruin and a desolation unto this very day."

And now thus says YHWH the God of Hosts the God of Israel: "Why are you committing a great evil against yourself, to cut yourselves – man and woman, child and suckling – off from Judah, so that no remnant will be left of you? You anger me with the deeds of your hands by offering incense to other gods in the land of Egypt where you have come to reside, so that you will cut yourselves off and become a curse and a reproach among all the nations of the land. Have you forgotten your ancestors' evildoing, and the evildoing of the kings of Judah and the evildoing of his [their?] wives, and your evildoing and the evildoing of your wives, which they did in the land of Judah and the courtyards of Jerusalem? They have not been subdued until this day, they have not been afraid, they have not followed my teaching and my laws which I have placed before you and before your ancestors."

Therefore thus says YHWH of Hosts the God of Israel: "Behold I set my face against you for evil, to cut off all of Judah. And I shall take the remnant of Judah who set their faces to come to the land of Egypt to reside there. They shall all meet their end in the land of Egypt: they shall fall by the

A DEBATE ON THE MEANING OF DISASTER (continued)

sword and meet their end by hunger, they shall die small and great by the sword and by hunger, and they shall become an oath and a desolation, a curse and a shame. And I shall visit those who dwell in the land of Egypt as I visited Jerusalem, with the sword, with hunger, and with plague. There will be no fugitive or remainder of the remnant of Judah who are coming to reside there in the land of Egypt or to return to the land of Judah to which they long to return and dwell there: for they will not return, except as refugees."

Then all the men who knew that their wives offered incense to other gods, and all the women standing there – a great crowd – and all the people who dwelt in the land of Egypt in Pathros, answered Jeremiah, saying: "The word that you spoke to us in the name of YHWH, we will not listen to you, but we shall surely carry out the word that has come from our mouth, to offer incense to the Queen of Heaven and to pour out libations to her as we did, we and our ancestors, our kings and our princes, in the cities of Judah and the courtyard of Jerusalem. Then we had our fill of bread and we lived well and saw no evil. But from the time that we stopped offering incense and pouring out libations to the Queen of Heaven we have lacked everything; we have met our end through the sword and hunger." [The women added:] "And do [only] we offer incense to the Queen of Heaven or pour out libations to her? Was it without our husbands that we made her cakes (?) in her image and poured out libations to her?"

(Jeremiah 44:1–19)

land of Egypt as [he] visited Jerusalem, with the sword, with hunger, and with plague" (44:12−13). All this had been standard prophetic teaching for generations; the Book of Jeremiah is full of passages that contain this message or one very like it.

But the response of Jeremiah's hearers is remarkable indeed. In this chapter, and nowhere else in the Bible, a prophet's audience answers him back. There are stories in scripture where crowds mock a prophet or simply ignore him, but here Jeremiah's audience tells him exactly why they intend to disregard his plea: when they worshiped other gods, they say, "we had our fill of bread; we lived well and saw no evil. But from the time that we stopped offering incense and pouring

out libations to the Queen of Heaven we have lacked everything"
(44:16–18).

The point at issue between Jeremiah and his hostile audience is very
specific. The prophet does not accuse them of neglecting the worship
of YHWH, their ancestors' God, nor do they threaten to abandon that
worship or deny that Jeremiah is indeed a prophet of YHWH speaking in YHWH's name. On such matters they are in full agreement.
Furthermore, there is no disagreement at all as to the basic cause of
Judah's exile: these people have been driven into exile by an angry
god. The disagreement concerns only one question, but a question of
fateful importance: which is the angry god? Jeremiah, speaking on
behalf of YHWH, accuses the people of having provoked the anger
of the ancestral God of the covenant by worshiping other gods alongside him. The people respond that they have made those other gods
furious by neglecting their worship at YHWH's (that is, Jeremiah's)
insistence. These survivors of catastrophe, huddled together in Egyptian exile, cannot agree on what has led to their awful situation and
so cannot decide what to do about it now.

The debate that unfolds in this chapter was a very old one. It seems
that for much of their early history, the people of Israel maintained
a kind of easygoing loyalty to their covenant with YHWH. Never
doubting that YHWH was their particular national god, they also paid
honor to other divine beings as circumstances appeared to indicate.
When King Solomon, ruler of a significant kingdom, entered into
diplomatic marriages with the daughters of nearby monarchs, he
built shrines where these women could honor their native deities, and
he joined his wives in the worship of these foreign gods. The biblical
writer strongly disapproves of these actions (see 1 Kings 11:1–9), but
to Solomon himself this was just the natural thing to do. The common
people, for reasons that were equally obvious to them, continually
paid honor to the storm god Baal and to other forces of nature that
were conceived as living gods. The laws of the Torah and the historical
books of scripture fiercely condemn this behavior, but the biblical
writers needed to repeat this condemnation time and time again,
over many generations, because the people would not abandon their
ways.

The insistence that all worship must go to a single god seems to
have arisen among a movement of religious visionaries, the prophets.

Perceived as YHWH's personal representatives to the nation, the prophets portrayed their god as a jealous god, a deity unwilling to share divine honors with any other, and the Bible almost invariably reflects the prophets' point of view.[4] The most famous of the early prophets was Elijah "the Tishbite" (1 Kings 17:1; nothing is known of his origins, not even his father's name). According to scripture, this man suddenly emerged out of the wilderness of Transjordan and began to roam the countryside, predicting fearsome drought as the outbreak of God's fury. Mixing thunderous denunciation with miracles of healing and sustenance, he wandered the land in a wild, primitive costume and attracted the hatred of King Ahab but the respect and fascination of the people of the land. After three years of drought, Elijah organized a contest between himself and the prophets of Baal: each side would prepare a sacrifice but bring no fire, and the god who took his own offering would thereby prove himself to be the real god, the only God deserving of worship and loyalty. Elijah's God, YHWH, won this contest by sending down fire from heaven. YHWH (and Elijah) were acclaimed by the crowded onlookers, the prophets of Baal were massacred, and the drought ended with a massive downpour of rain.[5]

But the people's loyalty was short-lived. Elijah's disciple, Elisha, had to keep up the struggle, and after them the great literary prophets Isaiah, Jeremiah, and Ezekiel kept on denouncing the people's inconstancy for generation after generation. Jeremiah's dispute with his listeners in Egypt took place nearly 300 years after Elijah's famous contest, and the terms of the debate had not changed.

Why should this have been necessary? The Bible recounts that Israel's God had demanded exclusive worship from the days of Moses in the desert, from the very beginning of Israel's covenant with him, but this was a partisan view, for centuries the view of a struggling minority. The bulk of the populace felt that the prophets' demand was simply absurd: why make all the other gods angry just to satisfy one? That view comes to the fore in only one chapter of the Bible, so modern readers can easily misjudge its prevalence in ancient times.

It should be noted that the people who asked that last question were not debating the idea of monotheism at all; the argument concerned a related notion that is often called *henotheism* or *monolatry*, the insistence that one single deity should receive all worship. True monotheism insists that there is only one God: there are no others whose anger must be feared. But Jeremiah's antagonists were deeply convinced that the other gods were real, and careful examination of the prophet's rebuke suggests that he did not dispute this conviction; he only insisted that the other gods were weaker than YHWH and presented no danger to YHWH's followers. In the prophets' view, YHWH demanded that his followers refuse to honor any rival gods and assured them that he would protect from harm all those who obeyed this demand. This was not a matter of theological abstraction: the demand was for loyal action, not correct opinion. Marriage too depends on loyalty, not on abstract beliefs about whether other men or other women exist, and it has already been noted that many biblical writers compare the covenant to a marriage. If the Israelites' worship of other gods was a kind of adultery,[6] this was a matter of wicked action, not foolish opinion.

The central religious issue that divided the Israelites for centuries thus begins to emerge more clearly. A group of hard-line radicals (for so they must have appeared) insisted that Israel's national covenant with YHWH absolutely forbade the worship of any other divinity, while the bulk of the population resisted this demand, preferring to maintain the other gods' goodwill while not neglecting their specific obligations to YHWH. Initially, as reflected in Jephthah's negotiations with the Ammonites, YHWH was one among equals, but as Israel began to assert itself against its neighbors this parity turned into rivalry and competition. The story of the Exodus, while set in an earlier time, reflects this conception: YHWH's victory over Pharaoh was also, and perhaps even more importantly, a triumph over Pharaoh's gods. However, when the rivalry became absolute, when YHWH became a jealous god who brooked no companionship at all, many people became unwilling to comply.

Many apparent assertions of monotheism throughout the Bible may actually reflect the aggressive rivalry just described. When the Torah insists that "YHWH is God in heaven above and on the earth beneath: there is no other" (Deuteronomy 4:39), but also recounts that YHWH "executed judgment upon the gods of Egypt" by killing the Egyptian firstborn (Numbers 33:4), the first claim begins to sound like a boastful repetition of the second. In Isaiah 44:6, YHWH boldly claims, "I am first and I am last; besides me there is no god," but elsewhere (41:21–22) the other gods are challenged to present their credentials in a fair trial: let them try to predict the future or perform wondrous deeds "so that we can know that you are gods." In such a context, when YHWH then boasts that "you come from nowhere and your deeds from zero" (41:24), this is not a denial of the other gods' existence but of their right to be considered divine: they may exist, but they are "nothing." This is not yet monotheism; this is the defiant boast of (the followers of) one god among many, a proud god who promises to defeat any rival who dares to come forward.

But Jews of later ages surely did believe that no other gods but their own are real, so how did monotheism arise? What led the people of Israel to such a radical conclusion? There is a hint about the answer to this question in the narrative of biblical history. The historical books of scripture describe a development that would recur every few generations: the appearance of a religious reformer who would attack the nation's tendency to idolatry and demand the removal of previously acceptable customs. For example, the Torah relates that when "fiery serpents" invaded Israel's encampment in the desert, Moses himself crafted a similar creature out of bronze or copper and set it up to view: "if a [living] serpent bit a man, he gazed upon the copper serpent and lived" (Numbers 21:9). One might have thought that the copper serpent's association with Moses gave it legitimacy, but years later the reforming King Hezekiah destroyed it, even though he knew that Moses himself had made it, because "the people of Israel had offered it incense, calling it *Nehushtan*."[7] Over the centuries, many objects of veneration were thus excluded from the life of the nation, until finally only one God was left.

Modern scholars will probably never be able to trace this development in any detail, but a pair of contributory factors, one internal and one a reaction to outside events, can be identified. The internal factor was a product of the basic covenant notion, already discussed, that every nation has its own special god(s). This meant that religion was a key element in what today would be called *identity*: you were what you worshiped. As the diverse tribes of Israel nurtured an ever-stronger shared national identity, an ever-stronger loyalty to YHWH as national god was both an important symptom of this development and an important force driving it along. Rejection of all things foreign became a sign of Israelite pride, not least in times of crisis, and this included rejection of all foreign gods. Eventually all gods other than YHWH were considered foreign, not only the national deities

of other nations but also international gods like the storm god Baal
or the fertility goddess Ishtar/Astarte (in the Bible called *Ashtoret*).
Scripture repeatedly emphasizes the foreign origin and the foreign
connections of gods other than YHWH. Jeremiah ties the worship of
such gods to the threat of exile; if the people insist on worshiping
other nations' gods, they will wind up having to worship those gods
in the other nations' lands.[8] Monotheism thus became a by-product
of patriotism (or *xenophobia*), of the wish to strengthen Israel's identity by purging its life of elements that were felt to be of foreign
origin.

But still the question remains: this process of ongoing exclusion
did not have to result in the denial of the other gods' very existence.
Would it not have been enough to insist that Israelites simply avoid
any dealings with them? Certainty is not possible, but outside events
may have had a decisive influence on the outcome of these developments. A Babylonian army destroyed the Kingdom of Judah and
the holy city of Jerusalem during the lives of two great prophets,
Jeremiah and Ezekiel. Facing this calamity, the nation's leaders had to
consider the usual explanation for such events: that the Babylonians'
gods had been stronger than their own and had overcome YHWH's
attempts to protect them. At an earlier time, an Assyrian general
had made precisely such a mocking claim while besieging Jerusalem
(see "The Assyrian General's Taunt"). That siege had failed, but the
idea haunted later generations: could any other god be stronger than
Israel's? Could YHWH's protection fail them at a critical moment?
The prophets' answer was to deny this possibility. If YHWH's people
have suffered disaster, it must be because their own God has inflicted
this punishment upon them for their sins against him. The other so-
called gods are not YHWH's rivals: if anything, they are his agents
and servants. They are surely no more than that.

Now people sometimes treated a king's ministers as if they were
actually the king himself. This could be a useful habit. The king himself was often so far away as to be invisible, a mere name, which
other, more local officials invoked to justify their own power. It could
not hurt to treat such officials with deference: they were the ones
with real power over ordinary people and their daily lives. But if
this were true of the human agents of a human king, could not the
same be said for the heavenly agents – sun, wind, and so on – who

THE ASSYRIAN GENERAL'S TAUNT

The Assyrian general known as Ravshakeh spoke these words to the people of besieged Jerusalem, inviting them to surrender and not rely on the unreliable promises of their king and their god. Every nation has a god, he said, but none of the other gods had withstood the great might of Asshur: why did the people of Judah think their god was any better? The king implored the would-be conqueror to speak in Aramaic rather than "Judahite" so that the people would not understand his frightening message, but, of course, he ignored the plea: his whole intention was to frighten them! The Israelite hearers were so haunted by these words that Scripture records them not once but twice; the modern reader can only try to imagine the terror they must have produced in their hearers.

...and do not listen to [King] Hezekiah, for he will mislead you, saying "YHWH will save us." Did the gods of the nations indeed save each his land from the hand of the King of Assyria? Where are the gods of Hammat and Arpad? Where are the gods of Sefarvaim, Hena, and Ivva? Did they save Samaria from my hand? Who of all the gods of the lands saved their lands from my hand that YHWH will save Jerusalem from my hand?

(2 Kings 18:32–35; see also 19:10–13)

were messengers and creatures of the one true God? The forces of nature have great power over our lives, and for centuries it seemed only prudent to treat those forces with the same deference that one offered to human servants of high rank. This kind of thinking lay behind Israel's adoption of the religious veneration of nature that was so important throughout the ancient Near East.

In the human arena, however, this same habit can lead to regrettable situations. Local officials were often more important in people's lives than the distant king; from time to time, flattered by the attention he received, a royal minister might rebel against his monarch and attempt to carve out a small territory or even to seize the throne for himself. The heavenly bodies, being perfect creations, would never rebel against their sovereign, but human attention was often deflected from a more abstract high god and focused instead on these concrete representatives of the high god's might; after all, they were more easily grasped and more easily approached. Over time, the prophets became increasingly worried that such a deflection was destroying Israel's covenant with its God; they strove with growing passion to prevent the veneration of any being other than YHWH himself.

This course of development explains otherwise perplexing biblical phrases. Certain texts acclaim YHWH as "God of gods" (e.g., Deuteronomy 10:17; Psalm 50:1). Such an acclamation makes no sense at all if no other gods exist, but it perfectly describes a dominant God who has appointed subordinates to run the world and has delegated the worship of those subordinates to other nations (see Deuteronomy 4:19; 29:25). Israel, privileged to worship the only god who was God (see 1 Kings 18:39; Psalm 18:32), thus asserted its honored position among the nations of the world. The very frequent divine title *Lord of Hosts* also probably refers to the hosts of heaven, of whom Israel's God YHWH was conceived to be the commander-in-chief.

This linkage between theology and national pride ultimately gave rise to monotheism. Constant belittlement of the other nations' gods finally led to a refusal to call them gods at all. Psalm 82 describes a fascinating scene in which God (unnamed) gathers the other gods in council, only to denounce them for failing at their tasks. Like any dissatisfied employer, he dismisses them from their posts:

> How long will you judge wickedly and favor evil people?.... I had treated you as gods, all of you, children of the Highest, but you will die like (any) man, you will fall like one of the princes. (Psalm 82:2, 7)

In the Book of Daniel, the latest of the Jewish scriptures to be written, the nations' gods are called *princes*, guardian angels,[9] and it appears that they continued to function in the way the people had long imagined, each defending the interests of "his" nation, though now in a subordinate role under the true God's constant scrutiny. Thus the world remained full of unseen superhuman beings, and the heavenly world remained thickly populated. Only one thing had changed: the heavenly hosts could no longer be called gods. That dignity had been taken away from them by their own commander, the one true God, YHWH, the God of Israel.

But if no one other than YHWH had the right to be *called* a god, that could only mean that no one other than YHWH *was* a god. Just

MONOTHEISM OUTSIDE ISRAEL?

In addition to the religious faith of Israel, the ancient world saw the development of several other monotheistic or near-monotheistic conceptions. The classical Greek philosophers came to understand that the forces that people labeled gods were actually manifestations of a single divine power that governs the world. They expressed this insight in different terms. Aristotle (384–322 BCE) famously defined God as the "unmoved mover," that is, the only self-sufficient power capable of acting on other beings without itself requiring energy from an outside source. His teacher, Plato (427–347 BCE), conceived of God as "the One," the ultimate unity that embraces the diversity of earthly phenomena. Earlier still, Xenophanes (565?–470 BCE) caustically noted that different human races depict their gods in their own image, and suggested that if horses had gods they would all have four legs. In fact, he said, the one true god is without shape and invisibly rules the world from a place beyond human ken.

None of these thinkers, even the skeptical Xenophanes, objected to the polytheistic religious practices of their societies. In their view, the multiple gods and goddesses of Greece represented aspects of the one true divinity, various dimensions of the divine that ordinary people encounter as they live their lives. For them the abstraction later called monotheism could not sustain the hopes and fears of ordinary humans and had to be kept in reserve for contemplation by the intellectual elite. In later centuries, this elitism attracted the critical attention of Jewish writers: the first-century CE writer Philo (see Chapter 6) wrote that some philosophers achieve true piety through contemplation, but the whole Jewish nation is guided to this achievement by its very way of life (*On the Virtues*, 65).

At a much earlier time, the Egyptian Pharaoh Amenhotep IV (also called Akhenaton: 1367–1350 BCE) created a monotheistic religion before the nation of Israel ever existed, but nothing came of it. The young ruler became fiercely devoted to Aton, god of the sun-disk, and attempted to shut down all the other temples of Egypt. Images of the other gods, even their very names, were erased from inscriptions, and the worship of Aton (with whom the god-king himself was associated) was installed everywhere. However, Akhenaton died young, perhaps by violence, and the various priesthoods of Egypt, not least the priests of the other sun-gods, abolished his reforms and sought to eradicate his memory.

Modern writers have speculated that memories of this episode lingered in Egypt and influenced the thinking of the young Moses, who was being raised in the royal palace, but this account requires that we accept the biblical story of Moses as essentially historical. More likely the present narrative is a much later distillation of folk memory, and the dramatic story of Moses being drawn from the Nile by a princess who gave him a royal education (see Exodus 2) is probably legend. Similar stories can be found in almost every culture in the world, and even within Scripture many heroes are distinguished for the remarkable circumstances of their conception, birth, or early childhood. In addition, to assume that accurate memories of Akhenaton's project persisted for 100 years or more, when all the priests of Egypt had been laboring the whole time to bury such memories in oblivion, is most unwise. The connection between Akhenaton and Moses has fascinated scholars and novelists for generations, but it is not likely a reflection of historical reality.

It should also be noted that numerous inscriptions and hymns from the ancient Near East address one deity or another in extravagant language that comes close to sounding like monotheism: phrases like "you only do we worship" or "trust in…, not in any other god" are addressed to numerous deities over many hundreds of years. Are these expressions of monotheism, albeit monotheism that failed to take root? Probably not. It is more plausible to see such language as flattery (one might speak in the same tone to a powerful official) or self-praise by the worshipers deflected onto their god (compare 2 Samuel 7:22–23). The prophets' own comparison of the covenant to a marriage is instructive here: when young people, newly in love, address each other as "the only one for me," this surely does not mean that no other potential lovers exist, only that the speakers would not cheapen their passion by pursuing them.

as there can be only one king, so too there can be only one God, and this was Israel's God, YHWH. The king can have many servants, some of them very powerful, and so too YHWH had a large retinue of ministers, agents, and the like, *but none of them was a god*. Belief in angels and demons and spirits of all kinds remained widespread, but now such underlings were carefully distinguished from the divine king himself.[10]

Thus Israel's monotheism developed as a distinctive feature of its national identity and way of life. Recognition of other gods became a form of treason for those who belonged to the covenant, *but this had no necessary implications for the beliefs or the practices of other people.* In the eyes of many, other nations might continue to honor their own ancestral gods for the same reason that Israel honored its God, though prudence dictated caution when facing YHWH's overwhelming power.

Other Israelites thought differently, of course: they strongly felt that it was wrong to allow people to worship non-gods when the true God, the only proper object of veneration, was available to the whole world. It was a cruel deception to leave idolaters trapped in error, and it was an insult to God to allow them to approach mere creatures as divine. These two attitudes, one leading to quiet acceptance of religious diversity and the other encouraging active missionizing, both found support in the heritage of Israel's ethnic monotheism. Both found advocates among Jews (and Christians) of later centuries; both enjoy eloquent support even today (see "Monotheism Outside Israel?").

3

The Book and the People

THE PRECEDING CHAPTERS HAVE RELIED HEAVILY ON INFOR-
mation found in the Bible, but the Bible itself, the book now in our
hands, has not yet appeared in the story. What is the Bible? How did
Judaism and then Christianity come to be based on this book? What
does it mean for any religion to be based on a book? Other ancient
religions were not grounded in books at all; why did Judaism go
down a different path?

As before, it will help to begin with certain narratives. A report in 2
Kings 23 describes an incident that took place in Jerusalem during the
reign of King Josiah (640–609 BCE): in the course of a major renovation
of the Temple building, a book was found that caused a revolution in
the life of the nation (see "King Josiah's Book"). The book contained
(or was said to contain) teachings of Moses himself, the founder of
Israel's religion, and the people saw they had been living in violation of those teachings for untold generations. King Josiah set out to
enforce these previously unknown teachings and placed them at the
foundation of national life; for this act he was remembered as a king
who "returned to YHWH with all his heart and with all his soul and
with all his might, according to all the teaching of Moses; there was
never another like him" (2 Kings 23:25).[1]

No previous narrative in Scripture records such use of written
material. At an earlier time, King Hezekiah (died 686 BCE) had carried out a similar reform, and scripture gives him similar praise,[2] but
there is no hint that his efforts had been inspired by a scroll. Previous books of scripture make abstract reference to a written version
of Moses' teachings, but these may reflect later conceptions, from
the time after such books had begun to circulate. Josiah's reform is

KING JOSIAH'S BOOK

This is the story of King Josiah's religious revolution, grounded in a mysterious book of Instruction (Torah) discovered during renovation of the Temple. By comparing the agenda of the revolution with the contents of the Book of Deuteronomy, modern scholars have concluded that it was a version of that book that the priest Hilkiah brought to the king.

In the eighteenth year of King Josiah's reign, the king sent Shaphan ben Atzaliah ben Meshullam the scribe to YHWH's house, saying: "Go up to Hilkiah the high priest and have him add up the silver brought into YHWH's house which the gatekeepers have collected from the people. And let them give it to the workers who are assigned to YHWH's house, and let [the supervisors] give it to the workers in YWHW's house who are working to strengthen the building – the woodworkers and the builders and the stonecutters – to buy wood and hewn stone to strengthen the house. But do not keep an account with them of the money given into their hand, for they are working in faith."

And Hilkiah the high priest said to Shaphan the scribe, "I have found the Book of Instruction in YHWH's house," and Hilkiah gave the book to Shaphan, and he read it. And Shaphan the scribe came to the king and brought the king a report; he said, "Your servants have emptied out the money found in the house, and they have given it into the hand of the workers assigned to YHWH's house." And Shaphan the scribe told the king, saying, "Hilkiah the priest gave me a book," and Shaphan read it before the king.

And then, when the king had heard the words of the Book of Instruction, he tore his clothes. And the king commanded Hilkiah the priest, and Ahikam ben Shaphan, and Achbor ben Micha, and Shaphan the scribe, and Asaiah the king's servant, saying, "Go and inquire of YHWH on my behalf and on behalf of the people and on behalf of all Judah about the words of this book that has been found, for YHWH's wrath is great and has been kindled against us since our fathers did not listen to the words of this book to do all that has been written about us."

So Hilkiah the priest, and Ahikam and Achbor and Shaphan and Asaiah went to Huldah the prophetess, the wife of Shallum ben Tiqvah ben Harhas the keeper of the [royal] garments – she resided in Jerusalem, in the Second Quarter – and they spoke to her. She said to them, "Thus has YHWH, the

God of Israel, spoken: Say to the man who sent you to me, 'Thus said YHWH: Behold I am bringing evil onto this place and its inhabitants, all the words of the book which the King of Judah has read, because they abandoned me and offered incense to other gods so as to anger me with all the doing of their hands, so my anger has been kindled against this place and will not be extinguished.'" And as to the King of Judah who sent you to inquire of YHWH, you shall say to him as follows: "Thus says YHWH the God of Israel [concerning] the words that you heard: Since your heart softened and you submitted before YHWH when you heard what I spoke about this place and its inhabitants becoming a desolation and a curse, [since] you tore your garments and wept before me, I too have heard, says YHWH. Therefore, behold I shall gather you to your fathers and you will be gathered into their graves in peace; your eyes will not see all the evil that I am bringing onto this place." And they brought the matter back to the king.

So the king sent and they gathered to him all the elders of Judah and Jerusalem. The king went up to the house of YHWH, and all the men of Judah and all the inhabitants of Jerusalem with him – the priests and the prophets and all the people from small to great – and he read in their hearing all the words of the book of the covenant that was found in YHWH's house. And the king stood by the column and made the covenant before YHWH: to walk after YHWH and to keep his commandments and his testimonies and his enactments with all [his] heart and being, to fulfill the words of this covenant which are written in this book. And all the people stood [to join] the covenant.

And the king commanded Hilkiah the high priest and the secondary priests and the guardians of the threshold to remove from the shrine of YHWH all the vessels made for the Baal and the Ashera and all the host of heaven, so they burnt them outside Jerusalem, in the Kidron fields, and he carried their dust to Bethel. And he put an end to the "priests" whom the kings of Judah had installed to offer incense at the high places in the cities of Judah and around Jerusalem, to those who offered incense to the Baal and the sun and the moon and the constellations and all the host of heaven. And he moved the Ashera from the house of YHWH to outside Jerusalem, to the Kidron brook, and burnt it at the Kidron brook and ground it to dust, and cast its dust onto human graves. And he demolished the houses

KING JOSIAH'S BOOK (continued)

for the male prostitutes that were in YHWH's house, where the women would weave houses for the Ashera. He brought all the priests from the cities of Judah and defiled the high places where the priests had offered incense – from Geva to Beersheba – and he broke apart the high places at the gates at the entry of Joshua the prince of the city, at a man's left at the city gate. Indeed the priests of the high places did not go up to the altar or YHWH in Jerusalem, but they ate unleavened bread among their brethren. And he defiled the Tofet in the Valley of the Son(s) of Hinnom, so that a man could no longer put his son or daughter through the fire for Molech. And he stopped the horses which the kings of Judah had installed for the sun at the entrance to YHWH's house, in the chamber of the eunuch Nathan-melech in the (. . . ?), and he burned in fire the chariots of the sun. And the king demolished the altars on the roof of the upper-story of [King] Ahaz which the kings of Judah had made, and the altars which [King] Menasseh had made in the two courtyards of YHWH's house, and he had them carried off from there and he cast their dust into the Kidron brook. And the king defiled the high places facing Jerusalem to the right of Destroyer's Mountain which Solomon King of Israel had built for Ashtoret the detestation of the Sidonites and for Kemosh the detestation of Moab and for Milkom the abomination of the children of Ammon, and he shattered the ceremonial stones and he cut down the Asherim and he filled their places with human bones. And he also demolished the altar in Bethel, the high place [by] which Jeroboam ben Nebat had led Israel into sin; that altar too and the high place he demolished and burnt and ground into dust, and he burnt the Ashera.

. . . And the king commanded all the people, saying "Celebrate the Passover to YHWH your God, as is written in this book of the covenant," for no Passover like this one had been celebrated from the days of the judges who had judged Israel, and through all the days of the Kings of Israel and the Kings of Judah. For in the eighteenth year of King Josiah this Passover was celebrated to YHWH in Jerusalem . . . in order to fulfill the words of the Instruction written in the book that Hilkiah the Priest had found in the House of YHWH.

(2 Kings 22:3–23:24; but compare 2 Chronicles 30)

the earliest recorded historical situation in which such a book can be found.

Yet, no one in this narrative appears surprised that the teachings of Moses should have been written down. This may be a sign that written books of *Torah* ("Instruction") were already familiar, or perhaps it reflects a moment in Israel's history when the production of written sacred texts was suddenly a widespread activity: the first edition of the prophet Jeremiah's words was compiled just a few years later.[3] Modern readers can simply note that by the time the First Temple was destroyed, the people of Judah were familiar with the idea that Moses' teachings could be found in a book, and that they accepted the idea that the nation's life should be based on that document. Moreover, there is every reason to suppose that when the nation's leaders were carried off to exile in Babylon they brought Josiah's book with them, and also any other such writings that they could find. They would surely have wished to do this, and later developments would otherwise be very hard to explain.

*   *   *

In 539 BCE the city of Babylon was overrun by the Persians, and for the next two centuries the Persian Empire dominated the Near East. Scripture records that the victorious King Cyrus almost immediately allowed the exiles to return to Judah and rebuild their Temple, though it naturally was taken for granted that sovereign power would remain in his hands.[4] Led by the Temple priests, the people of Jerusalem and its surroundings began to rebuild the way of life that Nebuchadnezzar had nearly destroyed.

The next great turning point occurred during the seventh year of the Persian King Artaxerxes,[5] when a scribe of priestly ancestry named *Ezra* arrived in Jerusalem bearing a letter of royal appointment. The biblical text goes out of its way to emphasize Ezra's distinguished priestly descent, tracing his parentage generation by generation all the way back to Aaron, the brother of Moses and Israel's first high priest. In the same breath the text also identifies Ezra's other claims to distinction: he was a scribe "proficient in the Teaching [Heb., *Torah*] of Moses which YHWH the God of Israel had granted," and furthermore "the king had given him . . . everything he asked" (Ezra 7:6).

THE ORIGIN OF A PROPHETIC BOOK

The actual literary origins of most of the books of scripture cannot be recovered. Jeremiah, however, has left us a brief narrative of his own first attempt to collect his prophecies and publish them. In this narrative, the prophet instructs his secretary, Baruch, to assemble his orations (he does not say how they had been preserved) and deliver the book thus created to King Jehoiakim. The king, however, does not like what he hears when the book is read, and he burns it. As a result, Jeremiah must immediately begin the task of preparing a second, expanded edition, and that revised collection probably developed into the book now found in modern Bibles. It seems that in ancient times the collection circulated in several versions: most intriguingly, the Greek Bible offers much the same material as the Hebrew one, but in a strikingly different order. Scholars differ as to the historical process through which such differences arose.

In the fourth year of Jehoiakim ben Josiah King of Judah, this word came to Jeremiah from YHWH: "Take yourself a scroll and write on it all the words which I have spoken to you concerning Israel and Judah and all the nations, from the day that I [first] spoke to you, from the days of Josiah until today. Perhaps the house of Judah will hear all the evil that I am planning to do to them, in order that they turn each man from his evil path and I forgive their trespasses and their sins."

So Jeremiah called Baruch ben Neriah, and Baruch wrote onto the scroll at Jeremiah's dictation all YHWH's words which he had spoken. Then Jeremiah commanded Baruch, saying, "I am confined and cannot go to YHWH's house. You go, and read YHWH's words from the scroll which you wrote at my dictation in the hearing of the people at YHWH's house on a fast day; read them also in the hearing of all of Judah which will have come from their towns. Perhaps their plea will fall before YHWH and they will turn each man from his evil path, for the furious anger which YHWH has spoken concerning this people is very great." Baruch ben Neriah did everything that Jeremiah the prophet had commanded him, reading YHWH's words from the book at YHWH's house.

In the fifth year of Jehoiakim ben Josiah King of Judah, in the ninth month, the entire people in Jerusalem and the entire people coming to Jerusalem from the towns of Judah declared a fast, so Baruch read the scroll of Jeremiah's words in YHWH's house (in the chamber of Gemariah ben Shaphan the scribe in the upper courtyard, at the new gate of YHWH's house) in the hearing of all the people. And Michaihu ben Gemariah ben Shaphan heard all of YHWH's words from the scroll, and he went down to the king's house, to the scribe's chamber, where all the princes were sitting: Elishama the scribe, and Delaiah ben Shemaiah, and Elnathan ben Achbor, and Gemariah ben Shaphan, and Zedekiah ben Hananiah, and all the [other] princes. And Michaihu told them all the things he had heard when Baruch had read the scroll in the people's hearing.

All the princes sent Yehudi ben Nethaniah ben Shelemiah ben Cushi to Baruch, saying, "Take the scroll from which you read in the people's hearing in your hand and come," so Baruch ben Neriah took the scroll in his hand, and he came to them. They said to him, "Please sit down and read it in our hearing," so Baruch read to them. When they heard all these things each man expressed fear to his companion, and they said to Baruch, "We must tell the king all these things."

Then they asked Baruch, "Tell us please, how did you write these things at his dictation?" Baruch said to them, "He would recite these things to me out loud, and I would write them onto the scroll with ink."

The princes said to Baruch, "Go hide, you and Jeremiah; no man should know where you are." They went to the king in the court while they put the scroll in the chamber of Elishama the scribe; they told all these things to the king. The king sent Yehudi to take the scroll, so Yehudi took it from the chamber of Elishama the Scribe and he read it in the hearing of the king and the hearing of all the princes standing beside the king. The king was sitting in the winter house in the ninth month, and a brazier was burning in front of him. So every time Yehudi would read three or four columns [the king] would tear them off with a scribe's razor and throw them into the fire on the brazier, until the entire scroll had been consumed in the fire on the brazier. The king and his servants who heard all these words showed no fear, nor did they tear their clothing; Elnathan and Delaiah and Gemariah entreated the king not to burn the scroll, but he did not listen to them. The king commanded Yerahme'el the king's son and Seraia ben Azriel and Shelemiah ben Avde'el to capture Baruch the scribe and Jeremiah the prophet, but YHWH hid them.

After the king had burned the scroll with the words that Baruch had written at Jeremiah's dictation, YHWH's word came to Jeremiah, saying: "Take yourself another scroll, and write on it all the original words that were on the first scroll that Jehoiakim King of Judah burned. And as for

THE ORIGIN OF A PROPHETIC BOOK (continued)

Jehoiakim King of Judah say, 'Thus says YHWH: You burned this scroll, saying, "Why have you written in it that the King of Babylon will surely come and destroy this land, causing man and beast to come to an end in it?"' ...

So Jeremiah took another scroll and gave it to Baruch ben Neriah the scribe, and he wrote on it at Jeremiah's dictation all the words of the scroll that Jehoiakim King of Judah had burned in fire; and he added to them many more words like those.

(Jeremiah 36:1–29, 32)

SCRIBES

Strictly speaking, the word *scribe* designates someone who can write, a rare skill in the ancient world. The earliest examples of writing that have survived tend to reflect certain specific environments, chiefly those of temples and royal bureaucracies: in both of those settings the official scribe was an important personage.

In the course of time, scribes became an important professional group even among ordinary people. They prepared personal correspondence and various legal documents (certificates of sale or gift, marriage and divorce papers, acknowledgments of debt, etc.) for persons who could not write these for themselves, and over time these early professionals developed a large body of legal expertise. Soon even people who might have prepared their own documents relied on scribes instead; scribes knew the proper wording of such materials and supplied a product that could withstand official scrutiny. By virtue of their ability to write, scribes thus became the main carriers of legal expertise in the ancient Near East.

One way to guarantee the acceptability of a particular document is to make it similar (or identical) to others that have already been accepted by authoritative officials; this consideration tends to produce uniformity in the formulation of such materials, and thus also in the legal conceptions that underlie them. Archeologists of the ancient Near East have found remarkable stability in the wording of legal documents from widely separated locations over a period stretching more than 1,000 years. Scribes knew how things were done, and scribes did them the same way for a very long time.

The Bible reflects important aspects of ancient scribal culture. Of course, the very existence of ancient books is due to scribal activity. In addition, however, biblical law (and to some extent even later rabbinic law) stands firmly in the international legal heritage of Near Eastern scribes. Judean legal documents from the early centuries CE that have been discovered by archeologists similarly reflect the standard scribal formulations of Hellenistic and imperial Roman law.

The scriptural Book of Kings depicts royal scribes as high officials. The scribe Shaphan, who helped to publish the Book of Moses in the days of King Josiah, was no mere secretary, just as the secretaries who form an American president's cabinet are no mere clerks. The same can be said of Shaphan's son Gemariah, or Elishama "the Scribe," or Baruch ben Neriah, who was secretary to the prophet Jeremiah; these men helped Jeremiah prepare the first collected edition of his prophecies, and they were all important figures in the public life of their time (see "The Origin of a Prophetic Book").

This combination of impeccable lineage, religious book learning, and royal support enabled Ezra to carry out a revolution in the nation's life.[6]

Two biblical passages shed light on the nature of that revolution. Ezra 7:12–16 provides a copy of the royal letter that Ezra carried (see "The Torah Comes to *Yehud*"). It is impossible, of course, to verify the accuracy or even the authenticity of this document, but most scholars have accepted the letter as genuine, and it warrants attention here. The letter recognizes Ezra's expertise in "the law of the god of Heaven" and grants him wide authority over the territory of Yehud (the official Persian name of the district) on the basis of that expertise. How did the king[7] come to hear of Ezra in the first place, and why did the king suppose that expertise in this law should be a prerequisite for Jewish leadership? The text answers neither question, but it appears that high-ranking members of the exiled Judahite community in Babylon[8] had access to powerful royal officials and brought Ezra to their attention. Such well-connected exiles from Judah must

THE TORAH COMES TO *YEHUD*

The following documents, both discussed in the text, shed great light on the process by which the Torah book came to be the legal foundation of the Yehud settlement. The first presents the letter of appointment from King Artaxerxes that put Ezra, with his book, in charge of the district. The second tells the story of Ezra's first presentation of the Torah to the people in Jerusalem. It frankly describes their shock at hearing rules they had never learned, and it concludes by describing a celebration of the Festival of Booths, a rite previously unknown to them, almost for the first time since the Exodus from Egypt.

I. The King's Letter

Artaxerxes king of kings to Ezra the priest, scribe of the law of the god of heaven.... I have commanded that anyone in my kingdom from the people Israel and its priests and Levites who offers to go with you to Jerusalem may go. For you are appointed by the king and his seven counselors to inspect Yehud and Jerusalem according to the law of your god which is in your hand, and to deliver silver and gold which the king and his counselors have contributed to the god of Israel whose dwelling is in Jerusalem, and [also] any silver and gold which you find anywhere in the province of Babylon through the contribution of the people or the priests, which they contribute to the house of their god which is in Jerusalem. With this money, therefore, you shall without fail purchase bulls, rams, lambs, and their [associated] flour-offerings and their drink-offerings, and you shall offer them on the altar which is in the house of your god in Jerusalem. With the remaining silver and gold, you and your brethren may do whatever seems good: act according to the will of your god. Vessels given to you for the service of your god's house are to be delivered before the god of Jerusalem. The remaining needs of your god's house which you must provide can be given from the king's treasury.

I, King Artaxerxes, have commanded all the treasurers that are [in the province] Across the [Euphrates] River that "whatever Ezra the priest, scribe of the law of the god of Heaven, asks of you must quickly be done, up to one hundred talents of silver or one hundred *kor*s of wheat or one hundred *bath*s of wine or one hundred *bath*s of oil or salt without written [requisition or limit]. Anything commanded by the god of Heaven must be performed diligently for the house of the god of Heaven, for why should

[God's] anger fall on the king's realm or his sons? And you should be aware that no tax of any kind may be levied upon any of the priests or the Levites or the singers or the gatekeepers or the Temple-servants or the [other] servants of the house of this god."

And you, Ezra, by the wisdom of your god that is in your hand appoint judges and magistrates who will judge the whole people in Beyond the River, all who know the laws of your god; those who do not know you shall teach. Whoever does not practice the law of your god and the law of the king must without fail be taken to judgment, whether by death or by banishment [?] or loss of property or imprisonment.

(Ezra 7:12–26)

II. The Assembly in Jerusalem

When the seventh month arrived...the entire people gathered as one man in the open plaza facing the Water Gate, and they told Ezra the scribe to bring the scroll of the Teaching of Moses [by] which YHWH had commanded Israel. So Ezra the priest brought the Teaching before the congregation, man and woman, anyone who could listen and understand, on the first day of the seventh month. He read from it, in front of the open plaza that faced the Water Gate, from dawn until midday, opposite the men and the women and those who could understand, and all the people's ears were [directed] to the scroll of the Teaching. Ezra the scribe stood on a wooden tower that they had made for this....And Ezra opened the scroll in sight of all the people (for he was higher than all the people), and when he opened it all the people arose; and Ezra blessed YHWH the great God, and all the people responded "Amen, Amen" while they raised their hands and bowed, prostrating themselves with their faces to the ground before YHWH....

Nehemiah and Ezra the priestly scribe and the Levites who were explaining to the people said to all the people, "Today is holy to YHWH your God [see Leviticus 23:24, Numbers 29:1]; do not mourn and do not weep," for all the people wept when they heard the words of the Teaching. And he said to them, "Go, eat delicacies and drink sweets, send portions to anyone who has nothing prepared, for today is holy to our Lord; do not grow sad, for joy in YHWH is your strength." ... So all the people went to eat and drink and send portions and to make great rejoicing, for they understood what had been made known to them.

THE TORAH COMES TO *YEHUD* (continued)

On the second day, the heads of the family groups of all the people and the priests and the Levites gathered to Ezra the scribe to ponder the words of the Teaching. They found written in the Teaching that YHWH had commanded by the hand of Moses that the children of Israel should live in booths during the festival of the seventh month, and that they should announce and spread the word in all their towns and in Jerusalem: "Go out to the mountains and bring [branches with] olive leaves and oilwood [?] and myrtle and palms and thickwood [?], to make booths as it is written" [compare Leviticus 23:40].

So the people went out and brought them, and they made themselves booths, each man on his roof or in their courtyards and in the courtyards of the house of God and in the plaza facing the Water Gate and in the plaza of the Ephraim Gate. So the entire congregation of those returning from the Exile made booths and dwelt in them, for the Children of Israel had not done so from the days of Jeshua bin Nun until that day: and there was very great rejoicing.

And he read in the Book of God's Teaching every day from the first day until the last; they celebrated the festival for seven days, and on the eighth day a closing festival, as ordained.

(Nehemiah 7:72–8:18; compare Leviticus 23:33–43)

themselves have believed that Ezra's scribal expertise was important to the well-being of the home community in Jerusalem, and they managed to obtain for Ezra a royal appointment to govern their homeland.

Being a scribe, Ezra naturally possessed a written copy of "the law of the god of Heaven," and when he arrived in Jerusalem to assume his office he arranged a public reading of that law (Figure 2). Another biblical passage (Nehemiah 7:72–8:18) describes that event (again, see "The Torah Comes to *Yehud*"). In later generations, religious tradition affirmed that Ezra's book was a scroll of the Torah, the same *Pentateuch* (a Greek word meaning "Five Books") now revered as containing the teachings of Moses and the word of God, but modern scholars are not convinced that this was so. The actual contents of Ezra's scroll remain unclear. Did the text contain only ceremonial instructions, and perhaps other rules and regulations, or also the vast narrative beginning of the Pentateuch that stretches

2. Ezra (or Moses?) reading from a scroll. A wall painting from the third-century CE synagogue at Dura-Europus in Syria, at the frontier of the Roman Empire. See Chapter 10 for more on this important site. (Photo courtesy of Art Resources, New York)

from the Creation through the Exodus to the revelation at Sinai, a book and a half out of the five? The present text does not say. In the chapter that follows the story of Ezra's public reading,[9] Nehemiah addresses the crowd and provides a summary of that great narrative, but many important elements of the story are omitted, and in any case, Nehemiah is not described as *reading* that account.

Moreover, were the rules even the same as those found later on? The narrative makes clear reference to the New Year festival (*Rosh ha-Shanah*) at the beginning of the seventh month and to the Feast of Booths (*Sukkot*) two weeks later, and it seems to cite Leviticus 23 when it describes the festival huts, but it entirely skips over the Day of Atonement (*Yom ha-Kippurim* or Yom Kippur), mentioned in the same chapter of Leviticus as falling between those holy days.[10] Does this mean that Ezra's scroll as yet contained no reference to this day, later the holiest of the Jewish year? Scripture contains no hint that Ezra's community observed Yom Kippur, though it is always possible that the narrator simply felt no need to include that detail in his story.

Just as the text does not describe what Ezra's scroll contained, it does not say how he obtained it. Later religious tradition maintained that small groups of learned and pious men had carefully preserved the sacred text since the days of Moses himself, but both Josiah and Ezra read their texts to people who were clearly unfamiliar with them. Tradition explained the shocked reaction of these audiences by saying that the masses had lost their knowledge of the teachings of Moses; on this view, it was Ezra's task to reintroduce the Torah to the people at large and to establish its rules as the official law of *Yehud*.

Many modern students, however, offer a different scenario. The Judahites who were taken into the Babylonian Exile were drawn from the upper levels of preexilic society.[11] In Babylon, these uprooted leaders worked to maintain their traditional way of life, and they looked for means of assisting this effort. One such means was to stress uniquely Israelite customs such as observance of the Sabbath every seventh day; this complete withdrawal from all economic activity was later recognized as a distinctive mark of Jewish identity, and it appears to have gained significance in the early postexilic age.[12] Another basic procedure would have been to assemble all the "teachings of Moses" (that is, the religious heritage of Israel) in a book that might then be distributed to the growing Jewish Diaspora in Babylonia and elsewhere. The great achievement of Ezra and those working with him was to take this book and make it the official law of the nation's ancient homeland.

Ezra himself emerged from high-ranking priestly-scribal circles, and it seems plausible (though it cannot be proved) that the book was produced in those same circles. There is no record of the stages of their work, but it can be surmised that they began by collecting all available written records from preexilic Judah: Josiah's book was such a document, as was the first edition of Jeremiah's prophecies, produced in the prophet's own lifetime.[13] Organizing all such materials into a kind of sacred library, they produced early versions of many books now found in the Bible. Where possible, they expanded these written materials by condensing oral traditions that had circulated for generations, setting these too in writing, and adding the new documents to the collection. Such traditions concerned both narrative and law, and much of this heritage found its way into the emerging Torah book as well, in the elaborate narratives of the Book of Genesis and in the detailed rules of purity and sacrificial ritual that are found in Leviticus and elsewhere. Most such lore, even in its unwritten form, had long been traced back to Moses, so it was only natural to ascribe the new, comprehensive document to him as well.

Thus Ezra brought Jewish life to rest on a book that derived its authority (as Ezra derived his own authority) from a decree of the king of Persia. Ezra and his associates no doubt saw the king as a mere pawn in God's plan for maintaining his covenant with Israel, but the power behind the book was the power of the Persian army, and the administration of the newly instituted law rested on a framework of Persian royal officials. This was a fateful combination. As long as both sides were content with the arrangement, the pious could disregard the foreign basis of their new government, while the king's officials, for their part, could pay no heed to their subjects' religious interests. Centuries later, however, when this agreement broke down, the result was persecution and war.[14]

* * *

Once God's instructions were found in a book, new religious practices and new types of religious leadership began to emerge. Ezra's own career illustrates this process. Ezra's initial presentation of the Torah took the form of an elaborate public ceremony: the scroll was read out to the people from a specially constructed platform, while Levite teachers explained the unfamiliar text to the assembled audience. The next day, however, a different kind of session took place. Now only "the heads of the family groups of all the people and the priests and the Levites" gathered together. Only a smaller group of community leaders sat down, with a more practical purpose in mind: "to ponder the words of the Teaching" and put these previously unknown rules into practice.[15] Knowledge of the book was now the essential preliminary to correcting the people's errors, and skill at explaining the book now became an important feature of leadership. The book could now both unify and divide them: all Jews everywhere could now revere the same sacred text, but dispute over interpretation could now lead to struggle for power. Those who could gain a hearing for their explanation of the Torah or, even better, those who could put their interpretation into practice, whether through force or conviction, became by that very fact the leaders of the Jewish people.

Of course, this outcome took centuries to emerge. There is no record of the Torah book in other parts of the Jewish world at this early date.[16] Since Ezra had carried the book from Babylon it was presumably known there, but scripture says nothing about its distribution or its authority among Babylonian Jews or indicates whether interpretations of the Torah differed from place to place at that early time;[17] no one even knows who was in charge of deciding such things. Whatever the process, however, the outcome is clear: book learning steadily gained in prestige and authority, and interpretive skill became the gateway to power and influence. Centuries later, a new model of rabbinic leadership would stand on this foundation.

* * *

It is instructive to compare Ezra's career with that of his contemporary, Nehemiah ben Hacaliah. Nehemiah was neither a priest nor a scribe: rather, he was the king's cupbearer, a high-ranking domestic servant (eunuch?) in the royal household. But this was no lowly task: what appears a minor assignment was actually a powerful office, because Nehemiah had daily access to the king, and he must have come from a distinguished Judahite family to have obtained such a post. When news reached him from his brother that the ancient holy city "lay in ruins, with its gates consumed by fire" (Nehemiah 2:3), all he had to do was ask the king to appoint him governor of *Yehud* with

INTERPRETATION WITHIN THE BIBLE

It has already been mentioned that the Bible is actually a collection of separate books written over a period of almost 1,000 years. It would not be surprising that later biblical writings sometimes interpret older materials in that same collection, and so indeed they do. Here are a few examples, two from the realm of ritual law and three (summarized more briefly) from the realm of religious thought.

1

In connection with the annual sacrifice of the Passover lamb, Exodus 12:9 contains a very clear instruction: *Do not eat it raw, or cooked in water, but roasted ... over the fire.*

The Hebrew word that designates the forbidden means of preparation ("cooked") comes from the root *b-sh-l*. However, in another treatment of the same matter, Deuteronomy 16:7 offers an equally matter-of-fact instruction: *You must cook [b-sh-l] and eat it in the place that YHWH your God will choose; and then in the morning you may turn toward home.* The same action that is forbidden in Exodus is simply taken for granted in Deuteronomy!

In later generations, people naturally wondered how the Torah really wanted them to proceed. In the last book of the Bible, 2 Chronicles 35:13 provides the following detail in describing King Josiah's Passover (see "King Josiah's Book"): *They cooked [b-sh-l] the Passover sacrifice over fire, according to the statute.* Of course, the statute seems to say the opposite, namely, that "cooking" is done with water and "roasting" is done over a fire. But the author of Chronicles was aware of the tension between the two Torah passages and added a quiet reassurance to his readers that a proper reconciliation of the conflicting texts had been achieved.

2

It appears that Ezra's contemporaries interpreted Leviticus 23:40–42 as an instruction concerning the construction of festival booths (see "The Torah Comes to *Yehud*"). In their view, such booths had to be built out of the materials listed in verse 40, and Nehemiah 8:15–16 reports that the people duly went out into the hills, collected the prescribed species of greenery, and built their festive huts. The author of the later Nehemiah text does not quote Leviticus but offers a paraphrase in which his identification of the required species is simply provided as the plain meaning of the earlier text.

This would all be unremarkable, except that later Jewish tradition interpreted those same Mosaic verses differently, as two separate instructions: the prescribed species were to be carried in special festive processions, but the booths could be constructed out of almost anything. In addition, while some of the species named in Leviticus and Nehemiah cannot be identified with confidence, it appears that later tradition identified the prescribed species differently than the interpreters in Ezra's time.

The scriptural text clearly indicates that Ezra's associates "gathered to Ezra the scribe to ponder the words of the Teaching," that is to say, they studied the text before them and worked out an accepted interpretation. The text does not describe the interpretive methods they used or the process by which they reached their conclusions. Later talmudic literature contains explicit exegeses of the relevant passages in Leviticus, but also does not explain why (or when, or by whom) the normative interpretation was first worked out or why (or when or by whom) it was finally accepted.

3

Genesis 32:24–32 tells the famous story of the patriarch Jacob wrestling with an unidentified man throughout the night. Jacob emerges lame from this mysterious encounter, and at dawn the man changes Jacob's name to Israel but refuses to reveal his own. Later interpreters took for granted that the "man," whom the text clearly identifies as such (*ish*), was in fact an angel. Why else was he so desperate to be gone before dawn? Why else refuse to tell his name? Who else would have the arrogance to change another man's name? Of course, there are possible answers to these questions, but the fact remains that Jacob's antagonist had been seen as an angel since very early times.

When the prophet Hosea alludes to this story (12:4), he simply takes for granted that Jacob's antagonist was an angel (*mal'ach*); the interpretive switch had already taken place before the Babylonian Exile!

4

The last chapter of the Book of Samuel (2 Samuel 24) tells a strange story of God's fury at King David after the Israelite ruler had ordered a census of his fighting troops. It is not strange that God should be angry at David for having wished this: the people of Israel had long believed that counting the folk was an affront to God and should be avoided, for had God not promised Abraham that his descendants would be as countless as the stars (Genesis 15:5), and had not Moses, when he wished to count the people in the desert, instructed each to bring payment of half a shekel and then counted the money instead (Exodus 30:11–16)? The surprising part is this: David took the census in the first place because he had been instructed to do so by God. *God was already angry at the people of Israel* (the reader is not told why) *and wanted a pretext to punish them*!

However, when this story is retold in the later Book of Chronicles (see Chapter 1, "What Is in the Bible?"), an almost verbatim repetition of the narrative differs in one crucial detail: it is not God who incites David to his foolish deed, it is Satan (2 Chronicles 21:1). Once again the reader gets no explanation as to why Satan should have done so, but the act is no longer surprising: Satan can be expected to cause trouble in this way. Through a subtle interpretive adjustment, the justice of God has been protected from challenge.

5

A striking example of explicit reinterpretation within the Bible itself can be found at Daniel 9:2, where the pious Daniel reports that he has been studying the prophet Jeremiah's prediction (25:11–12; 29:10) that Jerusalem would lie in ruins for seventy years and then be rebuilt. By the time the Book of Daniel was written (see Chapter 4), far more than seventy years had passed since the destruction of 586 BCE and the city was once more under oppressive foreign rule; the righteous of those days must have been asking how this could be: where was God's promise to the prophet now? At this key moment, the angel Gabriel comes to Daniel and explains to him that the prophet had really meant to speak of seventy *weeks* of years, that is to say, not 70 years but 490 (see Daniel 9:24). Through this remarkable act of reinterpretation, the pious of later years were spared the agonizing prospect that Jeremiah's word had gone unfulfilled.

authority (and provisions) to rebuild it. The king readily granted the request, and Nehemiah promptly set out.

Once in Jerusalem, Nehemiah appears to have carried out a program based on Ezra's lawbook.[18] On the day Jerusalem's rebuilt walls were dedicated, in a scene reminiscent of events in King Josiah's time, the ceremony included a public reading from the "Book of Moses." When laws excluding certain foreigners from "the congregation of God" were "found written there," foreigners were expelled from the community. Observance of the Sabbath was enforced, the Temple and the priestly tithes were regulated, marriages with foreign women were forcibly dissolved, and the women with their children were sent away.[19] Marriage to foreign women was Ezra's concern as well.[20] Many of these policies provoked the resistance of the populace. With respect to marriage in particular, the norm before the exile had been that full wives took on the legal status of their husbands (see Chapter 1), so the campaign of Ezra and Nehemiah to end mixed marriages must have struck the affected families as wildly radical.

Ezra and Nehemiah between them accomplished a double revolution. The prophets' opponents were dealt a ruinous blow. For hundreds of years, Israel's prophets had insisted that Israel revere only one God, but the masses of Israel, often under royal sponsorship, had kept on worshiping many. Derided or ignored, the prophets had won many battles but had never managed to win the war; even the great Jeremiah, at the end of his career, faced an audience who emphatically refused his appeal.[21] When the leadership of the nation was carried off, with the prophets among them, many must have been glad to see them go. The people left behind could go on worshiping YHWH and the deities of nature alongside him, just as their ancestors had done for generations, without having to face these fanatical "men of God" with their extravagant demands.

But now, by order of the king of Persia, a book containing the teachings of Moses, the greatest prophet of them all, had been declared the law of the land. To worship other gods now was to violate "the law of God and the law of the king." Resistance continued; Nehemiah had to fight his contemporaries, high-ranking priests among them, over one issue after another. But he won every battle, because power was now on his side.[22] People might go on complaining that the Torah's one-God policy was foolish or oppressive, but Jewish reverence for other gods could not long survive.

What was more, all these changes could be grounded in the Book of the Teaching of Moses: the other revolution was that the prophets' victory was enshrined in a *book*. King Josiah had proceeded differently; once Josiah had determined to carry out his reform, he had no further need for the book. The book inspired and lent weight to his royal authority, but he was the king, and he could have proceeded in any case. Ezra, on the other hand, had no authority at all beyond the book; even in his letter of royal appointment, his sole charge was to establish the book as the law of the territory and ensure that its instructions were obeyed. Ezra himself would soon be gone, but the power to command now issued from the scroll of Moses' teaching, and that scroll would exist long after he had passed from the scene.

Book in hand, migrating Jews could now carry the sacred center of their religion wherever they traveled. The Torah forbade construction of a Temple outside Jerusalem, but there was no limit on making copies of the Torah book itself. Prophecy was dying out, but every community could have its own scholars and scribes, every community could teach the book to its children, every community could study the book – without outside guidance if necessary – and apply its teachings as local residents (or their leaders) saw fit. Thanks to the book, Judaism became a religion that could travel to the ends of the earth, a religion that no foreign power could threaten by laying waste to a building.

In the course of time, Jewish life became inconceivable without the Torah. Earlier generations had brought their questions to the local priest or prophet,[23] but now the law of God could be "found written" in the Book, and now the scribe, not the prophet, would help the people determine the will of God. New, disruptive prophecies were neither required nor desired: the Torah of Moses was now enshrined in fixed, eternal form, to be read with care by all generations to come.

* * *

Alexander the Great conquered the Near East in a rapid campaign from 333 to 331 BCE. The conqueror died very young, but not before he had founded a city in Egypt that bore his name and became the royal capital of the dynasty of the *Ptolemies*. Alexandria grew into the largest, wealthiest, and most splendid city in the world, and Jews lived in Alexandria from its earliest days. Some were attracted from nearby Judaea by the kings' inducements to newcomers to help build the new capital; others were brought there as slaves but eventually were freed.

Around the year 250 BCE, in Alexandria, the Torah was translated into Greek. Many explanations have been proposed for this momentous project. Perhaps King Ptolemy wanted a copy of every known book in the Library he was assembling, or perhaps he needed a reference copy of the laws by which his Judaean subjects (Judaea was under Ptolemaic rule) were being allowed to live. The Jews themselves, however, told a different and quite remarkable story. Later generations recounted that the translation was carried out by thirty-five (or thirty-six) pairs of scholars; in later times the translation was called *Septuagint*, after the Latin word for "seventy." It was said that these teams were carefully isolated from one another, so none could see the work of the others; nevertheless, the people remembered that when the finished translations were compared they were identical, down to the last word, and such a remarkable outcome would surely have been impossible without God's own intervention.[24]

This story communicates the Alexandrian Jews' deep conviction that their Greek version of the Torah was a revelation from God, no less so than the Hebrew version from which it had been prepared. This feeling gave rise to an annual festival at Alexandria to celebrate the translation's publication; to the Greek-speaking Jews of the Hellenistic world, the giving of the Septuagint was a mark of God's generous love, no less extraordinary than the original revelation at Sinai.[25]

* * *

Persian rule over *Yehud* continued for another century after Nehemiah's career as governor, but very little is known about this long period of time. Ezra's establishment of the Torah as the law of *Yehud* apparently went unchallenged, and the succession of high priests apparently continued in orderly fashion, but no specific events are recorded for this interval, and any gradual developments in the life of the region are lost in the general lack of documentation.

One intriguing episode, however, did unfold in a far corner of the Persian Empire at Elephantine, on an island in the Upper Nile Valley, a military outpost of Jews who had been settled for some time. These Jewish soldiers were charged with protecting the Egyptian frontier from invasion out of the African heartland, and they had held this responsibility for a substantial period, each generation inheriting the task from the one before. For a long time, it seems, the local Egyptian population tolerated this alien military presence in their midst; these foreigners were, after all, protecting their homeland. In the late fifth century, however, these same Jewish soldiers were serving the interests of the Persian Empire, a foreign occupier.

Not much is known about the lives of these Jewish soldier-settlers, but one remarkable fact is clear: the Jews of Elephantine maintained the only known Jewish temple in the world at this time outside the Holy Land. Here the Jewish God, apparently called Yahu, was honored through familiar sacrificial rites, a situation that surely pleased the local Jews greatly but also greatly irritated the local priests of the Egyptian god Khnum: the temple of Khnum, otherwise the main temple on the island, felt intense pressure from this competitor from abroad. To make matters even worse in natives' eyes, these Jews' annual Passover festival cast the local environment of Elephantine (that is, Egypt) in a very bad light, and this festival was also notoriously marked by the slaughter of lambs, an animal considered sacred to Khnum.

Around 419 BCE, a letter from higher authorities ordered the local Persian officials to protect the Jews from interference as they celebrated their feast; the document does not say what was happening to make such a letter necessary or what the Jews had to do to obtain this protection, but clearly tensions were in the air. A few years later, the Jewish temple at Elephantine was altogether destroyed, apparently at the instigation of the priests of Khnum; after several years, during which appeals for help to the Jerusalem priesthood went unanswered, the sacrifices at Elephantine were partially restored,[26] but soon the rebuilt temple was again demolished, this time, it seems, for good.

Several features of this episode deserve comment. There is no sign that the Jews of Elephantine and their priestly leaders possessed copies of the Torah or even knew that such a book existed. The surviving correspondence between them and the authorities in Jerusalem never quotes or even mentions a sacred text, and the Jews of Elephantine practiced a way of life that actually disobeyed the Torah in important ways. The very existence of a temple outside "the place which YHWH had chosen"[27] violated a key requirement of the Book of Deuteronomy and undid the reforms which King Josiah had undertaken centuries earlier. Were the Jews of Elephantine unaware of those reforms because their ancestors had arrived in Egypt even before Josiah's time? That is possible, perhaps even likely, though no biblical writer shows awareness of their presence there. Did they simply presume that those reforms had been nullified by the Babylonian conquest? That too is possible. Did they believe Deuteronomy banned outside shrines only in the Holy Land, an interpretation that left them free in Egypt to do as they saw fit? Even that is possible: many Jewish schools of interpretation have limited the application of various Torah rules to the Jewish homeland in Palestine.[28]

Another element of the Elephantine Jews' religion would strike most modern readers as even more shocking: the Jewish god, here named Yahu, shared his Egyptian shrine with two female deities, Ashambethel and Anathbethel. Such associations of YHWH with other deities had been common in preexilic Israel, and here, in an isolated corner of the world, old patterns endured long after they had more or less disappeared in the homeland. No surviving record indicates whether the Elephantine Jews knew that others would have found this practice scandalous or how they would have justified it.

In short, the religion of the Elephantine Jews (can one even call it Judaism?) was nothing like the religion that the Book of the Teaching of Moses would have led readers to expect. And yet, these people were eager to celebrate Passover in the correct manner and invoked the Persian authorities' aid when the local population tried to interfere. They saw themselves as servants of Israel's god, they saw the people of Jerusalem as their cousins, and they saw the holy city as their ancestral capital and a source of religious guidance.

As the Jews of Elephantine struggled for permission to rebuild their destroyed temple, they tried to enlist the support of those cousins, but it appears that the Jerusalem priesthood was not very eager to help. At first, they made no response at all, so that three years later, when the people of Elephantine tried again, the petition went not only to Jerusalem but also to the leading family of Samaria. When finally the worship of Yahu was indeed renewed, the restoration was only partial: incense and vegetable offerings were permitted, but not the sacrifice of animals. Why were the Jerusalem priests so reluctant to support their fellow Jews, and why did the restoration remain incomplete? A likely answer is that the Torah was already known

THE SAMARITANS

In 722 BCE the Assyrians conquered the Kingdom of Israel and put an end to its sovereignty. According to the narrative in 2 Kings 17, the inhabitants of the land were carried off to Assyrian exile, and the Assyrians imported "people from Babylon, Cuthah, Avva, Hamath, and Sefarvaim" (17:24), similarly uprooted from their native lands, and settled them in the now-empty countryside of Samaria. The narrative goes on to report that the devastated country was overrun by lions, and this made the new residents afraid that they had angered YHWH, the god of the land, by worshiping him incorrectly. The king of Assyria ordered that a few of the exiled Israelite priests be returned to their homes to teach the newcomers "how to fear YHWH" (17:28), but the newcomers continued to serve their ancestral gods as well.

That is the Bible's dismissive, hostile account of the Samaritans. Clearly written from a rival Judahite viewpoint, this narrative depicts them as foreigners who were settled in the Promised Land by a foreign conqueror. Practicing a debased form of YHWH worship, they could not or would not abandon the idol worship they had brought with them from their countries of origin.

Centuries later, the Samaritans continued to maintain a distinctive religious identity. Samaria lies to the north of the Judaean heartland, and its inhabitants developed an alternative religious heritage, perhaps reflecting the customs of the northern tribes, just as Judaism reflected the heritage of the southern Kingdom of Judah. Relations between Judaeans and Samaritans were often tense or even hostile. In the days of Nehemiah, a son of the Jerusalem high priest was married to the daughter of the Samaritan leader, but Nehemiah expelled him from Jerusalem (Nehemiah 13:28), an act that sealed the bad relations between the two communities.

For much of the early Hellenistic period the Samaritans maintained a temple on Mount Gerizim, near modern Nablus (biblical Shechem), and they developed a version of the Torah in which all the implied references to Jerusalem (especially in Deuteronomy) were subtly reworded and applied to their shrine instead. Built shortly after the time of Alexander the Great, the Samaritan temple was destroyed by the Hasmonaean high priest Hyrcanus I; he claimed to be acting in retaliation for Samaritan cooperation with the hellenization program of Antiochus IV (see Chapter 4), but he was surely also motivated by the ancestral hostility between the two communities. The famous Gospel story of the good Samaritan (Luke 10:30–37) reflects

THE SAMARITANS (continued)

this hostility as well: nothing was more shocking to Judaean hearers than the idea of a Samaritan more virtuous than themselves. Under the Roman occupation, Samaria became a hostile buffer zone between the two Jewish districts of Judaea and Galilee. Pilgrims and others traveling between Galilee and Jerusalem were in constant danger of harassment and worse.

In later antiquity, Samaritan religion continued to resemble Judaism while remaining distinct from it. The Samaritans accepted the Pentateuch (but only the Pentateuch) as holy, though in a slightly different version, as already noted. The general rabbinic attitude toward them was that Samaritans can be trusted to follow only certain rules of the Torah, but to follow those rules with scrupulous care; it is difficult to know whether this was an outsiders' fantasy or an accurate description of Samaritan behavior.

The once-extensive Samaritan diaspora has almost entirely disappeared, but a modest Samaritan community continues to exist in modern Israel and the West Bank. The Samaritans honor their own line of priests and continue to recognize Gerizim as a holy mountain; at Passover time they continue to sacrifice a lamb (or goat) there.

in Judaea, and the leaders there were unhappy about supporting a flagrant violation of the Book's instructions. Another consideration, however, is that the Jerusalem priesthood was not unhappy to see a competitor go out of business. It is extremely improbable that Jews from elsewhere took the long journey to southern Egypt in order to worship at Elephantine, but perhaps the priests of Jerusalem thought that pilgrims from far away might be more willing to visit the homeland if no local shrine were available. The reduced worship that was finally allowed may represent a compromise: the Jerusalem leadership was ready to accept such activities at an alternative sanctuary but would not agree to support full restoration of a shrine apart from their own. Jewish solidarity on some matters did not always mean solidarity on everything.

Apart from the Elephantine correspondence, almost no documentary evidence survives from the time that Persia governed the Near East. After Ezra and Nehemiah were gone, *Yehud* apparently remained pretty much as those reformers had left it: the Torah book was the authoritative code, and the high priests in hereditary

succession were in charge of interpreting it. This arrangement continued to rest on royal authority, but later Persian kings did not intervene
in Jewish life. The Torah's insistence on strict separation from neighboring peoples and their customs continued to provoke resentment,
and probably some quiet resistance, from both leadership elements
and ordinary people in their private lives, but the situation appeared
stable, and no significant changes can be documented.

4

Crisis and a New Beginning

THE PERSIANS GOVERNED THE NEAR EAST FOR ALMOST EXACTLY 200 years: they conquered Babylon in 539 BCE, and they held power until a rapid series of spectacular defeats at the hands of Alexander the Great, King of Macedonia, from 333 to 331 BCE. After that, the Greek language and varieties of Greek culture dominated the eastern Mediterranean for almost 1,000 years, until the equally spectacular arrival of the Arabs and Islam in the seventh century CE.

Alexander kept the Persian system of dividing his kingdom into regions or satrapies and placing a trusted subordinate in charge of each; once active warfare had ended, many of his generals were appointed to these positions. He did take steps to implant Greek culture throughout the kingdom – he established settlements of active or retired soldiers in key locations, and he encouraged (or forced) his officers to marry high-ranking native women – but he may have been more concerned with maintaining stability and control than with starting a cultural revolution.

King Alexander made no move to interfere with the inner life of the Jewish (or any other) population now under his rule, but he did encourage large-scale immigration to the new city of Alexandria in Egypt. This new city soon became a royal capital, the largest city in the Greek world, home to the largest Jewish community anywhere. Here and elsewhere a Greek-speaking Judaism developed, flourished, and then almost completely disappeared; see Chapter 6 for further details.

As is well known, Alexander the Great died suddenly and very young, long before he had arranged a stable administration for his huge realm. He left no suitable heir, and after a period of intense, violent struggle among his generals and aides, his kingdom fell apart.

Most of Alexander's would-be successors were eliminated in the struggle, but after a generation of warfare a few survivors had established themselves as kings in their own right, each in control of one portion of Alexander's realm. Two of these new monarchs ruled over substantial numbers of Jews: *Ptolemy* in Egypt and *Seleucus* over much of the Asian portion of the old Persian Empire. Ptolemy's realm included Judaea as well as the growing capital at Alexandria, while Seleucus ruled over the exile community in Babylon, already several centuries old. About Babylonia in those early centuries almost nothing is known, but events in Judaea under Greek rule determined the character of Judaism for all time.

Like Alexander himself, Ptolemy I and his successors seem to have made no direct effort to change conditions in Judaea: the Torah remained in effect and the high priests remained in office. Nevertheless, unplanned changes began to appear in Jewish life. Greek officials continually passed through Jerusalem, and their presence began to affect the natives. People wishing to get the rulers' attention had to pick up at least a little Greek; those who wished to engage in large-scale commerce had to do the same. Those eager to enter royal service had to gain still greater fluency, and had to learn the complexities of court protocol and of life in the royal capital as well. The Greeks, for their part, did not hesitate to show off the brilliant superiority of their way of life,[1] and indeed, the achievements of Greek civilization were very impressive.

The result was a steady infiltration of *Hellenism* (that is, Greek culture) into the Judaean scene: this was especially true among wealthy, ambitious circles in Jerusalem, not least circles of high-ranking priests. Certain families learned to become comfortable with Greek ways, while others no doubt looked on with dismay at this departure from ancestral custom. Certain individuals rose to positions of power and honor, while others no doubt looked on with envy and resentment. In an age-old pattern, the countryside saw the city fall into wickedness (as they saw it), while anger and bitterness slowly mounted.

The historian Josephus[2] tells of one family named the *Tobiads* who gained the right to collect the taxes for all of Judaea and the surrounding territory.[3] This was an old family, used to wealth and power, which had managed to advance into the upper reaches of the Ptolemaic regime and marry into the high-priestly family at one and the same time. Josephus tells the story as a warning: on a trip to Alexandria one of the Tobiad brothers fell in love with a dancing girl, and this infatuation eventually led to the family's decline. Nevertheless, the account does reveal that Jews willing to compromise their national heritage were able to achieve riches and power on a previously unimaginable scale.

* * *

The Ptolemies and the Seleucids fought sporadically for control of Judaea, a valuable territory that straddled the border between their kingdoms; finally, in 198 BCE, the Seleucid monarch Antiochus III seized the territory for good. The new ruler offered firm assurances that the change in regime would have no effect on life in Judaea, and these assurances held as long as the conqueror was alive. When Antiochus died in 187 BCE, however, he was replaced by his son Seleucus IV, and things began to change.

The Second Book of Maccabees tells a strange story. King Seleucus sent his chief minister, a man named Heliodorus, to Jerusalem with instructions to enter the Temple there and remove funds that had been improperly mixed in with the Temple treasure.[4] At the entrance, however, Heliodorus encountered a huge mounted warrior covered from head to toe in solid gold armor who was accompanied by two resplendent youths. Facing these adversaries, Heliodorus and his entire entourage fainted dead away and had to be carried out of the sanctuary, and so the Temple was saved from violation.[5] Modern readers who come across this story are tempted to dismiss it as a fanciful legend, but in spite of its mythlike details it probably embodies the memory of a historical event. The raid must have disturbed and frightened the people of the time. Here was a new regime, a new royal dynasty ruling over Judaea, and after just a few short years in power, they had overturned an arrangement that had lasted for centuries. The king's agent had attempted to enter God's own house and steal from it, and only the appearance of God's own angel (for such it must have been) had prevented a disaster.

In 175 BCE, Seleucus IV was murdered by the same Heliodorus. He was succeeded by his brother, who took the throne as Antiochus IV; the dead king's son Demetrius was currently detained

THE APOCRYPHA

The Septuagint translation of the Torah began a process by which the Greek-speaking Jews of the Hellenistic Diaspora translated all their sacred writings into a language they could understand. This Greek-language collection eventually included materials that the emerging Hebrew-language collection of the *Tanakh* left out (see Chapter 1, "What Is in the Bible?"). The Hebrew texts became the Bible of the Jewish religion, while the Greek collection became the Old Testament of Christianity.

This situation persisted for well over 1,000 years, until the time of the Protestant Reformation in the sixteenth century. At that point, the Reformers, led by Martin Luther, concluded that there was something illogical about the claim that Christianity rested on the scriptures of Israel when in fact the Christian Old Testament included several books that the Jews themselves did not revere as holy! Protestants therefore removed those books from their Bibles or moved them to a special section of their own called the *Apocrypha*, from a Greek word meaning "items that ought to be hidden away." Thanks to their long history in the Christian Church, the documents in question were not actually hidden away; they were deemed worthy of careful study but were no longer placed in the same category of holiness as the biblical writings themselves. It must be kept in mind that these books, though Jewish in origin, were preserved through the Middle Ages by Christians and not by Jews; in fact, there are many passages that seem to show the alterations of Christian copyists.

The books of the Apocrypha are as follows:

1. 1 Esdras. An alternative version of the Bible's own narrative, starting at 2 Chronicles 35, including all of the Book of Ezra, and concluding with Nehemiah 7:72–8:13, rather abruptly in the midst of the verse. Only a long narrative of events at the court of the Persian King Darius in chapters 3–5 contains other material. The name *Esdras* is a Greek form of the biblical name *Ezra*.

2. 2 Esdras. A vision of the end of days said to have come to Ezra, here called a prophet (1:1). The book consists of a long Jewish exploration of the problem of evil as reflected in the Babylonian destruction of Jerusalem, though the book was probably written at the time of the later destruction by Rome. More explicitly Christian chapters have been added at the beginning and the end.

THE APOCRYPHA (continued)

3. Tobit. A romantic tale of the pious Tobit, who overcame great tribulations thanks to his faith. Tobit's son Tobias eventually marries Sarah, a pious widow all of whose previous husbands had died on their wedding night, and overcomes the demon that had been killing them.

4. Judith. The triumph of the beautiful, pious widow Judith, who rescues the Jews from conquest by the wicked Holofernes by offering herself to the Babylonian general but then getting him drunk and cutting off his head when they are alone.

5. Additions to the Book of Esther. The biblical text of Esther is famous for never explicitly mentioning God. The translators "corrected" this problem by adding several long prayers recited by the main characters of the story at key moments in the narrative. Other sorts of background information and elaboration are supplied as well.

6. Wisdom of Solomon. A set of philosophical musings in praise of Wisdom and fiercely hostile to idolatry, ascribed (like the biblical wisdom books of Proverbs and Ecclesiastes) to the ancient King Solomon.

7. Ecclesiasticus, or the Wisdom of Ben Sira. Joshua (Jesus) ben Sira was a wealthy resident of Jerusalem who around 200 BCE wrote a book of practical wisdom designed to guide the education of young men. The Wisdom tradition pervaded the Near East for millennia and underlies the biblical Wisdom books as well (see no. 6).

8. Baruch. A short set of orations ascribed to Baruch ben Neriah, the faithful secretary of the prophet Jeremiah (see Chapter 3, "The Origin of a Prophetic Book"). The sixth and last chapter is sometimes printed separately as the **Letter of Jeremiah**, allegedly sent by the prophet to the exile community newly arrived in Babylon.

9. Song of the Three Young Men. A long prayer and psalm of thanksgiving ascribed to the young Jews who were rescued from a fiery furnace during the persecutions of King Nebuchadnezzar. The poems are inserted into the Greek translation of Daniel 3.

10. Susanna. A short story about the piety of a young beauty who resists the seductive advances of hypocritical elders. It appears as an extra chapter in the Greek version of Daniel.

11. Bel and the Dragon. Another addition to the Book of Daniel, this one describing Daniel's successful unmasking of dishonest pagan priests. Also added to the text in the Greek version, the story makes reference to Daniel's escape from the lions' den in the Hebrew Daniel 6.

12. The Prayer of Manasseh. King Manasseh of Judah is described in 2 Kings 21 as the most wicked king that realm ever endured, but the retelling in 2 Chronicles 33:12–13 reports that Manasseh repented at the end of his life and composed a prayer of contrition. The Hebrew text only refers to this prayer, but the Greek text provides its text.

13. 1 Maccabees. A narrative of the persecutions of Antiochus and the Maccabees' heroic resistance. The book ends with the installation of Hyrcanus I in 135–4 BCE.

14. 2 Maccabees. Another account of those years, including some introductory material but ending with Judah's defeat of the general Nicanor in 161.

* * *

Many other Jewish writings from late antiquity have survived as well; these are often assembled into a collection called *Pseudepigrapha* ("falsely ascribed writings"), because many are presented as the writings of biblical heroes such as the prophets or the patriarchs or even Adam and Eve. These texts also were preserved by Christians throughout the Middle Ages.

in Rome as a hostage and was not able to succeed his father in the usual fashion. Under Antiochus IV the situation in Judaea rapidly disintegrated (even if the precise sequence of events remains unclear). The new king quickly replaced the incumbent high priest, Onias, with another, named Jason. Jason was Onias's brother, and thus from the legitimate high-priestly family, but nevertheless this was the first time in memory that a foreign monarch had removed a high priest from office and chosen his successor by royal appointment. To ordinary Jews of the time, this was a shocking interference in their religious lives, carried out by the brother of a king who had tried to remove money from their holy Temple. It appeared to many Judaeans that the new Seleucid rulers of their land meant to do them great harm.

Why did Antiochus do this? Did he not realize that his subjects would be horrified by such an action? It is possible that he did not; in the Greek world many priesthoods were offices of state, to be filled by appointment or election, and many priesthoods lasted for set terms and then expired. On his own terms, Antiochus may have seen his action as fully within the normal range of royal prerogative, and he may have seen the Jewish high priest as serving, like so many equivalent officials, at royal pleasure.[6] In addition, Jason may have offered attractive incentives, perhaps a guarantee of higher revenues, perhaps the suggestion that his brother's branch of the family was conspiring to bring back the rule of the Ptolemies over Judaea. If Antiochus had reason to suspect that Onias was plotting treason, then an immediate change in the local regime must have seemed urgently necessary. Whatever the king's reasons, the people reacted with shock. Onias refused to give up his office, and violent encounters between supporters of the two would-be leaders began to take place. Of course, the king took note of all this with alarm: he could not look easily on the spectacle of growing unrest in a territory on the border of his kingdom, especially when he suspected that the local leadership was harboring enemies of his interests.

Another important development contributed to the growing crisis, though its exact place in the sequence of events cannot be fixed. While a hostage at Rome, Antiochus had been impressed with his hosts' ability to rule a growing dominion by absorbing conquered neighbors into the Roman political system. The Roman practice of extending citizenship to defeated enemies (to be sure, in carefully regulated degrees of subordination) created large-scale political unity and gave others a stake in the well-being of the Roman state. Once in power, Antiochus set out to create a similar arrangement for his own large, diverse kingdom: he began to use Greek culture and the formal structure of the Greek city-state (*polis*) as the cement that would hold it together. Thus, when a group of wealthy Jerusalemites petitioned the king to restructure their city as a *polis* to be named Antioch in his honor,[7] he was only too happy to grant the request. It appears that the initial citizen list was limited to a few thousand people from the upper reaches of society; the rest of the people enjoyed no political rights at all.

Ancient Greek cities were governed by a common set of arrangements: the citizen assembly met periodically to pass resolutions and elect officials, while these leaders were supervised between assemblies by a standing council selected from the citizen body. In theory every Greek city was a sovereign entity, governed by its citizens according to any laws and policies those citizens saw fit to adopt. Cities had to accommodate the wishes of the monarchs within whose kingdoms they stood, but the kings were usually content to let local officials make local decisions and to allow the citizens of any *polis* to live as they chose as long as they caused no trouble. The founding of Antioch-in-Jerusalem thus amounted to a repeal of the Torah, or at least the cancellation of its formal authority: the people of the new Greek city were not compelled to violate the teachings of Moses, but they were now free to do so if they so chose. Ezra's work had been undone: his opponents, heirs to the opponents of the prophets, had triumphed at last.

The king's choice of Jason as high priest may be connected to these developments. With Jason's rise to power, opponents of the Mosaic heritage had taken control of Jewish life. The new leader was an enthusiastic admirer of Greek culture and quickly began to introduce changes into the life of Jerusalem; most particularly, to the shock of his contemporaries he built a gymnasium in Jerusalem that quickly became the local center of urban life.[8] Even worse, the leaders of the *polis* began to introduce changes into the Temple ritual, and the people were appalled.

Meanwhile, King Antiochus invaded Egypt and won decisively; he was about to do away with the Ptolemaic monarchy and add Egypt to his own kingdom when a Roman ambassador delivered a humiliating ultimatum and forced him to abandon the victory and return to his own country empty-handed. The people of Jerusalem, hearing that a king whom they hated had found misfortune in Egypt, mistakenly understood that he was dead and began to celebrate. The furious king, marching home with a humiliated army, passed through Judaea and found its inhabitants exulting over his death. Concluding that Judaea had become ungovernable and that the Jewish religion was the cause of the problem, he placed the territory under direct military rule. Appointing yet a third high priest, a man named Menelaus, who undertook to be more cooperative, the king ordered the abolition of traditional Jewish customs and the compulsory Hellenization of the Jewish religion. Pious Jews were ordered to worship idols. Circumcision of male children was prohibited on pain of death, and possession of scrolls of the Torah was declared a crime. The Temple itself was given over to the king's Syrian troops as their local shrine, and ceremonies were now performed in that holy place that biblical authors cannot even bring themselves to describe.[9] Outright persecution of the Mosaic way of life had begun; the king and his Jewish supporters were determined to bring a backward people into the cultural promised land of Hellenism.

* * *

The Book of Daniel was composed under the pressure of these terrible events. From the viewpoint of traditionally pious Judaeans, the Torah's promises had suffered a cruel reversal: where Moses had promised that loyalty to YHWH would bring prosperity while disloyalty would lead to disaster, the devout were now being destroyed for their faithfulness while apostates were gaining wealth and power under a Greek king's patronage. How could this be?

The Book of Daniel begins with some traditional stories, set in the courts of Babylonian and Persian monarchs, that tell of pious Jews who risked their lives to avoid transgressing God's law and were rescued from their enemies; the end of the book provides a detailed vision of the future culminating in the final triumph of the righteous and the terrible punishment of their tormentors, a final cataclysm that was to occur in the very near future. This vision is said to have been granted to Daniel in the first year of the Persian King Darius (that is, 522 BCE), but scholars have noted that its description of events in the supposed future is precisely accurate down to the time of the persecution under Antiochus IV, where it drops off in vagueness and guesswork. Clearly, the "vision" was composed at this time: the detailed predictions (written after the fact) lent weight to the anticipation of final vindication, and this anticipation gave encouragement to readers to endure a terrible time.

Hidden in this encouragement were some new religious ideas. The very idea that an angel could reveal the course of events centuries before their time meant that history was predetermined. The Jews' suffering was not punishment, as Deuteronomy insisted: events instead revealed the inexorable unfolding of God's mysterious plan. Victims of the persecution did not have to blame themselves (although many did): their task was only to remain steadfast under terrible pressure, to spurn all temptation to violate the Torah, to keep faith with God that their righteousness would not have been in vain. This refusal to see meaning in history was a retreat from the prophets' earlier confidence that all events have meaning as expressions of God's justice, but the events of their own time gave people no choice. They *knew* they had not been so wicked as to deserve what was happening to them now!

But if God's justice was not in fact to be recognized in events, then where and when and how would that justice assert itself? The latest books of the Bible offer a new idea to solve that problem: God's justice would be revealed in another world, after each life was complete and could be evaluated as a whole. The Book of Daniel contains the Bible's clearest allusion[10] to the idea of resurrection: all human beings will finally be restored to life and then judged as to the righteousness of the lives they had led. If this world cannot be a place where all people get what they deserve, another world must exist where the upright and the wicked will meet their proper destiny.

* * *

In the chaos of a country where armed gangs supported three different claimants to the high priesthood, and where royal officials were trying to abolish a cherished way of life while ordinary people were suffering and dying to preserve it, organized resistance began to emerge, and an obscure family of country priests came forth as its leaders.

The resisters seem to have been called *Hasidim* (Greek *Asidaioi*, English sometimes *Asideans*), or "loyal ones,"[11] and they were united in their fierce loyalty to the Torah of Moses and the religious discipline based on that Torah. As time went on and the persecution grew harsher, so did their refusal to yield to its demands. When possible, they fought back; when necessary, they gave up their lives. Fortified by a new kind of literature of which the Book of Daniel is typical, they were sure that God would not leave their suffering unrewarded or unavenged (see "Apocalypse").

People joined this growing army for any of several reasons. Some simply wanted the king and his supporters to stop harassing them; others were equally concerned to take back the Temple and restore its traditional rites. Some, probably few at first, saw an opportunity

APOCALYPSE

The Book of Daniel is the most important early example of a type of writing that has come to be known as *apocalypse,* after the Greek word for "revelation." These books depict the future in the form of a revelation granted by an angel to a pious hero. Scripture contains earlier examples as well, most notably toward the end of the Book of Zechariah, but Daniel's visions can be located precisely in their historical context, so they provide a useful starting point for examining this literature.

These books depart from the earlier scriptures in two noteworthy respects. In *form,* they continue to uphold the idea that the truly pious can hope to receive divine messages like the prophets of old, but now the source of those messages is an intermediary angel rather than God himself. This change suggests that God was increasingly seen as ruling the world through a throng of agents and representatives, just as the kings of the Hellenistic world (and then the Roman emperors) were seen as distant though powerful monarchs, approachable only through many levels of agents, bureaucrats, and ministers. Everything was done in their name, but ordinary people rarely saw them and could barely hope for their personal attention. God, of course, was never felt to be as remote or hidden as that; nevertheless, the idea began to spread that the world is full of God's agents, a kind of bureaucracy or a royal court of heavenly beings who actually perform the actions that are carried out in their commander's name.

In *substance,* apocalyptic writing differs from earlier biblical writings in that it has given up on understanding history. Deuteronomy confidently asserts that through historical events God rewards the righteous and punishes the wicked, and this idea was still widely accepted when the Babylonians destroyed Jerusalem (see Chapter 2, "A Debate on the Meaning of Disaster"). The Book of Daniel, however, is careful to avoid any such claim: as the persecutions of King Antiochus intensified, everyone could see that now it was those who violated the covenant who enjoyed wealth and power, while those who remained loyal to Moses and his teaching endured mounting sorrows. But now that was all right: what happens in this world is not a reward or a punishment but simply the realization of God's mysterious plan. The execution of God's justice will take place hereafter.

This type of writing remained popular among Jews for several hundred years. The books now known as 2 Esdras (or 4 Ezra) and 2 Baruch were written after the Romans destroyed Jerusalem again in 70 CE, and they apply this same manner of writing and thinking to the disaster of their own time. Fragments of many other apocalypses have survived as well.

As this way of thinking spread, it began to generate impatience for the promised end of history. Fervent eagerness for the end of the world was a natural response to seemingly endless suffering; fueled by the conviction that events were preordained and had no inherent meaning, expectation of the final resolution of Israel's painful history rose ever higher among groups of despondent Jews. Since the end of the world would mean the triumph of righteousness over evil, this eagerness often took the form of resistance to Herodian or Roman oppression: at the end of time, God would surely allow his true servants to overcome their enemies. Following the example of their Maccabean forebears, groups of the pious began taking up arms or just rioting in the streets of Jerusalem, confident that the reign of Satan was drawing to its close.

This enthusiastic readiness for cataclysm was an important ingredient in the Judaeans' willingness to start a war with the Roman Empire: the Maccabees had triumphed over the great kingdom of their time, and surely God would not allow his people to suffer defeat now. Not once but three times in less than a century the Jewish nation attempted to vanquish Rome by force of arms, and all three times their efforts ended in disaster; see Chapter 7.

to drive the hated Greek and Syrian idolaters from their land; others were eager to strike back at the oppressive Jewish elite who had been seizing their lands and their goods for generations and were now imposing religious outrage on their lives as well. All these groups shared a readiness to take up arms and fight their common enemy, supported by a deep confidence that the God of Moses would give them ultimate victory.

The *Hasidim* found their leader in an unexpected corner. In the village of Modi'in, about twenty miles northwest of Jerusalem, there lived an elderly priest named Mattathias. According to the report that came down to later generations,[12] a royal officer came into town looking for Jews ready to worship idols and offered a reward to any Jew who would do so. Mattathias not only refused the king's offer, he also killed a Jew who had accepted and the king's representative as well. Then, of course, he had to flee into the wilderness, where he gathered around him the beginnings of a guerrilla force to combat the persecution. This story was written at a time when Mattathias's descendants had become the rulers of Judaea and may contain an element of propaganda, but it is not implausible. Someone had to begin the struggle, and this may be how it happened.

Later writings also attribute a more radical innovation to the same Mattathias and his circle. The devout Jews' enemies[13] had figured out that law-abiding Jews would not take up arms on the Sabbath, even in self-defense, so naturally they attacked such Jews on that day and killed many of them. The pious fighters saw that this passivity was self-defeating:

> "If we all do as our brothers have done and do not fight against the gentiles for our lives and our laws, they will now quickly wipe us off the face of the earth." On that day they came to a decision: "If any man comes against us in battle on the Sabbath day, we shall fight against him and not all die as our brothers did in their hiding places."[14]

Thus Mattathias and his companions are credited with a far-reaching idea: in defending the tradition, they might have to modify it. Under rabbinic leadership several centuries later, this idea would be applied in previously unimaginable ways.[15]

Already an old man when the struggle began, Mattathias soon died. Leadership of the struggle passed to his son Judah, who was called "Maccabee," though no one is quite sure what that nickname meant. Judah became a popular hero, harassing the royal forces and protecting those who wished to go on living by the Torah. Judah and his father were not precisely defenders of religious freedom, though they are sometimes portrayed in that light today: Mattathias, while alive, had begun the practice of riding around the country-side, forcibly circumcising baby boys whose parents had neglected or refused to carry out this ancient rite.[16] Still, they won the loyalty and gratitude of the common folk of Judaea by defending the national way of life and guarding those who wished to preserve it. Judah's growing army won a string of victories against larger and better-trained Syrian-Greek forces, and gradually the king and his advisors abandoned their attempt to abolish traditional Judaism by force and withdrew their support from the radical Hellenizers who had taken over Jerusalem. These took refuge in the fortress of Jerusalem, while Judah and his followers entered the city and joyously rededicated the purified Temple to the God of their ancestors. This dedication, in the winter of 165–164 BCE, is annually remembered even today in the Jewish festival of *Hanukka* ("dedication"). The crisis was over. At around this time, Antiochus IV went off to the other end of his kingdom, to continue his late brother's project of removing suspicious funds from temple treasuries. He was killed in battle (this was surely God's vengeance!), and his young son became king as Antiochus V.

In spite of Judah's victory, the territory of Judaea remained under the sovereignty of the Seleucid kingdom. The king retained the right to appoint high priests and taxes continued to be paid, though the Torah was restored to its authority by royal decree. When certain Jewish groups continued the struggle, interested by now in overthrowing royal authority altogether, the monarchy did not willingly give up control. Attempts were made to win popular good will. The high priest Menelaus, hopelessly compromised by his support of Hellenization, was removed from office and put to death. A new high priest named Alcimus, acceptable to almost everyone, was installed in office on the understanding that traditional ceremonies would be maintained. But military attempts to evict the Greeks from Judaea were not tolerated. Judah himself, who did continue the struggle though hopelessly outnumbered, was killed on the field of battle in 161 BCE.

However, in the years following the rededication of the Temple, the Seleucid dynasty itself began to fall apart. At a key moment (162 BCE), Demetrius, son of Seleucus IV, escaped from Rome (perhaps with his hosts' connivance: "divide and conquer") and went back to Asia to reclaim his throne. Demetrius entered the kingdom, and a civil war between the two royal cousins began. An increasingly chaotic dynastic struggle went on for nearly a century, while rivals for the throne began to compete for their subjects' goodwill. This competition, skillfully exploited by the Maccabees, led to power for their family and freedom for the people of Judaea. When one would-be king offered the high priesthood to Judah's brother Jonathan

(152 BCE), the other soon ratified the appointment and added an offer of financial subsidy as well; the subsidy soon turned into full exemption from financial obligations to the throne, and Judaea was essentially an independent country. When Jonathan was murdered toward the end of 143 BCE, his brother Simon, the last of Mattathias's sons, was chosen to succeed him; this confirmed the Maccabees themselves as a new high-priestly dynasty. The family came to be known as *Hasmonaeans*, after a distant ancestor who was presumed to have given his name to the line.

Simon's accession to the high priesthood is noteworthy for another reason as well: at a key moment early in his term of office, his priesthood was confirmed by a formal resolution of the people of Jerusalem. Adopting a widespread Greek procedure, the people treated the high priesthood as though it were a civic office and declared through formal public resolution that by virtue of his previous contributions to the nation's well-being Simon should hold that office (see "The People Appoint Simon High Priest"). This procedure provoked a certain amount of anxiety: the people had never claimed this prerogative before, and the resolution provided that their decision might be overridden if a "true prophet" arose and designated some other priestly line.

The need for a true prophet had arisen once before: when Judah the Maccabee rededicated the Temple altar, no one knew what to do with the stones that had been defiled. They had for years been dedicated to the worship of Israel's God, but now they had been polluted by the "stupefying abomination." In the end, the stones were simply laid aside in storage, waiting for the time when a true prophet would come and advise the people what to do with them.[17] These incidents reveal another feature of the religious unrest that had engulfed Judaea: the people were living without prophetic guidance at a time when such guidance was desperately needed, but they had not yet accepted that direct Divine guidance at times of crisis had been taken away from them forever.

In a situation reminiscent of Ezra's, Simon thus occupied the high priesthood on a triple basis: by royal appointment, through popular resolution, and, of course, at the behest of the God of Israel. When Simon too was murdered, in 134 BCE, his son Yohanan (John), known

THE PEOPLE APPOINT SIMON HIGH PRIEST

Note: When the High Priest Jonathan was murdered in 143 BCE, his brother Simon, last of the Maccabean brothers, became his successor. That by itself would not be surprising: the family was a family of heroes, and no other plausible candidate for the office was available. However, the manner of his appointment was very surprising indeed: in addition to receiving appointment from the Seleucid king who technically still enjoyed this right, Simon was installed in office by vote of the people of Jerusalem. Never before had a high priest been elected. This was a standard procedure among Greek cities, but it was unheard of in Jewish history and had no basis in the Torah. It is striking that a family who had risen to greatness by defending tradition and resisting Hellenism nevertheless relied on this distinctly Greek mode of obtaining high office. The incident reveals the pervasive influence of Greek culture even on people eager to limit the effects of that influence.

Whereas: At a time when our land was repeatedly afflicted by wars, Simon son of Mattathias of the clan of Joarib and his brothers exposed themselves to danger and resisted their nation's foes, in order that their sanctuary and the Law might survive; they won great glory for their nation; Jonathan rallied his nation and became their high priest and then passed away; thereupon their enemies desired to invade their country in order to destroy it and violate their sanctuary; then Simon arose and fought for his nation and spent large sums of his own money, providing arms for the men of the army of his nation and paying their salaries; he fortified the towns of Judaea, including Beth-Zur on the border of Judaea, where previously there had been an enemy arsenal, stationing there a garrison of Jews; he also fortified Joppe by the sea and Gazara on the border of Azotus, previously inhabited by our enemies, settling Jews there; whatever was needed for removing impediments to pious Jewish life in those towns, he provided; observing Simon's fidelity and what he had accomplished and the glory which he proposed to bring upon his nation, the people appointed him their chief and high priest because of all these achievements of his and because of his righteousness and his uninterrupted fidelity to his nation, as he sought in every way to exalt his people; thereafter, during his time of leadership, he succeeded in expelling the gentiles from his people's land and in expelling the inhabitants of the City of David in Jerusalem, who had built themselves a citadel from which they used to go out and commit

THE PEOPLE APPOINT SIMON HIGH PRIEST (continued)

acts of defilement in the vicinity of the sanctuary and gravely impair its purity; Simon stationed in the citadel Jewish soldiers and fortified it for the sake of the safety of our country and our city; he built higher walls around Jerusalem; moreover, King Demetrius in view of all this has confirmed him as high priest and admitted him to the ranks of his Friends and conferred great distinction upon him; indeed, he heard that the Romans had given the Jews the titles "Friends and Allies (and Brothers)" and that they had treated Simon's ambassadors with honor – therefore, be it resolved by the Jews and the priests: that Simon be chief and high priest in perpetuity until a true prophet shall arise, and that he be commander over them (and that he have charge of the sanctuary) so as to appoint on his own authority the officials responsible for services, for the countryside, for armaments, and for fortifications, and that he have charge of the sanctuary, and that all persons obey him, and that all contracts in our country be drawn up in his name, and that he wear purple robes and gold ornaments. No one of the people or of the priests shall have the power to annul any of these provisions or to oppose any of his future commands or to convoke a meeting in our country without his permission or to wear purple robes or use a gold brooch. Whoever acts contrary to these provisions or annuls any of them shall be subject to the penalty of death.

(1 Maccabees 14:29–45; translation by
J. Goldstein in the *Anchor Bible*, slightly altered)

as well by the Greek name Hyrcanus, succeeded him as a matter of course.

* * *

What was the Maccabean struggle all about? The rebels were not simply hostile to all non-Jews or all aspects of Greek culture. Judah the Maccabee himself was quite ready to send Greek-speaking ambassadors abroad and forge treaties of friendship with the Romans and with the ancient Greek city of Sparta.[18] On the surface the issues revolved around religious practice: the right of individuals to live according to the teachings of Moses and the right of the nation to maintain those teachings in its central shrine. But what of those individuals who wanted to abandon the teachings of Moses or who preferred to modify the Temple ceremonies? Did they have the same right to act as they thought proper? The answer seems to be that in the view of the Maccabean fighters they did not. Heirs to the prophets, they were deeply convinced that the covenant nation has no choice but to fulfill its divine obligations, and that individual members of the covenant nation had no choice but to take part in that fulfillment. A key expression of the Maccabees' view of their situation appears very early in the semiofficial statement of their outlook, the *First Book of Maccabees*:

> At that time [the ascension of Antiochus IV], lawless men arose in Israel and seduced many with their plea, "Come, let us make a covenant with the gentiles around us, because ever since we have kept ourselves separated from them we have suffered many evils."... Some of the people took it upon themselves to apply to the king, who granted them liberty to follow the practices of the gentiles.... They joined themselves to the gentiles and became willing slaves to evildoing.[19]

These words have been ascribed to the Hellenizers by their enemies, but the point is clear: in the Maccabees' view, the wickedness of the others lay *in their wish to be more like other people*. In contrast, the Maccabean victory enshrined the opposite principle: *it is the essence of Judaism that Jews must not be like others. Jews who wish to become more like their neighbors must be stopped*. In the chapters to come, this book will examine various ways in which this principle was understood and resisted or put into practice.

5

The First Kingdom of Judaea

IN 104 BCE, THE HASMONAEAN HIGH PRIEST JOHN HYRCANUS was succeeded by his son Judah Aristoboulus; after only one year, Judah himself died and was succeeded by his brother Alexander Jannaeus. One of these brothers – it is not clear which – began using the title "king of Judaea." The kingdom lasted only a brief while – it was abolished under Roman occupation in the year 63 BCE – but these years represent a crucial interval in the history of Judaism.

The Maccabean state began insecurely. Over the 130's BCE, King Antiochus VII sat on the Seleucid throne. The last vigorous king of that dynasty, he barely missed reconquering the newly independent Judaea: Antiochus briefly reasserted royal authority over the territory but was unable to sustain his control. After that, the Jewish territory slowly expanded until finally (and briefly) the Kingdom of Judaea became a regional power in its own right, capable of influencing events throughout the region, sometimes even the royal domains of Syria and Egypt themselves.

That growth was propelled by an increasingly aggressive military policy. The Maccabean brothers, starting with Judah himself, had occasionally expelled the previous inhabitants of a border region and replaced them with Jews: the resolution installing Simon as high priest had specifically praised him and his brother Jonathan for this accomplishment.[1]

At a later point this policy changed in a remarkable way. When Judaean power was extended into a new region, the local inhabitants were not expelled but were compelled to become Jews themselves: they were forced to start living under Judaean law, that is, according to the Torah. To the rulers of the new Judaean state, this new policy offered several great advantages. Most obviously, the size of the Judaean nation steadily increased. This gratified the nation's pride and added to its military resources during the frequent crises of the time. It also avoided the creation of resentful gentile populations within the nation's borders; such elements posed the constant danger of instability and foreign attack and left the central home territory of Judaea less safe, not more. Finally, these forced Judaizations carried financial implications. The newly Jewish regions entered the Judaean economy, and in particular were added to the support network of the Temple in Jerusalem. People from these areas now joined the crowds of pilgrims at the great festivals. They also became subject to the Torah's laws requiring annual payments of harvest and livestock to the priests and the Levites. The new kings were also priests, and they managed to gather much of this revenue to themselves.

Had the newly absorbed populations resisted this dramatic change in their status, the new policy could have backfired disastrously: whole districts of Judaea would have been filled with people eager to betray their Jewish identity at the first opportunity. In fact, however, the Hasmonaeans' intentions were realized. These new Jewish populations soon became attached to the nation of Israel. One newly Judaized family, the Herodians, provided a new royal dynasty for Judaea after the Hasmonaeans were driven from power (see Chapter 7). Over 100 years later, when the territory exploded into rebellion against Rome, the new areas joined the struggle with no less energy than the Judaean heartland.

Alexander Jannaeus reigned from 103 to 76 BCE. He left two sons who differed greatly in temperament and ability: Hyrcanus, the elder, was ineffectual, while Aristoboulus was a forceful, driven man. It was clear that the younger brother would not willingly allow Hyrcanus to inherit the throne, so to avoid civil war it was decided that Hyrcanus would serve as high priest but that the rival brothers' mother, widow of the dead King Alexander, would continue to rule in her own right as queen of Judaea. Salome Alexandra ruled in this way for another nine years, until 67 BCE. When she died, civil war between the contending brothers soon began, and Aristoboulus quickly prevailed. He took the throne and the high priesthood for himself and forced his brother to retire from politics.

A bit later, in the year 63 BCE, the great Roman general Pompey was in Syria, putting an end to the Seleucid kingdom and setting up direct Roman control over its territory. Each of the Hasmonaean brothers sent a delegation to Damascus hoping to obtain Roman support.[2] According to Josephus, a third delegation accompanied those two and asked that Pompey rescue the people of Judaea altogether from a priestly dynasty that had become destructive and oppressive. The Roman declined this radical request; he restored Hyrcanus to the high priesthood but forbade him to use the title "king." Many conquered territories (though not where Judaism had become established) were removed from Judaean control. Aristoboulus was forced to abandon Jerusalem but continued to harass his brother, so Roman forces had continually to reenter Judaea and drive him away. The Maccabean kingdom was finished.

* * *

The *political* history of Hasmonaean Judaea is not especially re-markable. Arising during a period of opportunity when the great Hellenistic monarchies were in decline but the Romans had not yet come in force to the eastern Mediterranean, the country enjoyed a few generations of vigorous leadership and grew into a regional power. But Alexander Jannaeus ruled by harsh force and lost the willing loyalty of his people, and after his death the ruling family fell into internal disarray and squandered its resources in dynastic struggle. Thus, when Pompey and his army came into the area and established Roman rule over Syria, the Hasmonaean state was ripe for conquest and quickly fell.

The *religious* history of Judaea, however, set the course of history for the next 2,000 years, for the Jews and for all of Western civilization.

The supporters of Judah the Maccabee had formed a very loose coalition. Different elements among his supporters had joined his forces for diverse reasons (see Chapter 4), and many abandoned Judah's struggle as soon as their own purposes were achieved. As the Hasmonaean state took shape, moreover, many others who had supported the Maccabean campaign to the end began to oppose the new regime. Reasons for such opposition were also diverse. Some did not like innovations that the new high priests brought into the Temple, while others, impassioned by victory, began to advocate changes of their own that the Hasmonaeans resisted. Finally, it appears that many resented the Hasmonaeans' assumption of the royal title; kingship in Judaea was supposed to belong to the family of David, of the tribe of Judah that had given its name to the country, not to a priestly family of the tribe of Levi with no claim to royalty.

Religious dissension began almost at once. The high priest Alcimus, appointed as a compromise candidate when the persecutions were lifted in 165 BCE, provoked opposition by advocating changes in the Temple ceremonies; when he died of natural causes a few years later, many detected the hand of an angry God in his unexpected demise. The Seleucids left the high priesthood vacant for a few years in the hope that things would quiet down, but with the appointment of Jonathan, the first Hasmonaean high priest, unrest began once again to increase.

An intriguing document (4QMMT)[3] that was found among the Dead Sea Scrolls (see "The Dead Sea Scrolls I") appears to shed light on these early developments. The document appears to have been written soon after the Maccabees had purified and rededicated the Temple, and it contains a description of disagreements between the author of the text and certain unnamed authorities in the Temple.[4] The disagreements are numerous and detailed, and they touch on numerous topics in Jewish law, but they are respectfully presented; the document suggests that criticism of the new Temple regime began rather quickly but remained peaceful and collegial until frustration began to mount.

For generations, religious disputes of this kind had been kept in check by the fact of foreign control. The kings of Persia and then of two different Greek regimes were not interested in having a key border territory lapse into turmoil over issues that can hardly have made sense to outsiders. As the careers of Ezra and Nehemiah make clear, the general tendency was for the kings to identify strong leaders among the people and then support their authority with the implied threat of military intervention. Antiochus IV had attempted to continue that tendency, but he overestimated the backing of the Hellenizers whom he appointed as high priests, and then his attempt to restore order by force collapsed when the Maccabees won their astonishing early victories.

THE DEAD SEA SCROLLS (I)

The limestone hills that overlook the Dead Sea are full of caves, and in the fall of 1947 it was discovered that one of these caves had been used some 2,000 years ago to store parchment scrolls in big ceramic jars. The discovery triggered intensive exploration in the area near a ruin named *Qumran* where the first scrolls had been found. In the end, over half a dozen caves were found to contain writings and other materials, and a large settlement was found to have existed in the plain beneath those same hillsides.

Seven of the scrolls were nearly intact, and these were published rather quickly: those that had fallen into the hands of Jewish scholars in Israel were published by scholars at the Hebrew University, while those now possessed by Christian scholars were stored at the Rockefeller Institute in East Jerusalem, then ruled by the Kingdom of Jordan, and were published by them. The political situation in the Middle East meant that no public collaboration or sharing of materials between the two sides was possible.

One of the largest bodies of material, taken from the so-called Cave Four, had been trashed by ancient vandals and now existed in the form of many tiny scraps of parchment or papyrus, some containing no more than a few letters. These remnants were cataloged and tentatively assembled, a task that understandably took years, but came to light very slowly, as the original team of scholars (with some Jews added when Jerusalem was reunited after the Six-Day War of 1967) retained tight control over the material.

Finally, in the early 1990s, a number of concurrent but independent developments brought the entire body of Dead Sea materials into public view, although many documents still awaited careful scholarly publication. Much of the information in this chapter is drawn from the Scrolls, or from scholarly investigations of the Scrolls and their background over the past half century.

Now there was no outside restraint at all. The new monarchs themselves were Jews loyal to the covenant of Moses, and their situation recalled that of the last preexilic kings of Judah: groups and individuals with various religious opinions naturally wanted the entire nation to follow their teachings, and they all sought to use royal authority to bring about that outcome. Religion and politics became inseparable:

the "loyal ones" had overthrown one wicked high priest, and now they were willing to try again.

By the early first century BCE, conflicting religious movements had begun to appear in the country. Some of these strike the modern observer as interested mostly in wealth and power, but even groups of this kind developed distinctive religious teachings to justify their customs and attitudes. Others were driven by a definite religious vision, with a specific understanding of the Torah and its requirements and a developed image of the way all Jews ought to live; such groups too, even when driven by sincere piety, were often drawn into the struggle for power.

The historian Josephus (see "Josephus") repeatedly names three such groups as having dominated the scene: the Sadducees, the Pharisees, and the Essenes. In order to hold his Greek readers' interest, he misleadingly describes them as though they were akin to schools of Greek philosophy, but he provides enough information (especially when that is combined with information from other sources) to give a sense of what these groups were probably really like.

The Sadducees were the party of the priestly aristocracy; their name is almost certainly derived from *Zadok*, a high priest in the days of King David.[5] From the time of John Hyrcanus, all high priests were affiliated with this group; during her brief reign, Queen Salome Alexandra transferred her support to the Pharisees, an act for which she was warmly remembered in later generations, but her sons did not follow her example. As one might expect of an aristocratic party, the Sadducees were not especially numerous, but they enjoyed power out of proportion to their number.

A useful insight into the Saducean view of Judaism can be drawn from a story told (in two rather different versions) by both Josephus and the Talmud. One year during the Festival of Tabernacles, a high priest poured the ceremonial water on his feet rather than on the altar, so the crowd assembled in the Temple stoned him with the citrons they had brought for the celebration ("The Water Libation and the Citrons" explains the background for this story). Assuming that the priest committed this outrageous provocation on purpose,[6] why would he have done such a thing? What did he think was at stake? Another passage in Josephus provides the necessary clue: the

JOSEPHUS

When Judaea rebelled against Rome in 66 CE (see Chapter 7), a young priestly aristocrat named Joseph ben Mattathias was appointed military commander in one of the northern districts. As his name suggests, this Joseph had a family connection to the Hasmonaean dynasty, a source of great pride to him even though the family had lost its throne a century before. He was also, it seems, headstrong and self-indulgent, though very clever and a good leader as well. According to his autobiography, Josephus had passed his early years as a kind of religious searcher, spending a few years with each of the major religious groupings of his time, but now, of course, the situation demanded military skill and loyalty more than intellectual curiosity.

It appears that Josephus aroused suspicion almost at once, perhaps on account of the way he had spent his earliest adult years. A move began among leaders of the fledgling rebellion to remove him from his post, and the young Josephus needed great cleverness and eloquence to preserve his command and his reputation. (Of course, his own writings are our only source of information concerning these events.) In fact, however, at a key moment in the early stages of the war, and under extremely unclear circumstances, Josephus did change sides, and he spent the rest of the war trying to induce his fellow Judaeans to surrender to the Roman Empire before catastrophe overtook them. There was no surrender, and catastrophe did occur: in 70 the holy city of Jerusalem, together with its Temple, was destroyed. Josephus could portray himself as a patriot who had tried to spare his nation this awful fate, but many people then and since have viewed him as a traitor. After the war, Josephus moved to Rome under sponsorship of the new Emperor Vespasian, and he spent the rest of his life writing books of Jewish history. Four of his works survive.

The Jewish War was published quite soon after the war, and contains a detailed history of Judaea starting with the time of the Maccabees and concluding with the end of hostilities in 73 or 74. A preliminary version of this work may have been published in Aramaic, the author's native language, but the surviving version of the *War* and nearly all of Josephus's others writings are in Greek. The book seems intended as a kind of public relations document, seeking to convince the world that the Jews are a productive nation that had briefly fallen under the sway of ruffian upstarts, and seeking to convince the Jews that the Romans were not their enemies but had been given no choice but to destroy that outlaw regime.

The Jewish Antiquities appeared some two decades later, and contains a history of the Jewish people starting with the creation of the world and ending at the outbreak of the war in 66. Josephus did not repeat his account of the war itself. The first half of the work consists largely of a summary of the entire Jewish Bible, including the extensive legal sections of the Pentateuch. The purpose of this was to demonstrate that the Jews were an ancient nation and thus entitled to preserve their ancestral customs. The book thereby provides a treasure trove of early Jewish interpretation of scripture. The later portions often repeat parallel sections of *The Jewish War*, but subtle changes and sizable additions give some idea of changes in Josephus's own views over a crucial generation.

The Life is a kind of appendix to the *Antiquities*, and offers Josephus's own version of the events in which he personally was involved.

Finally, toward the end of his life, Josephus published *Against Apion*, a very different sort of work. Here Josephus answers the numerous, mostly Greek or Egyptian-Greek critics of Judaism as a religion, defending his heritage against the slurs of its enemies and offering his own quite sharp critique of Greek polytheism. This book shows Josephus as a religious thinker and offers the strongest expression of his persisting loyalty to Judaism. Part of this work survives only in a Latin translation prepared several centuries after the author's death.

In light of Josephus's numerous purposes in writing his books, some of them partly incompatible and some of them clearly self-serving, scholars have differed widely on the degree to which his information can be trusted. For all that, however, a very substantial portion of the information now available about Jewish history in the 200 years before his death is derived from his writings. These must be handled with care and with a degree of suspicion, but the subject could not be studied at all without the materials he has provided.

Sadducees, he writes, refused to be bound by any Jewish custom not explicitly commanded in the Torah.[7] The water libation is not grounded in scripture; therefore, people felt that the high priest had revealed his disdain for the ceremony in an intentionally shocking fashion.

THE WATER LIBATION AND THE CITRONS

The Torah demands that every animal sacrificed on the altar be accompanied by an offering of wine (see Numbers 15:1–16), but there is no requirement anywhere in scripture for a ritual offering of water. Nevertheless, the custom arose to offer an annual libation of water during the autumn Festival of Tabernacles, and this water ceremony became one of the highlights of the year: a later rabbinic tradition reports that "anyone who has not seen the Joy of the Water-Drawing has not seen happiness in his life" (Mishnah Sukkah 5:1). The practice probably arose because a water ceremony at the very start of the rainy season struck many people as appropriate, and it probably earned its great popularity because of the jubilant celebrations that accompanied it.

Leviticus 23:40 instructs as well that proper celebration of the Festival of Tabernacles involves the use of citrons and other particular plant species; these were carried in processions and employed in other rituals, and that is why everyone in the Temple crowd was holding such a fruit when the high priest poured the water on his feet.

As noted, the water ceremony has no basis in scripture, and on that account it was known to face opposition from Sadducees. When a high priest poured the water on his feet, the people naturally saw this as disdainful rejection of a beloved tradition, and they struck out at him in their fury. The ancient sources do not actually indicate the priest's motivation; it is entirely possible that his hand merely slipped. However, the crowd's immediate and fierce reaction gives testimony to ordinary Jews' deep mistrust of their leaders, and their readiness to see in such an act the worst possible motives and attitudes.

This Sadducean attitude is often described as reflecting a dispute over the legitimacy of the so-called Oral Torah, but that was a rabbinic term that first came into use several generations after the Temple was destroyed (see Chapter 8); at this early time no organized body of unwritten teaching existed. Nor did the Sadducees insist on interpreting the Torah literally or on not going beyond its strict requirements: the Torah can be a difficult book, and it surely needed interpretation in places where its literal meaning was unclear or impractical. Instead, the dispute concerned the right of the priestly Temple authorities (who for a while were also royal authorities) to interpret the Torah as they saw fit and to issue additional decrees and policy decisions without restraint. The Torah instructs that cases that are too hard for local authorities must be brought to "the place that YHWH will choose, . . . to the priests the Levites, to the judge who will be in those days," and that the inquirers must not "turn aside from the judgment that they speak, [not] to the right or the left";[8] naturally the Sadducean high priests interpreted this passage as referring to themselves. Few high priests (if any) were legal experts in their own right, so they surely had secretaries and other officials who did the interpreting for them. But everything was done in their name, and no challenge to their authority was tolerated. In such a matter as the water ceremony, when a high priest did act on his own (or his advisors') judgment, he took it for granted that his decision would be respected: if he determined that the ceremony was foolish superstition or decided to disdain it for any other reason, he did not believe that popular expectation should force him to hide his opinion. The dispute over this religious ceremony thus concerned power, not theology; it serves as a reminder that in ancient Judaea, politics and religion could hardly be separate spheres.

In contrast to the Sadducees, who dominated the political life of Judaea, the Essenes seem to have withdrawn from that life altogether. Several ancient writers – Josephus, Philo,[9] and the Roman traveler Pliny the Elder – have left us descriptions of this group, but the descriptions do not always match. Josephus implies that Essenes and their families lived scattered among the villages of Judaea, while Philo describes people who had withdrawn from society and lived – men and women separately – in a desert community somewhere near the Dead Sea (Pliny claims to have visited that very community). Of course, it is possible to reconcile these portrayals: perhaps some Essenes joined the group fully and went to live in its desert head-quarters, while others tried to follow Essene teachings but remained in the outside world.

And what were those teachings? No ancient writer explains Essene Judaism in detail, but the general picture is of a group of people who strove for personal holiness with unusual rigor. They avoided the common causes of impurity,[10] they were famous for keeping their word, and they avoided violence and weaponry of any kind.[11]

3. Fragment from the Dead Sea Scrolls. This is the document known as the Messianic Rule or the Rule of the Congregation; it describes a banquet to be held "in the last days," over which the "Priestly Messiah" and "the Messiah of Israel" will preside. The photograph gives an idea of the difficulty involved in restoring and translating these fascinating documents. (Photo courtesy of Todd Bolen/bibleplaces.com)

Complete dedication to these goals demanded a kind of monastic existence, and many people, attracted by this objective but not quite able to live up to it, must have supported the group without fully joining it.

Knowledge of the Essenes has now been dramatically altered by the discovery of the Dead Sea Scrolls near Qumran in the Judaean desert (Figure 3). When those documents were first examined, scholars naturally tried to identify them with an ancient Jewish movement already known: it seemed very unlikely that a religious party or sect could have built the large settlement at Qumran and assembled a significant library of scrolls while completely escaping the notice of all ancient writers. Of course, that possibility must be kept in mind, but the majority of modern investigators have concluded (by a process of elimination) that the Dead Sea community was probably the very Essene headquarters that Philo described and Pliny claimed to have seen. In that case, what do the scrolls teach us about this group? "The Dead Sea Scrolls (II)" summarizes some of the most instructive documents from the Qumran collection, and the picture that emerges from those documents is as follows.

The Qumran community lived in the desert, where it awaited the imminent outbreak of God's fury against the corrupt priests of Jerusalem and their defiled Temple. Possessing no weapons, the community nevertheless saw itself as a kind of armed camp, the Children of Light, who were charged with the mission of protecting themselves against all impurity while they waited for God's intervention. Founded by priests, the group had by-laws that guaranteed that priests would remain community leaders. The Qumran community apparently followed its own calendar, different from the calendar, now normative for Jews, that was followed in the Temple; thus they must have celebrated many festivals on days that were regular workdays for the bulk of Judaea's population. (See "Calendar and Controversy" for more on the Jewish calendar in Second Temple times.)

The residents at the Qumran settlement were organized in a strict hierarchy, and high-ranking leaders evaluated the ordinary members every year and adjusted the rank of every individual. Many of the group's rules governed these procedures or the internal management of the community: there were rules for the scrutiny and acceptance of new members, for the proper selection of leaders, for the conduct of public meetings and other ceremonies. Other rules provided the community's interpretation of familiar aspects of Jewish life such as observance of the Sabbath. Rotating committees studied the Torah night and day, and the community believed that through such study, all of its rules and regulations had been derived from the holy Book by direct Divine inspiration and under the leadership of their founder, the unnamed Righteous Teacher (or Teacher of Righteousness).

The Qumran sect lived as a commune: applicants for membership remained under scrutiny for several years, and when finally accepted, they had to surrender their possessions to the group treasury. This meant, of course, that expulsion or even suspension from the group was a fearsome threat: people were sent out with nothing, while their previous oath to accept nothing from outsiders remained in effect.

THE DEAD SEA SCROLLS (II)

This box describes the major scrolls that were found more or less intact in Qumran Cave One. An additional scroll from Cave Four, *Miqsat Ma'aseh Torah*, is described in the text.

The only Qumran text that had previously been known is the *Damascus Covenant* (*CD*), also known as the *Zadokite Fragments* from the name used in the earlier edition. A version of this text was found in the Cairo Geniza, a storeroom containing medieval documents of all kinds that was opened to modern scholarship, chiefly by Solomon Schechter, in the late nineteenth century. The *Fragments* were initially published in a German edition (*Eine Unbekannte Jüdische Sekte* [*An Unknown Jewish Sect*], New York: Jewish Theological Seminary of America, 1970) by Louis Ginzberg.

The editors of the Qumran versions (several partial copies were found) used the title *Damascus Covenant* because these materials tell of a group of pious Jews forced into exile who wandered the desert for a generation before settling near Damascus. It remained unclear whether this narrative records the actual history of the sect, or provides a metaphorical explanation for their isolated life in the Judaean desert, or offers a vision of the eschatological future. Religious exhortation to remain true to the teachings of the group is combined in the text with a set of detailed regulations pertaining to various aspects of life (group discipline, Sabbath observance, etc.).

The *Community Rule* or *Manual of Discipline* (*1QS*) has a similar structure, combining rules of the group (governance, admission of new members, behavior at meetings, etc.) with a long introduction that portrays the world as a battleground between the two spirits of evil and righteousness. The text asserts that individuals, when born, are assigned by God to one or the other camp, so the community must have seen itself as the assembly of the upright awaiting God's final triumph while avoiding the corruptions of Judaean society. The text ends with a long hymn of gratitude for having been placed among the righteous.

The *War Scroll* (*1QM*; full name *The War of the Children of Light against the Children of Darkness*) brings the apocalyptic struggle to its final stages, describing a series of battles to be fought at the end of time. Each side will have its banners (the slogans are provided in detail) and its guardian angels; each will win some battles and lose others, though, of course, the forces of righteousness will prevail in the end. The outcome of this war will be influenced in part by the participation of a mysterious gentile nation known as the *Kittim*, which is mentioned in other scrolls as well. If this eschatological fantasy contains a reflection of current affairs, the Kittim were probably the Romans, who were now preparing for their final conquest of the former Seleucid territories.

More concrete information about the great struggle against God's enemies emerges from a type of document that the authors called *pesher* (plural *p'sharim*), or "interpretation." These documents provide detailed examinations of biblical books, especially books of prophecy, in which scriptural references or predictions are applied to the history or the current situation of the community itself. The *pesher* to the prophetic book of Habakkuk (*1QpHab*) speaks of a series of encounters between two unnamed persons, the Teacher of Righteousness (or the Righteous Teacher) and the Wicked Priest. References to these two mysterious individuals appear in other scrolls as well. The Teacher of Righteousness was apparently the founder of the group, a priest unhappy with the course of affairs in Jerusalem; he quarreled with the Wicked Priest, apparently the high priest of his time, and eventually had to escape into the desert to protect himself and his followers. The identity of the Wicked Priest remains uncertain, but he was most likely one of the early Hasmonaeans.

In general, the Scrolls hide their historical references behind epithets of this kind. A later Hasmonaean monarch (probably Alexander Jannaeus) is called the Lion of Wrath. A group whom the community did not like (possibly the Pharisees) is called the Smooth Preachers. Perhaps the authors adopted this technique in order to indicate that every generation has its Wicked Priest and its Righteous Teacher, but that idea cannot account for the large number of epithets that are scattered throughout the Scrolls. Perhaps these epithets are a literary device designed to intrigue the reader, or perhaps the authors avoided naming their enemies out of sheer prudence.

One other scroll should be mentioned here: the Hymn Scroll (*1QH*), a set of psalm-like poems written in biblical Hebrew and reflecting the spirituality of the community and its founder. These hymns express deep and humble gratitude to God for having allowed the members of the community to be counted among the Children of Light.

CALENDAR AND CONTROVERSY

Every social organization needs a shared calendar to plan its activities and help maintain its cohesion. Professional sports leagues need to agree on which teams will play against one another on any given date; otherwise, the athletes won't know where to go. Americans have to agree to celebrate their country's origin on the Fourth of July; it would be extremely awkward if some insisted on that date while others preferred the Seventeenth of September, the date the Constitution was signed. Ancient Jews had a calendar as well (see Chapter 1, "The Biblical Calendar"), but in the days of the Second Temple this force for unity turned into a ground for bitter dispute. Two examples of this development can be examined here.

1. Leviticus 23 provides a brief summary listing of the festivals of the year. After treating Passover and the Feast of Unleavened Bread in verses 4–8, the text goes on to require the offering of a sheaf of new wheat "on the day after the Sabbath" and then to provide for another festival, the Feast of Weeks, fifty days after the presentation of that sheaf (verses 11–16). But which Sabbath was meant? Later rabbinic tradition began the count on the day immediately after the festival itself, that is, on the sixteenth of the month Nissan: by itself this was a reasonable idea, supported by the general flow of the biblical text, but that date might fall on any day of the week, in other words most likely not "on the day after the Sabbath" (in the usual sense of that word) at all. This interpretation was defended by pointing out that the festival was a day when ordinary labor was forbidden (see 23:7) and thus was a kind of Sabbath; nevertheless, many groups during the Second Temple period rejected this approach and insisted that the sheaf had to be offered, and the count had to begin, on the first day of the week. The second-century BCE *Book of Jubilees* (6:32–35) and the Dead Sea community insisted on a 364-day solar calendar; this meant that each date of the year always fell on the same day of the week, and the Feast of Weeks could always fall on Sunday. Different interpreters began the count from different Sabbaths – some the Sabbath before Passover, some the Sabbath during the week of the Festival of Unleavened Bread, some the Sabbath after that – but all those who used this calendar agreed that the fiftieth day had to be at the beginning of the week. The Mishnah (Menahot 10:3) reports that the Boethusians (apparently a group associated with the Sadducees) insisted that the sheaf should *not* be offered on the day after the festival,

but it also reports (perhaps fancifully) that the Temple proceedings openly rejected that view.

2. The Dead Sea *pesher* to Habakkuk, in its interpretation of Habakkuk 2:15, reports that the Wicked Priest once "chased after the Teacher of Righteousness to the house of his exile to swallow him up in his furious anger.... And at the end of the time appointed for rest, the Day of Atonement, appeared before them to swallow them up and cause them to fail on the Sabbath Day of Fasting" (*1QpHab* 11:7–9). The Wicked Priest was presumably the high priest in Jerusalem (see "The Dead Sea Scrolls (II)"); how did people not notice that he was missing from his post and chasing after his enemies in the desert on the most solemn day of the year? This mysterious report makes a lot more sense if we imagine that the Dead Sea community, with the Teacher of Righteousness at its head, followed a different calendar from the official Temple calendar; the sect may have been observing the Day of Atonement, but for the high priest it was an ordinary workday, perfectly suitable for desert raids and other kinds of political business.

Of all the dimensions of religious life, the calendar most lends itself to factional dispute because it is inescapably public in its function. If groups differ over details in the dietary laws, they can eat different foods. They can recite different prayers in their respective synagogues; they can favor different interpretations of biblical stories. They can celebrate holy days on different days as well, but only as private groups; the Temple, the great national center of the Jewish religion, could not celebrate the Feast of Weeks half a dozen times in order to satisfy different interpreters of an obscure passage in the Torah. The priestly authorities adopted one interpretation of that passage, set the festive date accordingly, and went about their business: others could celebrate whenever they liked, but not in the Temple. The authorities could ignore them or sense a threat and try to suppress their activities; reports about the Feast of Weeks do not say, but the Habakkuk *pesher* implies that they sometimes reacted with force.

The by-laws laid down penalties for a variety of offenses, not all quite so harsh, but Josephus reports that some unfortunates were reduced to wandering the desert and living off wild grasses.[12]

The *pesher* documents make clear that the members of the Qumran sect saw themselves as living fulfillments of ancient prophecy: in their view, specific verses in the Bible predicted incidents in the life of the Righteous Teacher or the history of their sect. This perspective, combined with the expectation of an impending Divine intervention, must have produced a very high level of religious excitement in the group: now more than ever, people had to hold fast to their destined role in God's plan. A little earlier, the Book of Daniel had also taught that in times of crisis the task of the righteous is to persevere:[13] the people of Qumran applied that idea specifically to themselves.

If the Qumran people were the Children of Light, then the wicked high priest of Jerusalem was the leader of the Children of Darkness. It is remarkable that this son of the Maccabees, heir to a family that had achieved greatness by defending the teachings of Moses from those who sought to uproot them, was now the target of such fierce anger. The Maccabees had established the principle that Jews must not seek to be like other people, and now the people of Qumran narrowed still further the field of righteousness: they refused even to be like other Jews! In the world of the Dead Sea Scrolls, the other nations hardly mattered at all, except as instruments of God's vengeance. The great struggle between God and his enemies was to be fought entirely within the framework of the covenant.

When the Romans destroyed Jerusalem, the Sadducees quickly disappeared. The masses had grown to detest the corrupt and arrogant high priests, and without the Temple there was no further need for them. The hereditary Jewish priesthood did not disappear,[14] but leadership passed to other parties. As for the Essenes, there is no record of their eventual fate. Qumran was destroyed by fire in the course of the great rebellion, probably by a Roman army searching for the last remnants of Jewish resistance: this may have been the occasion for concealing the Scrolls in the caves above the settlement. So the history of their community era ended in conflagration, just as those documents had predicted, but the new era was very different from the visionaries' expectations.[15]

* * *

It is very difficult to form a balanced picture of the ancient Pharisees, the third group whom Josephus describes, because our information about them comes from strongly biased sources: early rabbinic literature, which idealized the Pharisees (see Chapter 8), and the

Gospels of the Christian New Testament, which detested them (see most famously Matthew 23). Josephus's own description of the Pharisees varies from the early *Jewish War* to the later, rather more favorable picture that he provides in the *Jewish Antiquities*.

Josephus reports that the Pharisees were the most numerous of the three movements. According to all sources, the Pharisees were widely respected as religious teachers, experts in "ancestral tradition."[16] Modern writers have taken Josephus's phrase as referring to the later rabbis' Oral Torah, but this is almost surely an anachronism, as already mentioned. The point is not that the Pharisees went around spreading an organized body of unwritten teaching, but that ordinary Judaeans respected the Pharisees for their knowledge and piety, and therefore sought them out as teachers in many different situations. It was this reputation for piety that provoked the fierce resentment of many early Christians, because it was a style of piety very different from theirs (again, see Matthew 23).

What was the piety of the Pharisees? The name *Pharisee* is derived from an Aramaic word meaning "separation." Christian and rabbinic texts agree that the Pharisees took extreme care to maintain ritual purity in their everyday lives. This required separation from the causes of impurity and also from ordinary people, who were probably impure most of the time.[17] The rules of purity as laid down in the Torah identify a great many causes of impurity (Hebrew *tum'ah*) in everyday life. Certain causes of impurity, such as contact with a dead rodent, were simply unavoidable in the daily life of a Judaean farmer. Menstruating women were deemed impure, though this condition was entirely involuntary. Sexual intercourse left a couple impure, yet the Torah did not encourage celibacy, and in fact took for granted that sexual activity was a natural part of life. Even childbirth, which the Torah considers a blessing, was held to cause impurity.[18]

Precisely for this reason, ritual impurity carried no moral implication. It was taken for granted that most people were impure a lot of the time, and the Torah offered no criticism of this state of affairs. The only important consequence of finding oneself in a state of impurity was that one had to avoid any contact with the sacred: one could not enter the Temple; one could not have contact with sacrificial meat or other sacred foods or with the utensils used to prepare and eat these. To violate this prohibition was considered a terrible thing: the Day of Atonement, the holiest day of the Jewish year, seems to have originally marked an annual cleansing of the sanctuary itself from accidental, unknown violations of this fundamental rule.[19] Fortunately, most forms of impurity were easily removed through immersion in pools of water; when people wanted to visit the Temple or take part in a sacrificial feast, they underwent the necessary cleansing and then they were free to do as they wished. Most Judaeans needed to worry about all this only on special occasions (the priests themselves were surely an exception to this, and possibly most residents of Jerusalem); the rest of the time these complicated, restrictive laws played little or no role in their lives.

The Pharisees' innovation was that *they extended the rules of purity and impurity into their everyday lives. They ate ordinary meals as if these were sacrificial feasts. No one could be pure all the time, but this became the focus and the goal of their religious lives.* This commitment required people to master a great many complicated rules, and it demanded a high degree of attention to countless minute details. It also unavoidably caused a degree of separation from people who were unwilling or unable to maintain this rigorous discipline, and this possibly explains the strong feelings of other people toward the group. Some honored the Pharisees and tried to emulate them; others honored them without trying to be like them; still others, the Gospel writers among these,[20] disliked the Pharisees' isolation and viewed it as an expression of self-righteousness and religious snobbery.

Unlike the Essenes, the Pharisees did not guard their purity by withdrawing from national life. According to Josephus, there were Pharisees in every village and thousands of them in Jerusalem. Under the Hasmonaeans the Pharisees consistently worked to spread their influence, though Queen Salome was the only monarch of the dynasty who sided with them against the Sadducees. (For this reason she was remembered very warmly in later rabbinic teachings, while the family as a whole was recalled with a certain reserve.) Josephus reports that on King Herod's death, leaders of the Pharisees were able to organize huge public demonstrations against the Romans (on King Herod "the Great," see Chapter 7); he wants his readers to understand that even when the Pharisees were excluded from circles of power, their influence over the masses could not be ignored.[21]

These three groups originated and flourished during the brief independence of the Hasmonaean kingdom. Even taken together, however, they represent only a small percentage of the populace. Most Judaeans belonged to "the people of the land," the unaffiliated majority who followed the rules of the Torah as best they could without becoming involved in partisan disputes over fine points and elaborations of the kind just outlined. They avoided those actions that the Torah forbids, and they performed those actions that the Torah requires. They celebrated the great festivals, in Jerusalem when they could and at home when they could not. They married as custom dictated and raised their children as they too had been raised. Local customs surely varied from place to place. Individuals' compliance with the complicated rules of tithing or purity and defilement varied according to their temperament and local expectation. But enough was held in common that Judaea had a distinct and identifiable national culture, based on a revered holy book and held together by the exclusive worship of a single national God.

6

Diaspora and Homeland

THE WORD *DIASPORA* (GREEK FOR "SCATTERING") DESIGNATES the members of a nation or ethnic group who live outside their nation's original territory. Sooner or later most nations generate a diaspora, though smaller communities tend to blend into their surroundings and lose their distinctive identity. A Jewish Diaspora has existed since the Babylonian Exile, if not earlier;[1] in fact, since early in the Common Era, a majority of world Jewry has lived outside the Land of Israel. No history of the Jews or of Judaism is complete without an examination of this ancient widespread phenomenon.

When the Assyrians conquered the Kingdom of Israel in 722 BCE, they displaced its entire population and settled the land with foreigners who had similarly been removed from their homes.[2] The ultimate fate of these Israelite exiles has never been determined. They probably mingled with the peoples of the territories where they were settled and lost their national identity (this was the Assyrians' purpose), though some may have wandered back and merged into the surviving kingdom of the tribe of Judah.[3]

The fate of the Babylonian exiles of 597 and 586 was different. The first set of transfers took place about ten years before the final defeat. This earlier group of exiled leaders naturally stayed in touch with their homeland, because Judah remained an independent if subjugated kingdom.[4] In this way a pattern was created that the second, larger exile group could simply continue. Moreover, the Babylonian conquerors did not simply empty out the land and then fill it with newcomers, as the Assyrians had done; they carried the Judahite leadership off to Babylon, where they would be less likely to plan rebellion, but left the bulk of the population on the land in order to minimize disruption and keep the territory economically productive. As a result, the uprooted Judahites (Hebrew *yehudim*, hence "Jews") never lost contact with their fellow Israelites who remained in the ancient homeland.

The exiles settled down in Babylon and built a secure life there.[5] The Babylonians, for their part, supported these efforts (after all, this too would discourage the tendency to make trouble) and even provided an honorable stipend to surviving remnants of the royal House of David.[6] The exiles remembered their lost homeland with intense longing (see Psalm 137:1–6), but they now made lives some-where else and soon felt themselves at home; when Ezra the scribe made his famous trip to Jerusalem (see Chapter 3), he had trouble finding Levites to come with him (Ezra 8:15–20).

It is very difficult to reconstruct the life of the exile community: its size, its geographic distribution, its inner organization, or its religious practices. However, it is highly suggestive that when Ezra emerged from Babylon with a copy of the Book of the Teaching of Moses and brought that book to *Yehud*, it was apparently unknown to the people already there (again, see Chapter 3). This fact, together with the dif-ficulties Ezra and Nehemiah faced as they tried to put the Torah into practice, suggests that some of the religious issues of the preexilic period had not completely faded away.

What did those difficulties concern? Both Ezra and Nehemiah report that many Judahite men had married foreign women, and the new leaders forced those men to send their wives away.[7] Nehemiah had to contend with Jews who were defying other reli-gious norms as well: wealthy Jews were illegally demanding interest from poor brethren who needed loans,[8] the high priest had allowed an Ammonite to take up residence in the Temple, the Levites' tithes had been neglected, the Sabbath was routinely violated.[9] All this suggests that Ezra and Nehemiah had brought with them from Babylon a set of religious expectations and requirements that were more severe than the accepted standards in *Yehud*; these expectations were encoded in Ezra's Torah book, a book seemingly unfamiliar to the people of Jerusalem and one they appear to have been uneager to accept. The same groups who had for generations resisted the prophets' plea to abandon other gods, and who may well have been glad to see the conquerors remove those troublesome people from the scene, now resisted the new leaders' imposition of a little-known but highly demanding book of rules.

In Babylon, however, those same pious circles had developed a way of life that centered on teachings handed down in Moses' name. These teachings contained a wide variety of stories, ethical insights, social regulations, and the like, but more particularly, they included a set of social and ceremonial practices that helped (and may have been designed) to maintain a distinctive Israelite identity. These practices (circumcision, observance of the Sabbath, prevention of social tension through a ban on usury, and so on) had no equivalent in the culture of the surrounding population, and in the new Diaspora situation they must have been deeply valued by a community struggling to maintain its heritage. The people in *Yehud*, however, lived among their own people in their own land and took their identity for granted; many of them apparently failed to see the benefit of these restrictive regulations and had to be forced to respect them. The books of Ezra and Nehemiah reflect constant tension between the groups of returning exiles and those already in the land. Some of the local populace, especially in the outlying regions, were foreigners who felt no tie with the people of Israel. In *Yehud* proper, however, the antagonists were fellow Israelites, other Jews who did not harbor feelings of covenant obligation of the sort the new leadership believed they should. This problem persisted for generations: it was the root cause of the breakdown of order in the days of the Maccabees.[10]

While still in Babylon, Ezra had become learned in the Book of the Teachings of Moses, but we know nothing about the manner of his education. He had kept the record of his priestly ancestry all the way back to Aaron,[11] but we know nothing of priestly families' role in Babylonian Jewish life. Did priests serve as community leaders even in exile? If priests were not the community leaders, who were? We do not know. Nehemiah's family connections earned him a position of high rank in the royal court, but we do not know how this came about. The House of David kept genealogical records for at least 200 years after the fall of Jerusalem and perhaps even longer, but we cannot describe their role in the community. Did they enjoy authority or only empty honor? Were they possibly just ignored? (Given the careful record keeping, the last seems most unlikely.) Whom did they marry? Who provided their livelihood? At a much later time, officials

claiming to have descended from the old royal family bore the title
exilarch and served as hereditary leaders of Babylonian Jewry, but
there is no trace of such officials before the second century CE. When
did this office originate and how? Were the exilarchs of later times[12]
really descendants of the House of David? These are all questions
that scholars cannot answer today.

Nevertheless, it is clear that the Jews of Babylonia did establish a
stable and enduring way of life. Each generation raised children who
carried the heritage forward. When the first rabbis began to arrive
in Babylonia some 800 years after the exile, they found a vast Jewish
population waiting (perhaps ambivalently) to receive them.[13]

* * *

The other early Diaspora arose in Egypt. Earlier biblical writings view
Egypt as a place to be avoided, presumably on account of the memories of enslavement associated with that very name,[14] but nevertheless, a group of Judahite refugees fled southward ahead of the victorious Babylonians and settled there in several different locations.[15]
The ill-fated Jewish temple at Elephantine also bears witness to the
long-standing Jewish presence on that island in the Nile.[16]

The history of those early settlements cannot be reconstructed, but
Jewish life in Hellenistic Egypt (that is, after the time of Alexander the
Great) rapidly flourished. Jews lived in Alexandria virtually from the
time of its founding. Some were apparently brought there as slaves
or prisoners of war;[17] others migrated voluntarily, in response to the
founders' offer of generous incentives to those willing to settle in the
new capital. The Jews eventually formed one of the largest ethnic
minorities in the city, possibly numbering as much as 40 percent of
the entire population.[18]

Other Diaspora settlements quickly emerged as well. Some of
these settlements preceded the Macedonian conquest, as the Persian monarchs often transferred large groups of Jews to outlying
provinces – sometimes benignly, in the hope of strengthening these
territories, and sometimes as punishment for rebellion or resistance
to royal authority. Jews could be found in every major city in the eastern Mediterranean. The Seleucid capital, Antioch, quickly housed a
substantial Jewish community, as did the cities of Hellenistic Asia
Minor. By the time of Cicero and Julius Caesar (mid-first century

BCE), several tens of thousands of Jews lived in the city of Rome. Here too many had probably first arrived as enslaved prisoners of war and eventually received their freedom.

Jews tended to achieve a high level of cultural integration into these diverse environments. They spoke the local language, perhaps in a distinctive dialect but probably not: technical terms such as *Sabbath* that were required for Jewish religious life were simply imported from Hebrew.[19] They dressed like other people; their food habits resembled their neighbors', and so did their means of livelihood. To be sure, these dimensions of daily living were also regulated by the Torah. Jews' food habits were like those of other people, but at the same time they avoided eating pork. They earned their living like other people, but on the Sabbath they were absent from the marketplace.

Over the course of time, Jews in Alexandria mastered the forms of Greek culture to the point of contributing to that culture themselves. The first known Alexandrian Jewish philosopher, a man named Aristoboulus, who lived in the second century BCE, labored to show that biblical anthropomorphism need not offend refined philosophical thought. Indeed, he claimed that all of Greek philosophy is no more than an echo of the teachings of Moses![20] Another Alexandrian Jew of the same time with the biblical name Ezekiel was a poet who wrote tragedies in the classical mode. Ezekiel's characters, however, were not Greek gods or heroes but figures from the Bible: the most famous and the best preserved of his works was a retelling of the Exodus in the form of a tragic drama. Full of long speeches, and replete with scenes not found in scripture, the *Exagogê* was apparently intended for real performance,[21] but no record of an actual production has come down to us.

The most famous Alexandrian writer was the philosopher *Philo*. Scion of an exceedingly wealthy family, Philo received the finest education available; having achieved mastery of both Greek and Jewish literature, Philo became passionately convinced that Greek wisdom and the teachings of Moses (that is, the Torah) contain the same set of truths *as long as each is properly understood*. He then devoted his life to composing an elaborate, philosophically refined explanation of the Torah in the light of this conviction. Since the Torah surely does not appear on its surface to be philosophically refined, consisting as it does of stories about long-dead people along with very detailed rules of behavior, Philo necessarily concluded that the surface meaning of the Torah must be supplemented through a search for deeper truth: the Torah must be read as *allegory*, a text that seems to concern one subject but in fact concerns another. "Philo: The Torah as Allegory" provides a few examples of Philo's allegorical readings. Philo justified this approach through extravagant praise of Moses' wisdom. Not content to depict Moses as a mere secretary writing scripture at God's dictation, Philo describes him as a man so wise that his own thoughts had a kind of divinity. One could do no better than to base one's life on the teachings of such a sage, but no literal or surface reading could do justice to those teachings, hence the need for the elaborate allegory that plumbed their depths.

Philo's own writings reveal that other Jews in Alexandria differed from this approach. Philo repeatedly mocks those who were content with the surface meaning, who were satisfied to tell stories about the patriarchs and obey the instructions left by Moses. In Philo's mind this was to be content with far too little, though (like any Greek philosopher) he was ready to admit that most people could do no better. At the opposite extreme, in a famous passage Philo disputes with those who saw no point in observing the Torah's laws at all once they had achieved the insights those lessons were designed to convey.

Philo criticized this attitude on two grounds. For one thing, it was naive; it reminded him of people who considered the mind more noble than the body and therefore stopped eating! This view was also selfish. To look for the deeper meaning of the Torah while completely disregarding the surface was to leave the masses behind and cut off one's ties to community, as though these seekers after the pure truth had "neither city nor village nor family, no association with people of any kind, . . . seeking after naked truth" while they lost track of things that most people hold dear. Long-established customs have a claim on everyone. It is all right to contemplate the mysteries of the number seven, but the rules of the Sabbath should be upheld as well. The great festivals are symbols of joy in God, but they should be celebrated as well. Even the sanctity of the Temple would be lost if only the inner meaning of things received our attention.[22] For all his spiritual profundity, Philo could not allow the daily richness of Jewish life to be destroyed in this way.

PHILO: THE TORAH AS ALLEGORY

In order to find meaning in the narratives of Genesis, Philo interprets each of the characters as representing a general type of personality or religious experience; the stories themselves can then be read as shedding light on the nature of such personalities or experiences. Thus Abraham, Isaac, and Jacob, the three ancestors of the people of Israel, were all men of virtue, but they achieved virtue by different means and represented different types of religious personality: Abraham achieved virtue through learning, Isaac represented the rare individual who was virtuous by nature, and Jacob managed to attain virtue by dint of constant effort. He was the "man of practice," in contrast to his grandfather, the "man of teaching."

Philo then applies this typology to the narrative details of Genesis and interprets those details accordingly. Jacob wrestled with an angel (Genesis 32:23–33) because the struggle for virtue is an unending combat. Abraham and Jacob both received new names from God (Genesis 17:5; 32:29) because they became new men through the achievement of virtue; Isaac, virtuous by nature, did not require such a mark of transformation. However, Abraham was the man of teaching; once he had learned virtue, he did not forget his lessons. Therefore, once Abraham received his new name, the Torah never mentioned his old one (Abram) again. Jacob, on the other hand, was the man of practice; like all athletes, he was constantly in danger of falling out of shape and losing his newfound abilities. Therefore, Jacob's new name, Israel, and his original name appeared almost interchangeably in the last third of the book.

The laws of the Torah are similarly mined for abstract lessons in ethics, psychology, or theology. The Sabbath comes every seven days because of the special qualities of the number seven, qualities that Philo expounds for pages at a time. The only animals permitted for food are those that chew their cud (Leviticus 11:3): this is a reminder that no true learning can take place unless the student repeatedly coughs up the lesson and chews it over some more. Likewise, all permitted animal food species have split hoofs to remind us that all of life is a series of choices between right and wrong (*On the Special Laws* 4.106–109). The Torah commands that a man with two wives must acknowledge the special rights of his first-born even if the less-loved wife is the mother (Deuteronomy 21:15–17); to Philo, this teaches the lesson that we all prefer pleasure over the quest for virtue, but we must acknowledge nevertheless that the "offspring" of the quest for virtue have a greater claim on our lives and our goods, while children of the love of pleasure come after (*Allegorical Interpretation of the Laws* 2.48).

This is an excellent example of Philo's method, based on careful attention to the actual details of scripture but approaching those details with remarkable freedom of interpretation. If there were no significant difference between the change of Abram's name and that of Jacob's, why would the first take hold without slipping back, while the other appears in constant danger of being undone? If these changes of name contained no lesson for our own lives, why would we want to read about them at all? Why should some foods be allowed and others forbidden? Surely there must be some intrinsic meaning to the distinction. Why should the week be seven days long? It cannot literally be true that the all-powerful Creator needed six days to create the world or that he was tired after all that labor and had to rest; surely the great lawgiver had something else in mind when he wrote those words.

Philo casually mocks the literalists, but he earnestly pleads with the radical philosophers. He can sympathize with their way of thinking, but he cannot accept its consequences and he hopes that on further reflection they too will back away from far-reaching conclusions. A touching passage from his writings helps explain this attitude. He too had once luxuriated in solitary contemplation of the cosmos and had lived alone, so to speak, in the presence of God, but "the great sea of political [or civic] concerns" had swept him away, barely able to keep his head above water. Philo is probably referring to the communal responsibilities that unavoidably fell to him as the child of a distinguished family.[23] He warmly remembers the earlier time when he was free of such distractions, and he envies those Jews who still are free to pursue such interests, but he cannot bear to think that people may abandon Jewish life altogether in their search for pure abstract truth. To Philo, the need to serve his people and the desire to isolate himself in pure contemplation presented demands in constant tension: his life was an endless effort to keep those demands in balance.

Throughout the Diaspora, Jews faced a struggle similar to this one. Striving to feel at home in the places where they lived, fully integrated into their economic and cultural surroundings, they also struggled to maintain a distinct religious and political identity. Their neighbors were skeptical: if they wished so dearly to be accepted as full members of society, why would they not live according to society's rules? Most particularly, why would they not extend the simplest of courtesies and honor the city's gods?[24] Throughout antiquity Jews worked to overcome the hostility behind such questions. Accused of hating the mass of humanity,[25] they responded that they bore no ill will to anyone but were forbidden by their own law to honor other gods. It did not help, of course, that ancient Jewish literature is full of open contempt for idols and the people who worship them. These writings were available for anyone to read, though it appears that few non-Jews actually bothered to track them down.

This tension had a political dimension as well. Josephus provides long extracts from documents in which Roman officials instruct Hellenistic cities, mostly in Asia Minor, to stop harassing their Jewish residents, or in which Hellenistic cities, no doubt under Roman pressure, pass resolutions in which they promise to end such harassment.[26] At issue were matters like the Jews' right to observe the Sabbath in accordance with their traditions, their exemption from compulsory military service, and their right to a gathering place of their own where they could practice their customary ceremonies. The frequency of these communications suggests that Greek interference was a recurrent problem for the Jews in these cities. Jews naturally sought the most favorable political status they could achieve, but Greeks (who thought of these cities as their own) considered the Jews to be a foreign ethnic group who happened to be living among them. The Jews' refusal to worship the civic deities was proof in Greek eyes that Jews were outsiders who had no claim on citizen rights, while the Jews explained this refusal away as technical compliance with the Torah's rules that should have no bearing on their loyalty or their civic rights. Mutual incomprehension on this critical matter was very deep and beyond repair. In general, relations between Jews and Greeks remained tense but peaceful. The numerous resolutions and interventions suggest that the problem demanded constant attention, but actual outbreaks of violence appear to have been rare.

When violence did break out, however, it could be terrible. In the years 38–41, a series of riots against the Jews (in a later time they would have been called *pogroms*) shook the great city of Alexandria. The Jews were rounded up in the amphitheater, where they were terribly mistreated. Many lost their lives. Synagogues were destroyed. The Roman governor at the time, Avillius Flaccus, seemed to be providing the rioters quiet political and material support, and Alexandrian Jewry feared for its very survival.[27]

Several factors contributed to this horrifying outbreak. The Greeks of Alexandria had long resented the Roman takeover of their city, once a Greek royal capital, in 31–30 BCE. In particular, they felt that the Romans had unfairly favored the Jews, and they fiercely disliked this.[28] The governor, Flaccus, saw an opportunity to win over the Greek population of the city by allowing them to vent their anger at the Jews. He also hoped by this to regain the favor of the new emperor, Caligula (reigned 37–41), whom Flaccus had not supported during the just-ended struggle for power. Caligula, for his part, also did not like Jews, because they resisted his claim to be a living god and would not put his statue in their Temple and their synagogues. It was in the aftermath of this horrifying crisis that Philo led a delegation of Alexandrian Jews to Rome to meet the emperor and try to moderate his dislike for them. They had little success.

In the end, Flaccus's mismanagement of the situation in Alexandria cost him his position and eventually his life. Shortly after meeting the Jewish delegation, Gaius Caligula himself was murdered by high-ranking Romans who could not abide his tyrannical lunacy. The crisis in Alexandria had subsided, and the new emperor, Claudius (reigned 41–54), issued a decree in which he aimed to establish a new, lasting stability (see "The Emperor Claudius and the Jews of Alexandria"). This decree put an end for good to Jewish attempts to gain citizenship in the *polis*. The emperor acknowledged that Jews had lived in Alexandria since its foundation. He recognized the Jews' right to maintain their distinctive way of life, and in time-honored Roman fashion he cautioned the Alexandrians to cease interfering with this right. At the same time, however, the emperor made it clear that Jews were foreigners living in the city and should not hope to overcome their present status as aliens. (It is significant that he addressed them as "Jews," that is, Judaeans, but their antagonists as "Alexandrians.") He sternly

THE EMPEROR CLAUDIUS AND THE JEWS OF ALEXANDRIA

In the year 38, the Greeks (and native Egyptians?) of Alexandria viciously attacked the Jews with the tacit support of the Roman governor, Flaccus; in the year 41, after Flaccus had been arrested and killed and the hostile emperor, Caligula, had also been murdered, the Jews violently retaliated against their attackers. The new ruler, Claudius, quickly took steps to calm the turbulent city and issued an open letter to the citizens of Alexandria expressing his hopes and his concerns. The emperor's letter covers many issues; only the part that specifically addresses the status of Alexandrine Jewry is translated here. Claudius addresses the citizens of Alexandria:

As to the question of responsibility for the riot and feud (or rather, if the truth be told, the war) against the Jews, your ambassadors, and particularly Dionysius son of Theon, made your cause most vigorously in the argument, but I did not wish to inquire [into this] too thoroughly. Still, I have in reserve an abiding indignation against those who renewed the outbreak, and I tell you directly that if you do not end this stubborn destructive enmity toward one another I shall be forced to show what a well-intentioned ruler is like when he is brought around to righteous anger. Even now, therefore, I solemnly enjoin yet once again that, on the one side, the Alexandrines behave gently and kindly toward the Jews who for many years have dwelt in the same city, and not offend the customary exercise of their honor to their god but permit them to maintain their customs as in the time of the god Augustus, which I also, having heard both sides, have confirmed. On the other side, I order the Jews not to strive unduly for any [advantages] beyond what they have enjoyed up to now; and not ever again, as though living in two cities, to send two embassies (something never done before!); and not to barge into games [that are] under the leadership of the gymnasiarchs or their assistants, but to take pleasure from what is theirs, enjoying an abundance of all good things in a city not their own; and not to admit or to invite Jews sailing down from Syria or Egypt (from which I would be forced to conceive worse suspicions). If they do not [behave as instructed], I shall go after them in every way as though they have aroused a kind of general plague for the whole world. If you both put aside these [present attitudes] and are willing to treat each other with kindness and good will, I too will care for the city in the highest degree, as the founders of my family had begun to do.

Claudius thus rebukes both sides for having contributed to the unrest, though not quite symmetrically: he urges or "enjoins" (Greek *diamarturomai*) the Greeks but "orders" (*keleuô*) the Jews to abandon their previous mutual hostility. He commands the Greeks to stop interfering with Jewish religious life, but he reminds the Jews (whom he does *not* call Alexandrines) that Alexandria is not their city, and he warns them to abandon their persistent attempts to gain the rights of citizens. Claudius is plainly annoyed with the Jews: he complains of their political disorganization (two delegations indeed!), he hints at suspicions that they intend further violence, and he warns them not to become a "general plague" infecting his whole empire. Nevertheless, he concludes on an optimistic note: if both sides learn to accept the arrangement that he has decreed – full religious rights but not citizen rights, for the Jews – he will reward the city accordingly.

Josephus quotes another document in which the emperor seems to grant the Jews precisely the rights he has denied here; see *Antiquities* 19.280–285. But the papyrus document is unquestionably authentic, so it must be concluded that Josephus's document is not, at least not in its present form.

An uneasy peace prevailed in Alexandria for several more generations, but in a later uprising (115–117 CE) the Jews nearly destroyed the city, and their community was all but wiped out in return. See Chapter 7.

instructed them to stop trying to achieve rights that were not theirs; in effect, he criticized them for causing so much bother, and he warned them to stop making so much noise before he became really angry. It quickly became apparent that the emperor intended this settlement to apply throughout the empire. Individual Jews might achieve local (or Roman) citizenship in recognition of their achievements or contributions, but the Jews as a group could not aspire to full civic equality in the many cities where they lived.

Thus, the Jews' political struggles reached an unstable conclusion. On the one hand, a protected and even privileged minority, on the other, forever excluded from political equality, most Jewish communities of the Greco-Roman Diaspora maintained their separate existence for centuries. The situation changed in the third century CE, when Roman citizenship was extended to all free residents of the empire,[29] and again during the fourth and fifth centuries, when the now-Christian empire began to exclude Jews from positions of power and honor. These later developments, as well as the later history of Babylonian Jewry, will be examined in Chapters 8 and 9.

* * *

In spite of the difficulties just outlined, however, the Jews became a visible and effective presence in the early Roman Empire, so that governments had to take account of the Jews' wishes and the Jews' ability to demand attention. However, the most striking evidence of successful Jewish adaptation to the Diaspora was the steady flow of newcomers into their communities. It is not clear that such people should be labeled *converts*. The English word suggests people who have undergone a powerful religious experience, and ancient "Jews by choice" did not always adopt that identity out of spiritual motivations: other factors might have included the desire to marry a Jew, admiration for the cohesion of Jewish communities or the generosity of Jewish philanthropic arrangements, philosophical attraction to Jewish monotheism, simple fascination with Jewish rituals, even awe at the power of Jewish magic. The Greek word *prosêlutos* simply means "newcomer," and the English derivative *proselyte* should be understood in that sense.[30]

Very little can be said about the procedures by which such people were accepted as Jews: these may have varied widely over time across the huge expanse of the Mediterranean Diaspora. In later times, rabbinic law standardized a process by which newcomers could attach themselves to the people of Israel,[31] but that process may not have been formalized until after the great wave of newcomers had ended. One thing, however, is clear: during the last generations before the Common Era and the first generations thereafter, many people who had not been born Jews took up Jewish identity and the Jewish way of life. The size of the Jewish population in the early Roman Empire cannot be explained in any other way, and the frequent complaints by Roman writers that the Jews were everywhere, and were stealing the flower of Roman youth, point to the same conclusion. This wave of newcomers began to slow down after the great Diaspora war of 115–117 and the Bar Kokhba disaster a few years later, but it did not entirely stop until the newly dominant Christian Church moved the emperors to ban conversion to Judaism on pain of death.[32]

Associated with the full proselytes was another category of persons whom rabbinic law never recognized but who seem to have formed an important presence in the cities of the Diaspora: these were the so-called godfearers,[33] individuals who took on some or even most of the obligations of Jewish life but never formally became Jews. Many factors may have blocked that final step: family resistance, civic pressure, residual fear of the gods, fear of the pain or embarrassment of circumcision. Still, the existence of large numbers of such people is additional evidence of the attractive power of Judaism in the Diaspora. Many Christians repeatedly visited synagogues, to the great displeasure of Church leaders (see Chapter 10), but it appears that the great majority of proselytes and godfearers were drawn from the ranks of polytheism.

7

A Century of Disasters

WHEN THE ROMAN CONQUEROR POMPEY ABOLISHED THE Hasmonaean kingdom in 63 BCE, the national culture (*Ioudaismos*, the way Judaeans do things) remained, and the nation's way of life began to replace the monarchy as the visible focus of national identity and pride. Much remained in place. The Torah could still be studied and obeyed, the festivals could still be celebrated, the priests in the Temple could still offer the required sacrifices. Pompey allowed the manageable Hyrcanus II to remain in office, not as king but as high priest and official head (*ethnarch*) of the Judaean nation. The defeated Aristoboulus was eventually brought as prisoner to Rome, where he nursed his pride and plotted recovery, but in many important respects the Roman conquest seemed to allow the people of Judaea to go on living as they had done before.

This arrangement lasted until the year 40 BCE, when Antigonus, son of Aristoboulus, returned to Judaea with a Parthian army[1] and expelled the Romans from the land. The unlucky Hyrcanus was carted off to Parthia, where his ear was sliced off,[2] while Antigonus took over the priesthood more than twenty years after his father had been forced to abandon it. The Romans were stunned by this disaster and turned for rescue to a political newcomer, a man named Herod. Herod's father, Antipater, was an Idumaean, from a territory south of Judaea proper that had been absorbed into the kingdom during its years of expansion, one of the many who had been forced to take on the Jewish way of life as a result of that expansion. Antipater had served for years as intimate advisor to the now-exiled Hyrcanus. He had demonstrated his usefulness (and his loyalty) to Rome, and now his son was offered the kingdom as a reward. The Roman Senate formally recognized Herod as king of Judaea; if he could only recapture the kingdom from its Parthian occupiers, it was his to rule.

It took Herod three years (and the help of a large Roman force) to accomplish this task, but by 37 he was master of Judaea. To enhance his legitimacy he married Mariamme, a Hasmonaean princess, and arranged for her younger brother to become high priest as Aristoboulus III. Herod ruled for over thirty years, until his death in 4 BCE. During his lifetime, Rome went through the last stages of its endless civil war and was transformed from a chaotic republic to a military despotism under the rule of a single emperor, but Herod survived the transition thanks to his great political skill and the Romans' desire for a friendly client kingdom at the eastern edge of their empire. Exploiting his good standing in the Romans' eyes, Herod built Judaea into a large and wealthy kingdom. Donations to the cities of Greece and elsewhere won him much gratitude, and by rebuilding the Temple in Jerusalem he turned that shrine into one of the great tourist sites of the world (Figure 4).[3] King of Judaea by decree of the Roman Senate, he went down in history as Herod the Great.

There was a notorious somber side to Herod's reign as well: everywhere he turned, he saw conspiracies against himself. Even his own family was not safe. His young brother-in-law, the last Hasmonaean high priest, soon died by drowning (by accident, it was said) in 35 BCE. In 29 he put his beloved wife and several sons to death because he suspected them of plotting against his life. Other sons were executed in subsequent years as well.[4] On his deathbed, Herod ordered that when he finally died, several beloved religious leaders should be executed as well; he was afraid that the people would greet news of his own death with celebration rather than mourning, and he was determined to prevent such joy. The order was not carried out.

Religious developments in Judaea under Herod mainly continued previous trends. The Sadducees and Pharisees kept up their rivalry. The settlement at Qumran was destroyed by an earthquake in the year 31 BCE and not rebuilt during Herod's lifetime, but the religious movement centered there seems eventually to have recovered its energies. It appears that *Jesus of Nazareth* was born toward the

4. The Western Wall in Jerusalem. When the Romans destroyed the Temple complex in 70 CE, the western perimeter wall remained standing. This location became a site for Jewish pilgrimage in the centuries that followed, and after the city was reunited in 1967 CE, it was turned into an important site of modern worship. The picture provides a glimpse of the *tallit* or fringed shawl and *tefillin* used in traditional Jewish worship; see Chapter 8, "The *Sh'ma*," for more information. (Photo courtesy of Todd Bolen/bibleplaces.com)

end of Herod's reign, but his career took place only several decades later.

* * *

During a period of mounting turmoil, many itinerant preachers traveled the countryside bringing word of God's impending visitation and urging their audience to prepare themselves for this great event. For some, preparation meant military readiness; for others, repentance and a more righteous way of life. The Roman occupiers found it hard to tell these types apart, and from their perspective both were dangerous. The Romans saw Jews in general as irrational and excitable – they never knew when a crowd of Jews would suddenly start rioting and throwing stones – and all these preachers (whatever their message) tended to attract excited throngs. Roman anxiety in Judaea was accordingly high, and especially so during festival periods, when Jerusalem was crowded and enthusiasm was at a peak.

Among these wandering sermonizers was a Galilean named Joshua (in Greek *Iesous*), who attracted a large following among the ordinary people of the land. It is hard 2,000 years later to reconstruct the precise themes of his message,[5] but they seem to have included a demand for moral purity[6] and righteousness in preparation for God's coming judgment. We cannot know whether Jesus directly said anything about the Romans, but his basic message implied a sharp critique of the corrupt and violent high-priestly regime in Jerusalem: neither the Roman nor the Jewish leadership can have been very happy over his growing popularity.

One Passover season, at the most tension-ridden time of the year, Jesus was rounded up and executed. Surviving information is sketchy and not entirely consistent, but most likely the Roman and the Jewish priestly authorities were equally happy to see him gone. Among his followers, however, the belief quickly spread that Jesus had overcome death: he had risen from his tomb, had briefly rejoined his followers, and then had ascended directly to heaven. This belief ultimately gave rise to a new religion, called *Christianity* from the Greek word *Christos*, itself a translation of the Hebrew *mashiach* or "anointed"; this name reflected the conviction, confirmed by his astonishing resurrection, that Jesus had been God's Messiah, a divine Savior whose mission was to put an end to the long history of human affliction.

At this time, most people in Judaea firmly expected that God would soon deliver them from their suffering through some spectacular action, and this expectation took various forms. The Qumran community (see Chapter 5) expected that God would soon destroy a corrupted Jerusalem and allow the Children of Light to assume their rightful place in the world, others awaited a supremely talented but otherwise normal human being who would evict the idolatrous Romans from the Holy Land, and still others located the cause of their misery in the general human condition and expected that God would soon put an end to death or the human inclination to sin. This diversity in expectation of the end led to corresponding diversity in the expectation of God's method: some supposed that the awaited redemption could occur within the framework of natural human events, while others, especially those who feared that the predicament was too deep for any ordinary human to resolve, thought that only God Himself or some other superhuman being could fix what was wrong.

Thus it was possible to think that the Messiah, God's own anointed, would be a mortal who would achieve astounding political or military victories and restore the freedom and the greatness of Israel, but it also was possible to dismiss such victories as provincial or ephemeral, unworthy of the majesty of God. Those who held this latter view expected the Messiah to do something far more consequential, perhaps to overcome death and offer eternal life, perhaps to overcome sin, offer total forgiveness, and resolve the endless human struggle with sin and guilt. No human being could do that; only God himself, though perhaps in human form, could accomplish it.

* * *

The final version of Herod's will provided for the division of his kingdom among several surviving sons, with *Archelaus* inheriting Judaea proper and the right to be called king. The sons converged on Rome, each eager to convince the Emperor Augustus to increase his share of the realm at his brothers' expense. In the end Augustus upheld the will, except that Archelaus was forbidden to call himself king. He was to style himself ethnarch of the Jews, as Hyrcanus II had done half a century earlier; another Judaean kingdom had come to an end.

Augustus removed Archelaus in 6 CE, on grounds of cruelty and incompetence, and the Romans absorbed Judaea directly into their empire. They began sending out imperial officials as governors of the province, and things went badly from the beginning. Judaea was not a wealthy or beautiful province, and the emperors sent their best people to territories where their skills would be most useful. By contrast, many of the Roman governors of Judaea were men of little talent or honesty, unsuited for the position they occupied. The regimes of Herod and Archelaus had already encountered violent resistance, and this problem now grew steadily worse.

In addition, Judaea was not a culturally sympathetic area. The Romans saw themselves as the chosen people of the gods, destined to unite the world under their benevolent rule. The Jews too, of course, saw themselves as the chosen people of the one true God, and naturally disliked the rival claims of their idol-worshiping conquerors. As a result, the natives resented their Roman overlords, while the latter considered Judaism a bizarre and irritating oriental cult. The occupiers refused to understand Judaism or respect Jewish sensitivities. The notorious Pontius Pilate, governor for ten years (26–36 CE), once tried to sneak military emblems (for which Romans had a religious awe) into the holy city of Jerusalem. The populace threatened to riot until the offending objects were removed, and declared that Pilate could kill them all if it came to that, so the governor backed down.[7] On another occasion, a Roman soldier assigned to keep order during a religious procession disrupted order instead by exposing himself to the crowd; the infuriated onlookers predictably rioted, and according to Josephus, 20,000 people lost their lives in the tumult.[8] On yet another occasion, a soldier tore up a Torah scroll out of spite;[9] the soldier was put to death, but the damage to Jewish–Roman relations was profound and could not be repaired. The people were increasingly on edge waiting for the next Roman outrage, just as the Romans anxiously awaited the next Jewish riot.

The worst episode of this kind took place in the year 38. The Emperor Caligula, a despot who took literally the standard proclamation that he was a living god, ordered that a statue of himself be placed in the Jerusalem Temple. Caligula had already come to dislike the Jews for resisting his claim to divinity, and when a Jewish mob in Jamnia destroyed an altar in his honor that non-Jews had set up to annoy them, the emperor retaliated by issuing his shocking demand. A huge delegation of Jews went to Petronius, the governor of Syria, and implored him to rescue them from the emperor's order. Petronius knew that Caligula could not be talked out of his desire, but he also knew that Judaea would explode at any attempt to carry it out, so he played for time and did nothing. The emperor saw that his instructions were being treated lightly and he ordered the governor to commit suicide, but he was himself assassinated before this command reached Petronius; thus the governor's life was saved and the emperor's order quietly set aside. Jews worldwide were jubilant at this narrow rescue, but they did not forget the horrifying demonstration that Roman power, when exercised callously or angrily, could threaten the innermost heart of their way of life.

Shortly after this episode, a brief change for the better raised hopes that Judaea might yet live in peace. The late King Herod had a grandson named Agrippa, who was sent to Rome for his education and there became the close friend of the future emperor, Caligula. On coming to power in the spring of 37, the new ruler honored Agrippa by granting him portions of Herod's old realm (not yet including Judaea proper) and allowing him to rule them as king.[10] A few years later, in 41, when Caligula was murdered, Agrippa (who happened to be back in Rome) played an important part in securing the throne for the new sovereign, Claudius. In exchange, Claudius expanded Agrippa's kingdom to the size of his grandfather's. It seemed that the anxieties and discomforts of direct Roman rule had been removed.

Agrippa had enjoyed a wild youth, but he assumed his new royal position in a calm and measured way. He showed great loyalty to the Temple through gifts and frequent sacrifice. His coins (at least in Judaea) avoided any display of offensive images. When challenged by religious hard-liners, he responded calmly and in good humor, and he slowly won the affection of his Judaean subjects. However, shortly after a spectacular appearance in Caesarea, he died young after a very brief illness.[11] The Romans withheld the throne from his young son, also named Agrippa, and this last experiment in Judaean sovereignty came to a sudden, unexpectedly rapid conclusion.[12]

The governors who followed were even worse than those who had served before Agrippa's brief reign. In the words of one recent writer, "it might be thought ... that they ... systematically and deliberately set out to drive the people to revolt."[13] In some cases impelled by greed and in all cases showing complete disregard for Jewish sensibilities, they brought the province to a state of virtually permanent rebellion.

Judaea had long been a restless province. From the earliest days of direct rule by Rome, a group of militants called *sicarii* ("daggermen")[14] had engaged in frequent acts of violent resistance to the new regime. Not content to wait for God to deliver His people from idolatrous foreign rule, militants set out to destroy that rule on their own and conducted unrelenting guerrilla warfare against Rome and its high-priestly supporters. By the time Agrippa I became king, Judaea had been gradually collapsing into chaos for years. His short reign seemed to offer a brighter future, but then the steady decline simply resumed. Government repression and popular resentment mounted side by side; barely twenty years after the king had died, the province was ready to explode.

The explosion, when it came, took both sides by surprise.[15] The last prewar governor of Judaea, Gessius Florus, was rapacious far beyond the standard that his greedy predecessors had set. In the spring of 66 CE, he raided the treasury of the Temple itself, an outrage not previously attempted since the days long ago of Seleucus IV, and the reaction was not only angry but impolite: unidentified persons organized a charitable campaign to raise funds for the seemingly penniless governor. Florus, enraged by this insult, seized Jewish dignitaries at random and had them crucified while he allowed his troops to ravage the city. The next day he brought his troops into Jerusalem again and had them begin once more to massacre the crowds, but this time the people overwhelmed the Roman detachment and drove the governor back to Caesarea. King Agrippa II, who was visiting the country, was unable to convince the populace to declare their loyalty, but a shaky peace was restored. However, rebel forces seized the desert fortress at Masada, and – most fateful of all – priests in the Temple suddenly abolished the daily sacrifice for the emperor, in fact refused all further sacrifices brought by or on behalf of gentiles. The offering for Caesar, which the emperors themselves had supplied, was the accepted substitute for the actual worship that non-Jewish subjects of Rome had to render; to suspend it was an act of open rebellion, a suspension of loyalty to the empire itself. The leadership tried to convince the people to abandon this defiance, but they failed; an armed force sent by King Agrippa likewise failed to impose order and was treacherously murdered while trying to retreat. Riots between Jews and non-Jews broke out in border cities where a mixed population had lived for generations in uneasy quiet. In Jerusalem, the high priest himself, known as a friend of Rome, was dragged from hiding and murdered. Revolution was underway; the people of Judaea had declared war, so it seemed, on the world (see "Who Made the Rebellion?").

The Roman governor of Syria, Cestius Gallus, assembled a larger force than had been marshaled thus far and marched on Judaea to restore order. He came as close as the suburbs of Jerusalem but then, after failing to capture the Temple mount in the heart of the city, he withdrew and headed back toward Syria. His army barely reached

WHO MADE THE REBELLION?

In the text it was suggested that it seemed that "the people of Judaea had declared war . . . on the world," yet this is most emphatically not the picture that Josephus tries to paint. In his narrative, the rebellion was always the work of small factions of hotheads (he calls them "brigands" and the like) who compelled a reluctant nation to undertake a hopeless struggle against the most powerful empire ever known. Was he right?

It is clear why Josephus sought to give the impression that he did: the Romans deeply resented the Jews' insolence in waging a seven-year rebellion against the empire, and the Jewish historian was doing everything he could to convince the conquerors (who were also now his employers) that the rebels were not typical of the nation as a whole. But do modern readers have any way to evaluate his claim?

Substantial elements in the Jewish population opposed the rebellion and remained loyal to the empire. Most of Judaea's ruling class fell into that category, and probably the people in the larger cities with significant Greek populations did so as well. This is not surprising: the ruling class depended on Roman support for their considerable privileges, and Jews in mixed cities knew the Romans would support the Greeks in any outbreak of violence, which meant that any rebelliousness on their part would have been fatal. Details in Josephus's narrative (if one is willing to trust him at all) support these conjectures: he provides a long pro-Roman speech by King Agrippa II as the war is about to start, he reports in horror the murder by a Jewish mob (as he saw it) of the high priest himself, and he describes the wavering and often the ultimate withdrawal from the war effort of the mixed cities of Galilee.

On the other hand, the *sicarii* had been active for decades, and urban guerrilla movements of that kind survive most easily when they enjoy at least the passive support of the wider population. Moreover, the war was originally provoked by a group of young Temple priests when they abruptly refused to offer the daily sacrifice for Caesar. Even if these were admittedly men of immature judgment who brought ruin on their people, they would not have acted as they did without some hostility of their own toward the empire and its representatives.

The Romans, for their part, seem to have held the nation responsible for the war, not just one limited group. The new *fiscus judaicus* was collected throughout the empire and deposited in the temple of Jupiter. When the war was over, Rome declined to permit reconstruction of the Temple. It is true that the Romans also declined to curtail the rights of Jewish communities in the Diaspora, both at the outbreak of the war and when it ended, but that seems to have been chiefly a policy decision designed to keep the violence from spreading. Judging from their literature, Roman hostility toward Jews sharply escalated after the war, and did not distinguish between "good" Jews and rebels.

Perfect certainty in this matter will never be possible, not least because Josephus himself is the main source of information. Nevertheless, it appears that the war, once underway, drew support from a wide spectrum of the population – not from everyone, but from many people in many sectors of the populace. When the war had reached its disastrous conclusion, many refugees carried their fierce hatred of Rome to nearby countries, most importantly Egypt and North Africa; another, equally disastrous rebellion broke out there less than fifty years later (see later).

its goal; a Judaean force surrounded the Romans, captured all their equipment, and all but wiped them out. By now it was mid-autumn, and the revolutionary party was firmly in control. A new high priest was chosen by lot, and regional commanders were sent out to prepare for the expected Roman onslaught. Galilee, where the empire would make its first attack, was entrusted to a young aristocrat named Joseph ben Mattathias. In time, the world would come to know him as the historian Josephus (see Chapter 5, "Josephus").

To replace Cestius Gallus, the Emperor Nero dispatched a seasoned general named Vespasian to take over the war. Vespasian assembled a huge army, and over the course of the year 67 most of Galilee fell into Roman hands: some towns surrendered voluntarily; some had to be subdued by the enormous Roman force. In response to this chain of setbacks, toward the end of 67 a civil uprising in Jerusalem unseated the Jewish notables, a combination of high-ranking priests and distinguished Pharisees, who had led the rebellion thus far. In their place, power fell into the hands of radical nationalists who had come to be known as *Zealots*. When the earlier leadership tried to resist the takeover, the Zealots unleashed a bloodbath and the city sank into chaos.

Vespasian was about to exploit this situation when he learned that Nero had fled Rome and disappeared (June 68). Over the next year, military activity in Judaea came to a halt as both sides waited for a new ruler to emerge: this was the famous "year of the four emperors," as one aspirant after another tried to take power in Rome and failed. The ultimate winner in this power struggle was Vespasian himself: the legions of the east proclaimed him emperor in July 69, and by the end of the year he was the master of the Roman Empire. Vespasian proceeded to Alexandria and then to Rome, while his son Titus was given the task of completing the reconquest of Judaea. By the spring of 70, only the capital of Jerusalem held out, and the city came under siege. On the tenth day of the Hebrew month Av (August) the Temple was captured and burnt. Josephus insists that the burning of the Temple was an accident of battle and that Titus and his officers did everything they could to save it; other ancient writers report that Titus himself commanded that the sanctuary be destroyed because the remaining Jewish forces had turned it into a fortification from which to continue the struggle. The total subjugation of the city took another month. Outlying fortresses, most famously the desert stronghold at Masada, held out (to no avail) for another few years (Figure 5). By the spring of 74 the war was over (see "Masada").

* * *

Judaea was a devastated country. Over 1 million Jewish lives had been lost.[16] Most of the workable farmland in the province was either ruined or in the hands of new Roman owners, chiefly soldiers rewarded for their valor in a difficult war. Like the economy, the political structure of Jewish life was destroyed. The former priestly government had been swept away, and Judaea was now under direct military occupation. The priesthood, now without function, would presently dwindle into a mere reminder of past greatness. The Temple was gone, and with it the lavish ceremonial that had attracted visitors from all over the world and made Jerusalem a wealthy city. The great festivals could no longer be celebrated as the Torah prescribed. Individuals seeking atonement for sin or purification after major defilement could no longer present the required offerings or perform the required ceremonies.

5. Masada. This isolated hilltop royal palace and fortress was the last hold-out of the rebels against Rome in 73–74 CE; the photo suggests the enormous challenges faced by those who built and those who destroyed the stronghold. It remains an important tourist site and a powerful symbol of the survival of the Jewish nation, ancient and modern. (Photo courtesy of Todd Bolen/bibleplaces.com)

As though to lift up the Jews' misery for the world to see, the Roman victors now enacted a measure that bore consequences for the distant future. For generations, the Temple had been supported by a modest annual contribution of half a *shekel* from every adult Jewish male in the world. For many Jews in the far-flung Diaspora, pilgrimage to Jerusalem was an impossible luxury, or a rare opportunity at best; nevertheless, thanks to this payment, every Jewish household in the world could feel that the public Temple sacrifices had been offered on their behalf and with their participation. The Romans went on collecting this money, but now it was paid to the temple of Jupiter Capitolinus in Rome! It was the act of a schoolyard bully: the god of the Romans was stealing lunch money (so to speak) from the God of the Jews, and the Jews could do nothing about it. This fund, called the *fiscus judaicus*, was maintained for centuries.

MASADA

The fortress known as Masada stood in the desert southwest of the Dead Sea, built atop a steep hill; the location was probably chosen because the summit of this hill provided a large plateau for construction rather than the more common sharp peak. Josephus reports (*War* 7.285) that the first building on the site was carried out by the high priest Jonathan, meaning either the brother of Judah Maccabee (served 152–143 BCE) or his great-nephew, King Alexander Jannaeus (reigned 103–76 BCE), and then greatly expanded by King Herod the Great early in his reign. Herod appears to have designed the location as both a palace where he could escape the summer heat and a desert refuge for times of crisis and danger. When Judaea became a Roman province the site was probably converted into a military encampment, but this cannot be known for sure.

When the rebellion against Rome broke out in 66 CE, a band of Zealots captured Masada and occupied the site until the end of the war. The fortress came under Roman siege in 72 but held out for over a year. According to Josephus (*War* 7), when the end was near, the Zealot commander Eleazar ben Yair gave a lengthy speech to his followers in which he convinced them to die with dignity by their own hands rather than surrender to their enemies. Eleazar's exhortation reflects Greek historians' standard practice of inventing speeches and ascribing them to historical personalities; it is a long and quite noble oration, but there is no reason to suppose that Eleazar actually spoke this way the night his fighters died. Josephus reports that all but a handful took their own lives; when the Roman soldiers entered the fortress the next day, they found its inhabitants already dead.

In recent times, the fortress at Masada has become a widespread symbol of Jewish military valor. New Israeli soldiers are brought to Masada to begin their military service. Writers often invoke Masada as a model of the Jews' refusal to bend to the world's wishes: sometimes this is portrayed as noble and inspiring; sometimes it is presented as a dangerous, suicidal impulse. Today Masada is one of the most popular tourist spots in the state of Israel.

But diverting the payment in this way created a new problem: who was obliged to pay? Before, the Jews had maintained their own shrine voluntarily. Now Roman tax collectors were going to have to enforce an unwelcome levy, and many Jews would no doubt try to avoid the obligation. In most cases, people had no choice: they were known to be members of the Jewish community and could not hide their identity.[17] But there were two kinds of borderline cases that needed to be decided: those who were born Jews but had abandoned their heritage and those who were born outside the Jewish community but had adopted its way of life. Which of these people would have to pay the new Jewish tax? Developments cannot be traced in detail, but the ultimate determination was of huge importance for the future of Judaism: the Romans began collecting the tax from anyone who practiced the Jewish religion, whatever his family background, and they began ignoring those of Jewish background who had clearly taken up the worship of other gods.

Several considerations contributed to this outcome. For one thing, religious behavior is always more or less visible. Did X open his shop on Jewish holy days or not? Was Y to be seen in synagogues on a regular basis or not? Did Z also go into other temples or not?[18] In addition, however, by defining Jewish identity as religious rather than ethnic, the Romans struck a blow at the Jews' hope for national recovery. From now on, Roman policy increasingly treated the Jews as a religious community, people who worshiped a particular God and maintained a particular set of customs but did not require political recognition of any other kind. Over the next generations, this policy would be strengthened even further, most notably when the province of Judaea received the new name *Syria Palaestina* (see later), a change that left the Jews with no officially recognized homeland anywhere in the world.

In the long run, these changes helped prepare the Jews for the empire's adoption of Christianity as its official religion, and for the growing tendency throughout the Western world to see religion as the key element in personal identity and the key determinant of loyalty and status. But in the short run, these changes were disastrous. If Judaism was to survive this catastrophe, it could do so only after radical adjustment to its new circumstances. The story of this adjustment, and the early history of the rabbis who accomplished it, will unfold in the last three chapters of this book.

*   *   *

Further catastrophes intervened before the adaptation of Judaism could really begin. In the year 115 CE, a fierce struggle broke out between the Jews of North Africa (Egypt and Cyrene) and their Greco-Roman neighbors. Beginning probably as a local disturbance that got out of hand, the conflict rapidly escalated into an all-out war between the Jews of North Africa and the Roman Empire. The war took on a messianic dimension. The Jewish leader, an otherwise unknown personage named Andreas or Lukuas, received the designation king and seemed to aim at gathering a huge Jewish army and marching across Africa in order to expel the Romans from the Holy Land. This force seems to have reached as far as Alexandria, where a two-year conflict led to the destruction of almost every pagan temple in the city but also the annihilation of the greatest Diaspora community the Jews had ever known. The devastation all across Africa was still reported by travelers a century later. Egyptian Jewry was virtually wiped out, as were the communities of Cyrene and Cyprus.[19]

What provoked the Jews to undertake this hopeless war? One cause seems to have been the deep mutual resentment of Jews and Greeks that had festered ever since Rome had conquered the Hellenistic world. This antagonism had exploded into terrible violence twice before, once in 39, in the time of Flaccus and Philo (see Chapter 6), and again in 66, when the Judaean war began. After the destruction of Judaea, escaped *sicarii* had blended into the Jewish population of Alexandria and other areas; for over a generation, with passionate reliance on the avenging anger of their God, they had fomented hatred of Rome and the Greco-Roman world,[20] and the result was disaster. Philo's allegorical approach to the Torah survived in Christianity but had no further echo in Jewish thought: the Greek-language Judaism of Philo and his forerunners never produced another major writer, and the great works of earlier days were preserved only by Christians. The Mediterranean Diaspora survived, but the center of the Jewish world shifted back to the Aramaic-speaking Near East – Palestine and Babylonia – areas where the new rabbinic movement was slowly rising to prominence.

That rise was interrupted yet one more time. In 132 CE, another terrible rebellion erupted in the Judaean homeland, this time under a leader named Simon ben Kosiba. This man's messianic aspirations led him to adopt the epithet *Bar Kokhba* ("son of a star"), an allusion to the messianic Torah-verse Numbers 24:17. Once again, the Romans were taken by surprise by the Jews' ferocity and the degree of their preparations. Huge arsenals of hidden armaments suddenly confronted the empire's legions, and once again it took several years until overwhelming Roman numbers crushed the Jewish fighters. Once again Judaea was devastated, and this time it never really recovered; the center of Judaism in the Holy Land now shifted north, to Galilee, where it flourished for several centuries, but the area that gave Judaism its name became a gentile territory. It has already been mentioned that the land even lost its Jewish name: from now on the empire called this province Syria Palaestina, that is, the part of Syria where Philistines had lived centuries before. In this way Judaea ceased to be the homeland of the Jews, except in their own memories and their own hopes.

Why did the Jews undertake yet a third hopeless campaign against the largest empire ever known? One reason, not to be underrated, was their undying religious faith. This was the people of the covenant, a nation on whom the Creator of the world had conferred generous and surely reliable promises. Surely such a nation would not have to endure centuries of oppression at the hands of those who worshiped flesh and blood! Surely God's gift of the land could not be thwarted by the ambitions of a nation of idolaters! If God's nation would only rise to defend his honor, surely he would not let them down.

But two more concrete factors must be considered as well. At some point in his reign, the Emperor Hadrian (reigned 117–138) instituted two policies that set the Jewish world on edge. It is not known whether these enactments helped to provoke Bar Kokhba's war or were issued afterward in punitive response.

One of these decrees announced a plan to rebuild Jerusalem as a pagan city, sacred to Jupiter, that would be called *Aelia Capitolina*, after that god and the emperor's own family.[21] This plan raised the prospect of losing the holy city forever: once an idol's temple was built where God's own shrine once stood, how could that site ever be holy again? It is not hard to see that fear of such an outcome might have driven the people of Israel to desperate action.

In addition, however, Hadrian proclaimed an additional decree that would have affected Jews everywhere. This rule was really aimed at Near Eastern fertility religions: these had begun to attract honorable Roman citizens with their lurid rites, most particularly a custom in which men would dedicate their own fertility to the god(dess) through voluntary self-castration. A lover of Greek culture, Hadrian admired the ideal beauty of the human body and could not abide this religion of self-mutilation, so he issued a blanket prohibition of all religious disfigurement of the male body. As drafted, this ban included the Jewish rite of circumcision. Hadrian may not have realized this and may not have intended this result, but once in effect the rule threatened the very survival of the Jewish way of life. In the days of King Antiochus, many had died for performing this rite; were those horrible days now to be repeated? Hadrian sternly enforced this rule against the "covenant of Abraham" once the war was over, but modern scholars have not fully determined when he first put it into effect. Very soon after the emperor's death, his successor, Antoninus Pius (reigned 138–161), specifically exempted the Jews from this edict and allowed them to circumcise their own sons, but circumcision of male converts remained technically illegal until the Roman Empire collapsed.[22]

As the second century CE neared its midpoint, the Jews were a battered people, partly stunned by the two enactments just described, partly decimated by wars of their own making. Out of this wreckage a new form of Jewish life, often called *rabbinic Judaism* after its novel form of leadership, emerged to set the history of an ancient religion on a different course.

8

The Rebirth of Judaism

WHEN BAR KOKHBA'S REBELLION WAS OVER, JUDAEA WAS ONCE
again a conquered territory under military occupation. In Roman eyes
the inhabitants were defeated enemies with no rights at all, and the
victors could have treated the defeated Judaeans in any fashion that
they wished: mass exile, total enslavement, even (had the Romans
seen any point in this) outright extermination. None of these terrible
things occurred, but the situation was dire just the same. Many lives
had been lost, and many Judaeans had been captured for the slave
market. For the last few years of Hadrian's reign a terrible suppres-
sion of Judaism raged in the old homeland. Those who engaged in
public teaching of Torah were put to death, often barbarously – the
most famous martyr was the venerable sage *Akiba ben Joseph*[1] – and
other traditional Jewish practices were banned as well. The emperor
died after a short while, in 138 CE, and his successor quickly ended
the persecution, but the memory of this oppressive time lasted for
generations.

As stability returned, however, the Romans prepared yet again to
restore some form of Jewish self-government in the subdued territory.
The Romans were probably guided by the awareness that the Jews
remained numerous and were famous everywhere for their determination to follow the Laws of Moses. Such a people could not easily live
under direct foreign control: no outsider could understand the Torah
and its ways in the necessary depth; any outsider would eventually
do something that offended them and begin a new cycle of resentment and violence. As before, therefore, it seemed wise to provide
the Jews with acceptable leadership drawn from their own people.
But the challenge in meeting this goal remained what it had always

been: to identify such leaders among elements whom the Romans too could trust. Without the Temple the priests were no longer useful. The danger of a new Zealot uprising continued to haunt the authorities. In the end, a new Judaean leadership based on wisdom and learning emerged, and came to bear the title *sage* or *rabbi*; this new aristocracy of the Torah enabled a threatened heritage to survive its crisis and then once more to flourish.

The origins of rabbinic leadership are obscure. A famous story in the Talmud tells of a leading sage named *Yohanan ben Zakkai*. During the first uprising, while Jerusalem lay under siege, Yohanan had himself spirited out of the encircled city under pretext of having died[2] and managed to gain access to the Roman general Vespasian. Yohanan predicted that Vespasian would soon become emperor, and when this prediction was fulfilled the new emperor offered the Jewish sage a gift in recognition of his prophetic skills. Among other requests, Yohanan said, "Give me Yavneh and her sages."[3] In later rabbinic memory, this is how the first rabbinic academy was begun; this is how the heritage of Judaism survived the disaster of 70 to begin a new era of growth.

What is the historical reality behind this story? The late Israeli historian Gedaliahu Alon has plausibly suggested that throughout the war the Romans used the city of Yavneh (Jamnia in Greek) as a kind of internment center for Jewish leaders who might be helpful once the fighting was over. These were people who had not compromised themselves too badly with either side: they had not openly taken up arms against the empire, nor had they blatantly collaborated with the occupiers in the years leading up to the upheaval. In Yavneh, a city near but not in the heart of Judaea, Jews and Greeks lived in an uneasy mixture: the presence of each group kept the other from causing much trouble. Yohanan and many others were transported there to live, and when the Romans were ready to start dealing with a new Jewish leadership, they found appropriate candidates ready at hand.

Yohanan himself is remembered in later rabbinic stories as a clever and imaginative leader, able to figure out which parts of pre-Destruction Judaism might be preserved, which parts had to be replaced, and which parts were hopelessly lost pending the restoration of the Temple and its rites. But Yohanan quickly disappears from our record; either he simply retired out of old age and exhaustion or he was displaced from the leadership by his well-connected successor, a sage named Gamaliel, who came from a long line of distinguished Pharisaic leaders.[4] An enigmatic report in the Mishnah[5] indicates that Gamaliel once missed an important deliberation because he had "gone to Syria to receive permission (or authority) from the governor." Modern interpreters are not sure what this means. What was going on? What did Gamaliel want permission or authority to do? Despite its vagueness, this brief text reveals something noteworthy: by the late first century CE, just decades after the Destruction, a leading rabbi, drawn from an old family of Pharisaic leaders, was in contact with the Roman governor of Syria/Palestine. This contact had to do with some kind of permission or authority that the governor was empowered to grant.

A new Jewish government slowly emerged. Community funds for administrative and charitable purposes were collected and disbursed by duly selected officials. Jewish judges, presiding over Jewish courts, heard cases on the basis of the Torah and Jewish tradition.[6] By the third century these dignitaries were appointed and supervised by a hereditary leader bearing the Greek title *patriarch* (Hebrew *nasi*, plural *nesi'im*); by the fourth century these patriarchs were men of high rank, the Jews' official representatives to the Roman authorities. It took a while for the new arrangement to become stable. Later tradition assigns the title *nasi* to leaders from the late first century on, but this is probably an anachronism.

The patriarchs were associated with a larger group called *hakhamim* or sages, who were known for their learning and their wisdom: these sages were the earliest rabbis. Not all of the earliest Jewish officials were drawn from these circles: many old, rich Jewish families expected positions of honor and authority on account of their wealth and ancestry, while the priests no doubt struggled to recover their former pre-eminence as well. The early sages seem to have been a diverse group striving to build communal solidarity under their own leadership. They shared a dedication to lives based on wisdom and learning, and now they began to seek formal recognition as leaders based on that dedication. Many of the earliest sages had been leading Pharisees before the war; the new group, while absorbing other elements as well, inherited the Pharisees' earlier reputation as masters of the national heritage.[7] Each teacher lived in his own village and taught his disciples there, though from time to time informal gatherings

WHO WERE THE EARLY RABBIS?

By the third century CE, rabbinic masters routinely depicted their movement as a continuation of that of the earlier Pharisees. The Mishnah-tractate *Avot* ("Ethics of the Fathers") begins with an elaborate chain of transmission for the rabbinic tradition (here called *Torah*) that begins with Moses, reaches the Pharisees, and then concludes with the leading rabbis of the first two centuries CE. Other passages in the Mishnah (Hagiga 2:2; Peah 2:6) seek to give a similar picture. Indeed, early rabbinic texts display a range of interests and concerns that closely match what is known about the Pharisees. In particular, much early rabbinic law has to do with the rules for tithing produce and the rules of purity – how to maintain or restore purity, how to preserve and prepare foodstuffs while protecting them from defilement – concerns that were also of great importance among Pharisees before the Temple was destroyed.

Josephus writes (*Life* 191; *Jewish War* 1.110; *Antiquities* 13.401) that the Pharisees were the largest and most popular religious movement in pre-war Judaea, respected by the masses for their learning and their piety; if this was indeed the case, any new movement arising from the ashes of the Destruction would naturally have wished to inherit that prestige. However, Josephus's picture of the earlier movement is not always so favorable, and the rabbinic "movement" itself was so small when Josephus was writing that he is unlikely to have thrown his weight behind it in such a fashion. Moreover, it is not clear that the earliest rabbis were as closely identified with the Pharisees as their successors wanted people to believe. Recent scholars have suggested that the early rabbinic movement began as a coalition put together from the remnants of several different prewar sects and groups; Pharisees were surely to be found among these people, perhaps even as their leaders, but lay and professional scribes, priests, and representatives of the landed aristocracy eventually joined as well. Tensions among these different elements continued to flare up, and rabbis in the Land of Israel continued to complain about "those appointed for money" until well into the talmudic period (J. Bikkurim 3:3 65d; *Sifre* 2.17). Nevertheless, the gradual spread of rabbinic influence over the Jews of Palestine in late antiquity suggests that the coalition held.

The economic concerns that are reflected in the Mishnah are chiefly those of independent small farmers. Much attention is paid to the proper tithing of crops and to proper observance of the sabbatical year, while little attention is paid to matters of international commerce or large-scale manufacturing. Mishnaic labor law seems especially concerned to protect smallholders from the excessive demands of those whom they employ. The Mishnah is aware of large cities but seems mostly addressed to townspeople and villagers; one passage (Berachot 9:4) suggests that anyone spending time in a large city offer a special prayer on entering and on leaving, as though such a place was especially frightening and dangerous. Rabbinic presence in the large cities, in particular the capital at Caesarea, cannot be documented before the third century CE.

All this suggests that the rabbinic movement began as a movement of rural sages of modest means, holy men known for their devotion to pious learning though not especially inclined to asceticism or poverty. There were exceptions, of course. Certain rabbis (Judah the Patriarch or the earlier R. Tarfon) were said to have been extremely wealthy, while others are described as very poor (R. Aqiva at the beginning of his career, or Joshua b. Hananiah, among the earliest sages at Yavneh). But overall, the economic interests of Mishnaic law seem to be those of the class of small freeholders, and that same element appears to have supplied most of the early sages.

Appendix 2 provides short biographies of selected early rabbis.

shared opinions and tried to achieve consensus on important questions. The earliest such meetings were said to have taken place in Yavneh, but at a later time the center of rabbinic activity shifted north to Galilee (see "Who Were the Early Rabbis?").

The sages had little organization, and there was little group control over the activities or the teachings of individuals. The gatherings of sages initially resisted the idea that one man should be their leader,[8] but eventually the patriarchs managed to establish a kind of limited monarchy. Enjoying the direct support of Rome, they dominated Jewish life in the Holy Land from the third until the early fifth century. They controlled appointments to public office and presided over the announcement of new rulings in Jewish law; a later tradition suggests[9] that at times they also possessed the exclusive or preeminent right to award the title "rabbi" to accomplished disciples, though it is not likely that use of the title in ancient times was ever formalized or regulated to such a degree. It seems more probable that ordinary people used "rabbi" as a general term of honor for those whom they considered teachers and that sages used the title informally as a way of paying respect to their colleagues.[10]

The early sages could rely on the loyalty of their disciples and other voluntary followers, but they had no mechanism to impose their rulings on the private lives of ordinary Jews: even synagogues, the main scene of rabbinic activity in the modern world, seem to have operated independently of formal rabbinic jurisdiction. In the court and marketplace, some rabbis enjoyed binding legal authority by virtue of official appointment, but in other sectors of life they had to depend on voluntary compliance with their teachings.

How, then, did they finally gain such compliance? How did it turn out that rabbinic teachings eventually shaped Jewish life nearly everywhere in the world? The spread of rabbinic teaching is hard to retrace in detail, but it is possible to identify certain factors that contributed to this outcome.

Rabbis' official role as judges kept them in the public view. Litigation was a frequent occurrence in ancient life, just as it is today, and a growing proportion of the judges in the autonomous Jewish courts were rabbis who found many opportunities to expound their views and communicate their vision of Jewish life. Rabbis also frequently adjudicated issues of inheritance and marital status. This enabled them to enforce their interpretations of Jewish rules of marriage and divorce even when people might otherwise have scorned those interpretations: if the rabbinic archivist would not register their marriage, their children might have trouble inheriting their estate (see "Marriage in Early Rabbinic Teaching").

In the long run, however, early rabbis' unofficial functions might have been more decisive. Famous for their dedication to a life of study and teaching, rabbis cultivated an image of themselves as holy men. Rabbinic texts are full of stories of rabbis who could heal the sick but also inflict injury or death through the "evil eye," rabbis who could plant whole crops and reap whole fields without even standing up but also devastate whole regions if sufficiently angered, and rabbis who could create whole animals out of nothing and then cook them for Sabbath dinner (see "The Power of Torah"). Rabbinic learning was largely unwritten and memorized (see later), and rabbis would rehearse their lessons as they walked along the road: the sight of a holy man mumbling powerful incantations (as they seemed)

MARRIAGE IN EARLY RABBINIC TEACHING

In the text, it was suggested that rabbinic officials might disapprove of a proposed marriage. Such disapproval might be caused by several different factors. For example, one of the parties might have ended a previous marriage through divorce, and the divorce might not have been carried out according to rabbinic norms. The Torah gives almost no information concerning divorce procedure (see Deuteronomy 24:1–3), but rabbinic law developed extremely detailed requirements for the preparation and delivery of divorce documents. Some of these requirements were simply prudent: procedures to make sure that the names on the document were really those of this husband and this wife, methods for confirming the identity of the witnesses, and so on. Other rules were derived by analogy from the rules for obtaining and releasing slaves. This style of reasoning has occasionally led observers to conclude that the husband owned the wife as people might own a slave, but this is a misunderstanding: see the following.

Other equally detailed rules concerned the case of the childless widow obliged to marry her late husband's brother (Deuteronomy 25:5–10); here too, well-meaning people might fail to comply with all the rabbinic requirements and find themselves in difficulty later on.

In both of the cases mentioned so far, the woman's situation was likely to be more painful than the man's; even men who had been improperly divorced could in theory just take a second wife. Other rules, for example those concerning marriages involving priests (see Leviticus 21:7, 13–14), might give rise to complications that would affect both parties equally.

Some rabbinic enactments sought to protect the interests of women. A man who had authorized preparation of a bill of divorce could not retract his authorization without informing his wife (see "Early Rabbinic *Taqqanot* and *Gezerot*"). Most significantly, every husband was obliged to pay his wife a significant sum on termination of their marriage; this was his own debt in case of divorce and the debt of his estate if he died and left a widow. The contract (*ketubba*) that created this obligation was so fundamental to the rabbinic understanding of marriage that the debt was created by rabbinic edict even in cases where no actual document had ever been drawn up. The institution of the *ketubba* was designed to protect older women from destitution and to discourage men from impulsively divorcing their

MARRIAGE IN EARLY RABBINIC TEACHING (continued)

wives. Other forms of marriage contract existed among ancient Jews, but this particular arrangement, which the rabbis ascribed to their early predecessor Simeon ben Shetach (see Appendix 2), became the foundation of the talmudic rules of marriage.

As in most premodern cultures, ancient Jewish marriages did not spring from romantic love. A fascinating set of documents, the family archive of an early second-century woman named Babata, was found in the Judaean desert. They reveal that most people in Babata's family had more than one marriage (though never at the same time!) and that people were acutely aware of the financial implications of marriage, inheritance, and issues of child support. Why did people marry? Men wanted heirs and legitimate sexual partners (Yevamot 63a), and women, especially those with small children, wanted protection and sustenance. In time most couples did form bonds of affection and loyalty, but these other, more concrete factors continued to dominate. Husbands always exercised significant power, not least economic power, over their wives, but women knew how to protect their own interests as well, and fathers (when they could) were careful to find advantageous marriages for all their children and to protect their estates from falling into the wrong hands.

Did the payment of money at marriage imply that in some way the husband had indeed bought his wife? Probably not, at least not by Roman times. The payment indicated that a contract had been formed, a contract with many (often unstated) clauses and obligations from each to the other that rabbinic law spent generations clarifying. In rabbinic law the husband enjoyed the huge advantage that only he could end the contract through divorce (at Elephantine, and probably elsewhere, either spouse could initiate divorce), but the *ketubba* arrangement created a very strong disincentive against his doing so. In any case, the clearest sign that the husband did not own his wife was that he could not sell her, as he could a slave, nor could his heirs should he die: at best, he could release her from her obligations to him by divorce or through his own death and send her back out into the marketplace as a free agent, to seek another husband or not, as she wished.

On rabbis' attitudes toward their own wives and families, see Chapter 9, "The Yeshiva and the Family."

THE POWER OF TORAH

Rabbis' reputation as holy men was based in part on the belief that their knowledge of Torah equipped them to perform wonders and control the powers of nature, death not least of these. The following texts portray these abilities at work. They reveal an important feature of early rabbinic Judaism and express an important belief that was widespread among Jews of the time, even if modern readers have difficulty accepting them at face value.

* * *

R. Huna had wine in a dilapidated house, and he wanted to get it out. He brought R. Adda b. Ahava, who continued to recite his learning until [R. Huna] cleared out [the wine]. After he left, the house fell down. (Ta'anit 20b)

The angel of death could not overcome R. Hisda, for he never ceased repeating his learning. [The angel] went and sat on the cedar tree of the academy and caused it to creak. R. Hisda fell silent [out of concern over the noise], and death overcame him. (Mo'ed Katan 28a)

R. Hanina and R. Oshaya sat a whole Sabbath Eve [that is, all day Friday] and studied the Laws of Creation; they created a third-grown calf and ate it. (Sanhedrin 67b)

R. Eliezer said, I have learned three hundred (or, three thousand) laws concerning the [magical] planting of cucumbers, and no one ever asked me about them except for [Rabbi] Akiva ben Joseph. He and I were once walking along the road and he said to me, "Master, teach me about the planting of cucumbers." I said something, and the whole field filled with cucumbers. He said to me, "Master, you have taught me about planting them; teach me about picking them." I said something [else], and they were all gathered into one place. (Sanhedrin 68b)

A certain student sat before R. Yohanan. On hearing his teaching he responded, "O Master you have taught well, for as you have spoken so have I seen." [The rabbi] responded, "O empty one, if you had not seen you would not have believed; you mock the words of the Sages!" He set his eyes on him and turned him into a heap of bones. (Sanhedrin 100a, Bava Batra 75a) must have left a deep impression on passers-by as they encountered him in the street.

* * *

The early history of the rabbinic movement is exceedingly hard to reconstruct. All available information comes from later rabbinic sources,[11] and these provide descriptions of the early days that seem full of anachronistic projection. Still, certain traditions possibly offer a glimpse into those early generations.

"Early Rabbinic *Taqqanot* and *Gezerot*" contains a selection of ordinances (*taqqanot*) ascribed to early authorities. Several appear to have been direct responses to the destruction of the Temple. Yohanan b. Zakkai reportedly transferred to the "provinces" certain rituals previously limited to the Temple and adapted the procedure for examining new-moon testimony to the changed situation. Others, however, such as the changes in divorce procedure ascribed to R. Gamaliel the Elder (or some other early authority) appear to be ordinary legal reforms not connected to the national disaster.

Similar to the *taqqanah*, the *gezera*, or edict, was another mode of rabbinic legislation. The most common use of *gezera* was to forbid an action or the use of some material that was permitted in strict law; such a prohibition was decreed in times of emergency[12] or when the authorities feared that the permitted action might too easily lead to violation of the Torah. As with the ordinances, it is not clear how widely these decrees were followed. The Talmud contains a rule that "the court may not issue a decree unless most of the public can follow it";[13] this rule (from a later period in any case) implies that "most of the public" was usually ready to obey rabbinic instructions, but that may have been wishful thinking. There is very little sign that rabbis could actually set public policy before the Middle Ages.

Then who did pay attention to these rabbinic enactments? None of these reports actually says. It seems unlikely that the sages inherited religious authority from the priests so smoothly that the entire nation just naturally accepted their decisions: there is plenty of evidence that rabbis' instructions were often defied or disregarded, and it is more likely that these *gezerot* and *taqqanot* were improvised arrangements designed to guide the rabbis' own behavior and that of their followers and disciples. Rabbis would have been happy to see their program

EARLY RABBINIC *TAQQANOT* AND *GEZEROT*

[*Leviticus 23:40 ordains that the Festival of Tabernacles should involve cere-monies involving palm branches and citrons along with other species; how-ever, the first half of the verse speaks only of the first day, while its last words say to celebrate for seven days. How can this be accomplished? The tradi-tional practice solved this problem by reaffirming the uniqueness of the Temple.*] Originally the palm branch (*lulav*) was carried in the Temple [for] seven [days of the Feast of Tabernacles] and in the provinces [for] one day. When the Temple was destroyed, Rabban Yohanan ben Zakkai ordained that the palm branch should be carried in the provinces for seven [days] in memory of the Temple.... (Mishnah Sukkah 3:12; Rosh Hashanah 4:3)

When the Near Year festival fell on the Sabbath, they would blow the ram's horn (*shofar*) in the Temple but not in the provinces. When the Temple was destroyed, Rabban Yohanan ben Zakkai ordained [them to] sound the horn wherever a court was located. Rabban Eliezer said, "Rabban Yohanan ben Zakkai ordained thus for Yavneh only." They said to him, "Whether Yavneh or any place that had a court." (Mishnah Rosh Ha-Shanah 4:1)

[*As long as the Temple stood and for a while thereafter, the new moon was determined by observation rather than mathematical formula. A spe-cial court questioned people who claimed to have seen the new crescent moon, and this body determined whether the claimed sighting had been authentic, that is, whether a new month had begun. The witnesses had to arrive before midafternoon, so that the priests and the Levites could pre-pare for the new moon sacrifices that would have to be offered at once if their testimony was accepted. Once the Temple ritual could no longer be performed, however, this precaution was unnecessary. Yohanan is said to have made further adjustments in the procedure as well.*] When the Temple was destroyed, Rabban Yohanan ben Zakkai ordained that [the court] might receive testimony concerning the new moon all day long. Said Rabban Joshua b. Qorha, Rabban Yohanan ben Zakkai also ordained that even when the head of the court was elsewhere the witnesses should always go to the place of the tribunal. (Mishnah Rosh Ha-shanah 4:4)

Originally [a man] might convene a court in a different place [from his wife's residence] and nullify [a bill of divorce without her knowing this]. Rabban Gamaliel the Elder ordained that people should not do so, for the sake of social order. Originally [a man] might change his or her name or

EARLY RABBINIC *TAQQANOT* AND *GEZEROT* (continued)

the name of his or her residence [in a bill of divorce and thus conceal his identity from people unfamiliar with the case]; Rabban Gamaliel the Elder ordained that [the scribe] should write "So-and-so and all names by which he or she is known" for the sake of social order. (Mishnah Gittin 4:2)

* * *

A tailor should not go out with his needle toward dark, lest he forget and go outside [after the Sabbath has begun], and not a scribe with his pen, . . . nor should one read by the light of a lamp. The teacher may check where his students are reading but he should not read himself [for fear that he will move or tilt the lamp, activities forbidden on the Sabbath]. These are among the laws pronounced in the upper room of Hananiah ben Hizkiah ben Gurion when they (?) went up to visit him: they counted, and the House of Shammai outnumbered the House of Hillel. (Mishnah Shabbat 1:3–4)

A man may plant pumpkin and gourd in the same hole so long as they are oriented in different directions: anything forbidden by the Sages [in this respect] was only decreed on account of what the eye might see. (Mishnah Kil'ayim 3:5; see Leviticus 19:19 for the ban on planting "mixed crops.")

widely adopted. They had no means of enforcing such decisions on those who preferred to be guided by other models, but other people surely saw what rabbis were doing, and sometimes rabbis' enactments were formally announced to the community at large; perhaps larger numbers of ordinary Jews began voluntarily accepting rabbis' authority in their personal lives. In the course of time, as rabbis did begin to exercise recognized public authority, these rules became binding on the entire Jewish community. But this process took several generations even in the Land of Israel, and centuries before it was complete worldwide.[14]

By the early third century, the patriarchal regime was firmly established in Galilee. The *nasi* of the time, a sage named Judah who is always called "Rabbi Judah the *Nasi*" (or "Rabbi Judah the Prince") to distinguish him from others of that name, is remembered as having achieved unusual greatness. A man of both wealth and learning, remembered as the personal friend of the emperor,[15] Judah gathered the power of appointment to office into his own hands and cemented the notion that rabbinic sages ought to be the guides of community affairs. His greatest significance, however, lies not in his political achievements, which did not last, but in his contribution to the religious heart of Jewish life, a book called the *Mishnah*. Chapter 9 will examine that contribution and its consequences.

* * *

The ancient rabbis may be compared to architects who have been commissioned to restore a once-splendid mansion destroyed in some disaster. Some of the old building can be repaired and some is damaged beyond repair, but even remnants of the lost portions can possibly be rescued and incorporated into the replacement structure. The challenge is to save as much as possible, and to blend the old and the new into a seamless whole.

The sacred traditions of Israel had just suffered such a catastrophe, and the rabbis' first task was to figure out what could be rescued and what was lost forever. They did this without public authority and without even being sure that anyone else was paying attention. They embarked on this project because their own lives as Jews would have been unbearable otherwise. Without the Temple much of the Torah could not be put into practice, and without national freedom the promises of the Torah seemed a mockery. How could the covenant endure?

The rabbinic sages saw that the Jewish calendar could be preserved, and in their hands the calendar remained almost unchanged from the one used during Temple times. Perfect continuity was impossible: the festivals could be celebrated on the traditional dates, but without an altar for sacrifice they could not be celebrated in the traditional fashion. Months could still be declared on the basis of eyewitness testimony that the new moon had been sighted, but the priestly court that had received and weighed such testimony would have to be replaced.[16] The *structure* of the calendar remained what it had been – the same festivals on the same dates, the same unbroken cycle of the week – but the actual *content* of the festivals – what it meant to celebrate them, how they were experienced – began to change. Without the annual sacrifice of a lamb, Passover began to lose its associations with spring. The holiday increasingly centered on the theme of national freedom, and this focus too began to shift from the distant

THE PRAYER "FOR THE MIRACLES"

This prayer is inserted into every daily service throughout the eight days of Hanukka; it also is added to the standard grace after meals. It is noteworthy for the absence of any reference to supernatural miracles; instead, it deems miraculous the very fact that the outnumbered, ill-equipped, and ill-trained Maccabean army was able to defeat a great Hellenistic kingdom, force its way into Jerusalem and the Temple, and restore the traditional mode of worship that had been displaced from there. The prayer does mention the lighting of lamps in the Sanctuary, but without any reference to the story, famous at a later time, of the small can of oil that burned for eight days instead of one. The prayer does not attempt to explain the eight-day length of the holiday, perhaps because all ancient Jewish dedication celebrations lasted for (seven or) eight days; see 1 Kings 8:65–66.

In the days of Mattathias ben Yohanan, the Hasmonaean high priest, and his sons, when the wicked kingdom of Greece rose up against your people Israel to make them forget your Torah and violate your gracious laws, in your great mercy you stood by them in their hour of trouble. You fought their fight, you supported their cause, you executed their vengeance. You delivered the mighty into the hands of the weak, the many into the hands of the few, the defiled into the hands of the pure, the wicked into the hands of the righteous, those who scoffed into the hands of those committed to your Torah. For yourself you established a great and holy name in the world, and for your people Israel you achieved a great deliverance and a liberation that has lasted to this day. Afterward your children entered the shrine of your House; they cleared out your Temple and purified your Sanctuary, they kindled lights in your holy courts, and they set these eight days of Dedication to thank and praise your great Name.

past (the triumphant exodus from Egypt lost its savor under Roman oppression) to the distant messianic future.[17] The summer Feast of Weeks began to lose its association with the ceremonial presentation of first fruits to God and turned into an annual celebration of the revelation of the Torah.[18] The newest major celebration, the Hasmonaean Festival of Dedication (*Hanukka*), also acquired new content. An ancient prayer "For the Miracles" (*Al ha-Nissim*) that is still recited on Hanukka presents the holiday as a straightforward celebration of victory and its aftermath (see "The Prayer 'For the Miracles' "). In the course of time, however, the Maccabees' worldly accomplishments were all but forgotten, and the holiday became associated instead with a most unworldly miracle: a little pot of holy oil that should have burned for only one day was said to have lasted for eight. This story, now widely familiar, appears in no ancient text earlier than the Babylonian Talmud (Shabbat 21b); its preservation there suggests that the rabbis had been looking for a new reason to maintain the commemoration after the original events had lost their meaning.

As with the festivals, so too with the formal structure of public worship. Without sacrifices, the rabbis began to create a liturgy of *word and gesture* to replace the lost worship of *gift and ceremony*. Synagogue worship had been developing for generations, but rabbis now began to standardize the practices that went on in such places.[19] The Mishnah reflects that process but does not supply the text of the early rabbis' prayers; modern scholars cannot tell whether those prayers had been composed from the very beginning of the process or achieved their present wording only after a time of improvisation and experiment.[20]

From an early time, the rabbinic liturgy centered on two elements: a three-paragraph recitation from the Torah known from its first word as the *Sh'ma* ("*Hear* O Israel: the Lord our God is One"; see "The *Sh'ma*" for the full text) and a sequence of eighteen (later nineteen) blessings combining thanks and praise to God with detailed requests for Israel's material and spiritual needs. This sequence came to be known as the *Tefilla*, or the prayer par excellence. (See "An Early Version of the *Tefilla*.") In synagogues that were guided by rabbinic leadership (and perhaps in others as well), these two elements formed the core of Jewish worship before the end of antiquity, and they functioned as replacements for the lost Temple sacrifices. *Sh'ma* was recited twice a day, in keeping with the rabbis' interpretation of the text itself.[21] One prayer was recited every morning and one every afternoon, at the same hours that the daily "constant sacrifice" (*tamid*)[22] had been offered in the Temple; at a later time, a third prayer was added at night to accompany the nighttime recitation of *Sh'ma*.[23] On the Sabbath and on the annual festivals an additional prayer was recited, corresponding to the "additional sacrifice" (*musaf*) that was offered on such days. Thus it could be imagined that the prayers of the synagogue had taken the place of the sacrifices, and indeed, the rabbis offered a homily on the biblical verse "we shall fulfill [the words

THE *SH'MA*

As noted in the text, the *Sh'ma* recitation consists of three paragraphs taken from the Torah. They read as follows:

Hear, O Israel: YHWH our God is One. You must love YHWH your God with all your heart and with all your being and with all your might. These words which I command you today must be on your heart: you must teach them repeatedly to your children, and you must speak of them when you are at home or on the road, when you lie down and when you rise up. You must bind them as a sign on your hand and have them as markers(?) between your eyes, you shall write them on the doorposts of your house and your gates.

(Deuteronomy 6:4–9)

If you indeed listen to my commandments that I command you today, to love YHWH your God and to serve him with all your heart and all your being, then I shall give your land rain in its season, early and late, and you will gather in your grain and your wine and your oil. I shall give grass in your field for your cattle, and you will eat and be satisfied. Take care lest your heart be seduced and you turn away to serve other gods and bow to them: then YHWH's anger will burn against you and he will shut up the sky and there will not be rain: the earth will not yield its produce and you will quickly be gone from the good land that YHWH is giving you. Place these my words on your heart and your very being: bind them as a sign on your hand and have them as markers(?) between your eyes, teach them to your children, speaking of them when you are at home or on the road, when you lie down and when you rise up, write them on the doorposts of your house and your gates. [Do this] in order that your days, and the days of your children, may be many on the land that YHWH swore to your ancestors he would give to them, [as many as] the days the heavens are over the earth.

(Deuteronomy 11:13–21)

YHWH said to Moses: Speak to the Children of Israel and say to them that for [all] their generations they shall make a fringe at the corners of their garments and place a blue thread upon the fringe. It will be your fringe, so that you see it and remember all YHWH's commandments and do them, that you not wander off after your hearts and your eyes which you wickedly follow. [Do this] in order that you remember and do all my commandments and become holy to your God. I am YHWH your God who brought you out of the land of Egypt to be a God for you: I am YHWH your God.

(Numbers 15:37–41)

According to a teaching in the Mishnah (Berachot 2:2), recitation of the first paragraph constitutes "accepting the yoke of Heaven" and recitation of the second paragraph means "accepting the yoke of the commandments": this interpretation probably arose because the second paragraph, unlike the first, stresses YHWH's commands and offers reward for obedience and punishment for violation. The sequence also leads worshipers to contemplate their general human situation prior to affirming their loyalty to the Jewish way of life and is replicated in the pair of blessings that are to be recited before the actual *Sh'ma*. This must be a message that the rabbis assembling the liturgy wished to convey.

When *Sh'ma* is recited liturgically, the biblical text is interrupted after the first verse by an additional proclamation: "Blessed be the name of his glorious kingdom forever!"

The Hebrew word *totafot*, here translated as "markers," probably means something like "headband." According to tradition these verses refer to *tefillin*, small boxes containing these very passages on a scroll that are worn on the arm and the head during certain prayers. The same double phrase appears twice in Exodus 13, a chapter also included in the *tefillin* scrolls.

The third paragraph singles out a particular Jewish ritual (the wearing of fringes) as representative of them all. Because that ritual is not practiced at night (you must "see" the fringes), there was some uncertainty (see Mishnah Berachot 1:5; see also Chapter 9, "The First Chapter of the Mishnah") as to whether it should be included in the nighttime recitation; this may be why the paragraph is recited third, out of sequence with respect to its place in the Torah. In the end, the section was retained because it concludes by affirming Jews' gratitude for having been rescued from slavery in Egypt.

of] our lips with bulls" (Hosea 14:3). The obvious interpretation that one who pledges a sacrifice must fulfill his pledge could no longer be accepted, for this was impossible now; the verse was now said to mean that one who offers sincere words to God is as if he had offered the costly sacrifice of a bull.[24]

Both of these daily recitals could be accomplished at the synagogue through participation in public worship, or in private if one were unwell, in a location where no synagogue was available, or just too busy. During the week most farmers and workers probably had no opportunity to attend public worship, but on the Sabbath

AN EARLY VERSION OF THE *TEFILLA*

The Tefilla *or* 'Amida *(lit., "standing" prayer) is a sequence of short* berakhot *(benedictions) that has served as the core of rabbinic worship since the first century. Each paragraph ends with a short phrase beginning "Blessed art thou," the standard formulation of rabbinic benedictions, and is preceded by a longer text elaborating the theme of that blessing.*

The following version is based on Emil Schürer, The History of the Jewish People in the Age of Jesus Christ, *revised and edited by Geza Vermes et al. (Edinburgh, T. & T. Clark, 1979), volume 2, pp. 460–461. It was found in a Cairo storeroom in the late nineteenth century and is undoubtedly very old; on the other hand, there is no ground to call it the original version or even to attempt reconstruction of any earlier versions from this text. This version appears to stem from the synagogues of the Land of Israel; modern Jewish prayer books use a longer version of Babylonian origin.*

You are blessed, Lord, God of our fathers, God of Abraham, God of Isaac and God of Jacob, great, mighty and fearful God, most high God who creates heaven and earth, our shield and the shield of our fathers, our trust in every generation. You are blessed, Lord, shield of Abraham.

You are mighty, humbling the proud; strong, and judging the violent; you live forever and raise the dead; you make the wind and bring down the dew; you provide for the living and make the dead alive; in an instant you cause our salvation to spring forth. You are blessed, Lord, who makes the dead alive.

You are holy and your Name is awesome, and beside you there is no God. You are blessed, Lord, the holy God.

Grant us, our Father, knowledge from you, and understanding and discernment from your Torah. You are blessed, Lord, who grants knowledge.

Lead us back, Lord, to you and we shall repent. Renew our days as of old. You are blessed, [Lord], who delights in repentance.

Forgive us, our Father, for we have sinned against you. Wipe out and remove our evil deeds from before your eyes. For your mercies are many. You are blessed, Lord, rich in forgiveness.

Look on our affliction and plead our cause and redeem us for your Name's sake. You are blessed, Lord, redeemer of Israel.

Heal us, Lord our God, of the pain of our heart; remove from us sorrow and grief and raise up healing for our wounds. You are blessed, [Lord], who heals the sick of thy people Israel.

Bless this year for us, Lord our God, and cause all its produce to prosper. Bring quickly the year of our final redemption; and give dew and rain to the land; and satisfy the world from the treasuries of your goodness; and bless the work of our hands. You are blessed, Lord, who blesses the years.

Proclaim our liberation with the great trumpet and raise a banner to gather together our dispersed. You are blessed, Lord, who gathers the banished of your people Israel.

Restore our judges as in former times and our counselors as in the beginning; and reign over us, you alone. You are blessed, Lord, who loves judgment.

And for apostates let there be no hope; and may the insolent kingdom be quickly uprooted, in our days. And may the Nazarenes and the heretics perish quickly; and may they be erased from the Book of Life; and may they not be inscribed with the righteous. You are blessed, Lord, who humbles the insolent.

May your mercies be showered over righteous proselytes; and give us a rich reward, together with those who do your pleasure. You are blessed, Lord, trust of the righteous.

Be merciful, Lord our God, with your great mercies, to Israel your people and to Jerusalem your city; and to Zion, the dwelling place of your glory; and to your Temple and your habitation; and to the kingship of the house of David, your righteous Messiah. You are blessed, Lord, who builds Jerusalem.

Hear, Lord our God, the voice of our prayer, and be merciful to us; for you are a gracious and merciful God. You are blessed, Lord, who hears prayer.

Be pleased, Lord our God, and dwell in Zion; and may your servants serve you in Jerusalem. You are blessed, Lord, whom we worship in awe.

We praise you, Lord, our God, and the God of our fathers, on account of all the goodness and grace and mercies which you have granted to us, and have done to us and to our fathers before us. And if we say our feet are

AN EARLY VERSION OF THE *TEFILLA* (continued)

slipping, thy grace, O Lord, succors us. You are blessed, Lord, the All-Good, you are to be praised.

Bring your peace over Israel your people, and over your city and over your inheritance; and bless all of us together. You are blessed, Lord, who makes peace.

Another name for the *'Amida* prayer is *Shemoneh Esreh*, or "eighteen," after the number of benedictions it originally included. Modern versions actually contain nineteen blessings, though the "extra" blessing cannot be singled out with certainty. In later days the blessing for Jerusalem was split into two, one for the rebuilding of the Holy City and for the speedy arrival of the messianic redemption. The Talmud also suggests (Berakhot 28b), however, that the blessing against apostates and heretics was added in the late first century to an already existing structure. The inclusion of "Nazarenes" in the preceding version should not be taken to mean that the additional blessing was originally directed at the growing Christian movement.

and festivals the entire community probably gathered. Modern scholars remain sharply divided on the question of whether women regularly attended public worship, and where those who did attend were expected to sit or stand.[25]

The prayer was constructed as a sequence of blessings or benedictions; the blessing (*berakha*; pl. *berakhot*) was the building block of nearly all rabbinic worship. A blessing or benediction contains two parts. The first part is constant, found in all cases, and invokes the majesty of God: "You are blessed O Lord (our God, King of the World)."[26] The second part reflects the occasion on which the blessing is being recited: enjoyment of food or drink, performance of an action demanded by the Torah (*mitzva*), encounter with a spectacular natural phenomenon, arrival of a fixed liturgical moment. By providing a *berakha* for designated situations, the rabbis transformed such moments into opportunities for religious experience. Celebration of a marriage was marked by reciting a prescribed set of *berakhot*, study of Torah was prefaced by reciting a prescribed *berakha*, and so on. Daily life – meals, worship services, family celebrations – was punctuated by the recitation of these usually brief formulas, and the major occasions of religious experience were put together by assembling *berakhot* into carefully organized sequences.

This approach to the life of prayer offers an excellent example of the early rabbis' conception of Judaism. On the one hand, the *berakhot* are short and simple; a single *berakha* takes almost no time, and even children can learn the ones most frequently needed in everyday life. Thus the rabbis saw to it that daily piety – the opportunity to invoke the presence of God in commonplace moments of life – was within the reach of anyone, and this style of worship has remained characteristic of observant Jews until modern times.

On the other hand, the total number of these liturgical formulas was considerable, and rabbinic masters devoted a lot of discussion to fixing the precise wording of each and the precise circumstances under which each was appropriate. People who failed to master this elaborate etiquette might achieve nearness to God in their own way, but in rabbinic eyes they would always be scorned for their ignorance. They would be deemed *ammei ha-aretz* ("people of the land"), worthy of very low rabbinic esteem.[27]

Incorporating a great quantity of material from the Bible, the rabbis developed other hymns and benedictions to surround these original elements and knit them together. They determined the proper times for reciting each prayer. They incorporated the public reading of scripture (and the sermon?) into the normal order of worship. They developed expanded liturgies for the weekly Sabbath and the annual festivals. By the start of the Middle Ages, the rabbinic prayer book was ready to circulate throughout the world and to assume its place as *the* Jewish prayer book into modern times.[28]

Together with these arrangements for public and private worship, the early rabbis invented entirely new rituals. For example, the Sabbath and holy days now began and ended with ceremonial drinking of wine, respectively called *kiddush* ("sanctification") and *havdala* ("separation"). Jews probably used wine to mark special occasions before rabbinic times,[29] but the rituals that became standard were of rabbinic origin; elaborate talmudic discussions as to the proper manner of performing these, discussions that show dispute on even basic points, suggest that they were new and not yet firmly established. Other Jewish rituals, many of much earlier origin such as the New

Year sounding of the ram's horn (*shofar*), the kindling of celebratory lamps at Hanukka, and the Passover meal (*seder*), underwent a similar process of standardization.

Rabbis strove for adaptation and uniformity in other areas of Jewish life as well. Marriage was an important institution for the maintenance of a stable Jewish community, and the sages worked at putting their own stamp on its character. Many, perhaps most, ancient Jews arranged their own marriages and negotiated their own terms free of rabbinic scrutiny, possibly free of any government regulation at all.[30] The rabbinic laws that regulate the mutual obligations – social, financial, sexual, and so forth – of husband and wife are very complicated, as such laws tend to be in many cultures, but there was no need to consult the authorities at all unless disputes arose. The complexities of rabbinic law, and the elitism those complexities nourished, could often be disregarded by those who found them uninteresting; couples (or their parents) could simply negotiate a dowry and any other necessary matters and set up house. Nevertheless, using older legal concepts and practices, the rabbis built an elaborate set of rules for the governance of marriage and married life, and during the early Middle Ages these became the operating rules for all Jews everywhere. Civil law took longer, but the rabbis of the Talmud developed a full body of rules for the transfer of property, compensation for damages, the interrogation of witnesses, and so on as well. Much of this legislation may similarly have became operative only during later centuries.

In general, it is hard to determine when rabbis actually gained the power to put all these rules into effect: for generations, people who wished to disregard rabbinic regulations or even to reject them openly were apparently able to do so. The process by which rabbis gained official power was gradual, depending on the attitude of the governing powers and the disposition of local Jewish communities in various locations. Until the Middle Ages, rabbinic authority (such as it was) remained limited to two countries, Palestine and Babylonia. But the rabbinic goal was to reshape every feature of Jewish life according to their own lights, preserving its continuity with the lost Temple-based Judaism while also overcoming that terrible loss so that a new form of Judaism might survive and even flourish.

It was the rabbis' great accomplishment eventually to convince most of the Jewish people to adopt that goal as their own and to accept rabbinic leadership in its pursuit. The great transformation of Judaism took place when the rabbinic sages came to be seen as models for all Jews to emulate, rather than as exceptional holy men who had managed to secure administrative power through the intervention of foreign rulers. But that transformation took place after the period this book describes; the acceptance of rabbinic teaching as the only proper basis of Jewish life marks the entry of the Jewish nation into the Middle Ages.

9

The Rabbis and Their Torah

AROUND THE YEAR 200 CE, RABBI JUDAH THE PATRIARCH changed forever the character of rabbinic teaching and learning by compiling the *Mishnah*, the oldest book of rabbinic teaching that survives to modern times. This text, divided into six *Orders* and subdivided into a total of sixty-three *tractates*, is half again as big as the Jewish Bible (see "The Contents of the Mishnah"). Each tractate contains a collection of rabbinic teachings on a specific theme, usually a topic of Jewish law. Some of these topics are obviously religious, as modern readers use that term (prayer, festival observances, sacrificial rituals, etc.), others concern ordinary material life (property and damage law, rules of testimony, etc.), and some straddle the boundary between these two realms (marriage, divorce, oaths and vows). The Mishnah did not quite embrace every imaginable aspect of Jewish life, but anyone who had mastered its contents was ready to become a teacher of Torah.

The Mishnah is overwhelmingly concerned with details of Jewish law, but it cannot easily be viewed as a legal code. As "the First Chapter of the Mishnah" shows, there is too much material that a code should not contain: unresolved disputes that give no clear indication of the actual law, stories and interpretations of scripture that have no clear legal point, and so on. It is more likely that the Mishnah was intended to accomplish what it accomplished in fact: the Mishnah became the first known standard training text for rabbinic disciples. A previous point can be repeated: anyone who had mastered the Mishnah's contents was ready to become a teacher of Torah.

Torah was the rabbis' name for the object of their dedication and the source of their powers (see Chapter 8, "The Power of Torah"), but

THE CONTENTS OF THE MISHNAH

Order One: Zera'im ("Seeds" or Agriculture)

Berakhot ("Blessings")

Peah ("Corner [of the field]")

Demai ("Produce That May Not Have Been Tithed")

Kil'aim ("Mixed Species")

Shevi'it ("Seventh [year]")

Terumot ("Heave-offerings")

Ma'asrot ("Tithes")

Ma'aser Sheni ("Second Tithe")

Hallah ("Dough-Offering")

Orlah (Fruit of Young Trees [lit., "foreskin"])

Bikkurim ("First Fruits")

Order Two: Mo'ed ("Appointed Time")

Shabbat ("Sabbath")

'Eruvin ("Mixture" [of Sabbath domains])

Pesahim ("Paschal Offerings")

Shekalim ("Shekels" [given to the Temple])

Yoma ("The Day" [of Atonement])

Sukkah ("[Festival] Booth")

Betzah ("Egg" [rules for cooking, etc., on festival days])

Rosh Ha-Shanah ("New Year")

Ta'anit ("Fast Day")

Megillah ("Scroll" [of Esther])

Mo'ed Qatan ("Minor Feast")

Hagigah ("Festival Offering")

Order Three: Nashim ("Women")

Yevamot ("Sisters-in-Law")

Ketubot ("Marriage Contracts")

Nedarim ("Vows")

Nazir ("Nazirite")

Sotah ("Woman [Suspected of] Going Astray")

Gittin ("[Divorce] Documents")

Qiddushin ("Consecrations" [i.e., betrothals])

Order Four: Neziqin ("Damages")

Bava Qama ("The First Gate" [of civil law])

Bava Metzi'a ("The Middle Gate")

Bava Batra ("The Last Gate")

Sanhedrin ("Sanhedrin")

Makkot ("Blows" [corporal punishment])

Shevu'ot ("Oaths")

Eduyyot ("Testimonies")

Avodah Zarah ("Foreign Worship" [idolatry])

Avot ([Teachings of the] "Fathers")

Horayot ([Incorrect] "Rulings")

THE CONTENTS OF THE MISHNAH (continued)

Order Five: Qodashim ("Holy Things")

Zevahim ("Animal Offerings")

Menahot ("Flour Offerings")

Hullin ("Nonsacral [slaughter]")

Bekhorot ("First-Born")

Arakhin ([Vows of] "Evaluation")

Temurah ("Substitution")

Keritot ("Extirpations" or Heavenly Punishments)

Meilah ("Misappropriation" [of sacred property])

Tamid ("Perpetual" [daily offering])

Middot ("Measurements" [of the Temple and its chambers])

Kinnim ("Nests" [bird offerings])

Order Six: Tohorot ("Purities")

Kelim ("Vessels")

Oholot ("Tents")

Nega'im ("Inflictions" [of leprosy])

Parah ("Heifer")

Tohorot ("Cleannesses")

Miqva'ot ("Pools" [for ritual immersion])

Niddah ("Menstrual defilement")

Makhshirin ("Fluids That Leave Foodstuffs Subject to Defilement")

Zavim ("Those with Flux")

Tevul Yom ("One Who Has Immersed That Day")

Yadaim ("Hands")

Uqzin ("Stems")

this ancient term no longer served merely to designate a book. Over the early centuries of the Common Era, rabbinic teachers developed the idea that Moses had not written down the entire content of God's revelation. Instead, he had conveyed essential teachings by word of mouth to selected disciples, in particular to his designated successor, Joshua, and so had inaugurated a chain of teacher-to-student transmission that had continued without interruption to the rabbis' own time. This Oral Torah was indispensable for proper understanding of the written Torah, and the rabbinic sages claimed to be the only heirs to this body of knowledge.[1] In rabbinic eyes Jewish life had no

THE FIRST CHAPTER OF THE MISHNAH

This sample extract from the Mishnah illustrates the character of the document as a whole, as discussed in the text.

Tractate Berakhot, Chapter One

1. From what time [may people] recite the evening *Sh'ma*? From the hour that the priests come in to eat of their *teruma*-offering, until the end of the first watch; [these are] R. Eliezer's words, but the Sages say, Until midnight. Rabban Gamaliel says, Until the first light of dawn. There was an incident when his sons came back from a feast. They said to him, "We have not recited *Sh'ma*." He said to them, "If the first light of dawn has not appeared, you are obliged to recite." And not only [in] this [case], but [in] every [case where] the Sages have said "Until midnight," the commandment [really applies] until the first light of dawn: the burning of fat parts and [prescribed] limbs [on the Temple altar] – the commandment [to do so applies] until the first light of dawn; all [sacrifices] which are to be eaten for [only] one day – the commandment [to stop eating does not take effect] until the first light of dawn. If so, why did the Sages say "Until midnight"? In order to keep a man away from transgression.

2. From what time [may people] recite the morning *Sh'ma*? From [the time one can] distinguish between blue and white. R. Eliezer says, Between blue and green. And he [must] finish it by sunrise. R. Joshua says, Within three hours [of sunrise], since it is the way of princes to arise at the third hour. One who recites from this hour forward has not lost anything; [he is] like a man reading in the Torah.

3. The House of Shammai say, In the evening all people [should] recline and recite, and in the morning, they [should] stand, as it is said, "*When you lie down and when you rise up*" (Deuteronomy 6:7). But the House of Hillel say, Every man reads in his [own] way, as it is said, "*And as you go along the way*" (*ibid.*). If so, why does it say, "*And when you lie down and when you rise up*"? – At the hour that people [generally] lie down and the hour that people [generally] rise up. Said R. Tarfon, "I once was traveling and I lay down to recite according to the opinion of the House of Shammai, and I endangered myself on account of robbers." They said to him, "You deserved to lose your life, since you violated the opinion of the House of Hillel."

THE FIRST CHAPTER OF THE MISHNAH (continued)

4. In the morning [one] recites two blessings before [*Sh'ma*] and one after it, and in the evening two before it and two after it, one long and one short. At a place where they said to lengthen, he is not permitted to shorten; to shorten, he is not permitted to lengthen. [Where they said] to seal off [a blessing, with the words "Blessed art Thou, O Lord"], he is not permitted not to seal off; [where they said] not to seal off, he is not permitted to seal off.

5. [People should] make mention of the Exodus from Egypt at night [as well as by day]. Said R. Eleazar b. Azariah, "Behold, I am as one seventy years old but I was never able [to prove] that the Exodus from Egypt should be mentioned at night, until ben Zoma offered this interpretation, as it is said, '*In order that you remember the day of your leaving the land of Egypt all the days of your life*' (Deuteronomy 16:3). '*The days of your life*' would mean the days; "*all the days of your life*" [includes] the nights." But the Sages say, "*The days of your life*" [means] this world; "*all the days of your life*" includes the days of the Messiah.

hope of religious fulfillment, and the Jewish people had no hope of redemption, without rabbinic leadership. This idea served as both motive and justification for a sustained effort to gain authority over Jewish life.

In the rabbinic understanding, Torah was first and foremost a set of God-given instructions, the commandments (*mitzvot*) by which the people of Israel had been instructed to live. To follow these commandments brought blessing; to live in violation of God's will brought disaster. This idea long predated the rabbinic movement, and the rabbis never departed from it.[2] Their own role was to clarify the Torah's rules, partly through careful text study and partly through knowledge of unwritten tradition, and thus to make sure that people followed them correctly.

At the same time, Torah was not limited to that system of rules. A life dedicated to Torah demanded constant immersion in the study and teaching of sacred traditions, and the name Torah designated a religious discipline that went far beyond the usual limits of law.

Torah was the rabbis' term for what people today might call Judaism or religion. Torah was a book and also a body of unwritten learning, but in addition Torah was a path to personal and communal holiness. Its rewards included the extraordinary powers that rabbis claimed to possess, powers even of life and death, along with all the other blessings, in this world and the next, that a just God had promised for those who followed and spread his word.

The phrase *Oral Torah* served to distinguish the rabbis' own teachings from the ancient words of scripture: the written Torah consisted of a fixed text, no longer subject to addition, subtraction, or change, while the rabbis' Oral Torah was constantly growing, each generation making its own contribution to the sacred heritage of Judaism. The phrase also indicated that rabbinic teaching was Torah, Divine revelation, no less sacred than the ancient books and endowed with no less authority. Any time a rabbinic sage offered a legal ruling, even an informal, nonlegal teaching or for that matter even a wordless gesture, his words and actions constituted Torah (see "'Torah' Embraces Everything"). This meant that Moses was not the only vehicle for the word of God and that the writings of Moses were not the only source of Divine wisdom; every rabbinic tribunal in every generation was the equivalent of the court of Moses himself, endowed with the same sacred authority in every generation.[3]

The rabbis' Torah was oral in another sense as well. Rabbis generally issued their legal rulings and instructed their disciples by word of mouth. Teachers and students may have kept written notes of their lessons, and rabbinic courts probably maintained written records of their decisions, but the actual teachings and rulings were given without reference to such materials. Such avoidance of writing was also found among other ancient intellectuals, most famously among certain Greek philosophers. It appears to have been rooted in the concern that authors can never be sure that their writings will be correctly understood once they are no longer present to explain them.[4] Only face-to-face contact, only the living presence of the teacher, can promise correct understanding; only the teacher in person can make sure that the students have learned their lessons well.

Grounded in these conceptions, the emerging rabbinic leadership was elitist but without hierarchy: in the rabbis' view, no one other than

"TORAH" EMBRACES EVERYTHING

These three brief stories illustrate the range of the concept Torah. They show that Torah included the most intimate aspects of bodily well-being, and they stress the importance of learning Torah (including those same intimate matters) from a living teacher, both through words and through careful observation of his behavior.

R. Huna said to his son Rabba, "Why do you not attend R. Hisda, whose teachings are so wise?" He answered, "Why should I go to him, since when I do go he engages in worldly talk? ... " [His father answered,] "He teaches matters of health and you call that worldly talk?"

(Shabbat 82a)

R. Akiva said, "Once I followed R. Joshua into the privy, and I learned from him three things." ... Ben Azzai said to him, "Were you that disrespectful toward your master?" ... He said to him, "This is Torah, and I must learn!"

R. Kahana once went in and hid under the bed of Rav. He heard him talking [with his wife] and joking and caring for his needs. He said, "It seems that [Rav's] mouth has never tasted such a spicy dish!" [Rav] said, "Kahana, are you here? Leave, it is not proper." He said to him, "This is Torah, and I must learn!"

(Berachot 62a)

If one has learned Scripture and Mishnah but has not served the Sages: R. Eleazar says, "Such a person is an ignoramus." R. Samuel b. Nahmani says, "Such a person is a boor." R. Yannai says, "Such a person is a heretic." R. Aha b. R. Jacob says, "Such a person is a Magus."

(Sotah 22a)

themselves had the right to guide Jewish life, but anyone (that is, any Jewish male) could aspire to become a rabbi, and no rabbi (except possibly the *nasi*) outranked another.[5] The concept Oral Torah thus embodied two basic assumptions: (1) rabbinic teaching represented a heritage faithfully transmitted over countless generations, and (2) any rabbi's version of that heritage had the same legitimacy, and the same authority, as any other's. The sages never clearly explained how a tradition could have been faithfully transmitted yet now exist in so many different versions, but these two assumptions can be found behind every ancient rabbinic text.

* * *

At around the same time that the Mishnah was compiled, rabbinic teaching spread for the first time beyond the limits of the Holy Land. Rabbinic sages, perhaps in flight from the devastation resulting from Bar Kokhba's uprising and the Roman oppression that followed, began to appear in *Babylonia* by the mid-second century CE and soon attracted small numbers of followers from among Jews native to the area. As the century advanced, contacts between the two countries increased. By the turn of the third century, several important Galilean sages were men of Babylonian origin, and finally, around 225, one of these Babylonians, a man named Abba,[6] who had studied with Judah the Patriarch, returned to his native land and established the first known rabbinic study-circle outside the Land of Israel.

In those days the political and administrative leadership of Babylonian Jewry lay in the hands of the *exilarchs*, men who traced their ancestry to the ancient royal House of David and based their claim to authority on this pedigree. These leaders came to value the sages for their knowledge of law and legal procedure, and they began to appoint rabbis or rabbinic disciples to various judicial and administrative positions; in this way, the growing circles of rabbinic masters gained a public role for themselves and acquired a measure of formal legal authority under the auspices of the hereditary exilarchs. For generations the relationship was unsteady: rabbis could not accept the idea of leadership based on mere ancestry without Torah learning, while the exilarchs often resented the arrogance (as they saw it) of mere functionaries.[7] Over time, however, the two ideologies (leadership through learning vs. leadership through ancestry) achieved reconciliation, not least because rabbis and exilarchs began to merge their families through marriage; only in the Middle Ages, however, did the two completely merge into a single regime for the Jews of Babylonia.

In both Palestine and Babylonia, rabbinic study increasingly centered on mastery of the Mishnah. Teachers would gather their disciples and work through each tractate paragraph by paragraph, explaining difficult words and passages, identifying (when they could) the scriptural basis for various rules, applying the rules to hypothetical situations, and reporting actual situations where a rule had been applied or disregarded. All this was carried out through direct teacher–student interaction, in keeping with the notion of Oral Torah. Written copies may have existed all along – this is hard to determine – but they do not seem to have been used in formal study sessions.

Teachers' explanations were soon being preserved along with the Mishnaic text itself; in an environment where memorizing was a much-cultivated skill, a huge amount of such material began to accumulate. As time went on, these explanations merged with the original Mishnah into a more complex body of teaching known as *Talmud* or *Gemara*, Hebrew and Aramaic terms, respectively, that both mean "learning." After a number of generations, this Talmud itself was compiled into a set of books.[8] There are two Talmuds: the so-called *Jerusalem Talmud*, actually produced by rabbis in northern Palestine around the year 400, and the *Babylonian Talmud* dating from a century or two later. The Babylonian Talmud became the basis for all later forms of Judaism: aside from the Bible itself, it is the most influential Jewish book ever written.

In form, the Talmud is a very extensive commentary on selected tractates (slightly more than half) of the Mishnah. *Commentary* is really not the right word: the Gemara is more like the record of a very leisurely, rambling conversation. Since the Talmud emerged from a culture of face-to-face discussion, this is not surprising. It is easy to imagine how a session would start by reciting a paragraph of Mishnah and proceed through explaining and applying its contents in assorted real or hypothetical situations. It is also easy to picture frequent digressions to tell stories, offer moral guidance, explore scripture, respond to students' questions, or talk about anything else the teacher saw fit to mention: students now, or those who can remember their student days, will quickly recognize that modern classrooms are often not very different. The Talmud's treatment of any single paragraph could be very brief or could go on in its final written version for over a dozen pages; a single phrase might give rise to hundreds of words. Eventually, however, the discussion always returned to the base text; when no one had anything left to say, the teacher simply went on to the next paragraph of Mishnah and the process started all over again.[9]

As the Gemara accumulated, rabbinic masters in Galilee and especially in Babylonia began to transform the study of Oral Torah into a new intellectual discipline. Earlier rabbinic teachers, the rabbis of the Mishnah and their immediate successors, had chiefly been interested in questions of substance: What does this word mean? What is the law in this case? As time went on, however, a new way of thinking, a growing interest in questions of logic and argumentation, began to develop alongside this one: *Why* was the law decided this way rather than some other? *Why* do we follow this master and not that one, and *why* was the rejected opinion preserved at all? *Why* was this verse, rather than that verse, chosen as decisive in this case? *How* do those who embrace one opinion answer the claims of those who support some other, and *how* does that other group answer back? It was no longer enough to know *what* your teacher had said: you had to know *why* he had said that and not something else, *why* he had interpreted a certain biblical passage one way and not another, *how* he could have said a certain thing in one context when he had reportedly said something else in another. If two people were quoted as having issued a certain ruling, you had to know *why* the Talmud had bothered to cite both. Were they really the same? Did the later authority not know that a predecessor had already decided this issue?

Such questions were of little interest to ordinary Jewish men and women. While the rabbinic scholars of Babylonia increasingly transformed Torah into a complex intellectual realm, other Jews, in Babylonia, throughout the Diaspora, and probably in the Land of Israel as well,[10] went on independently trying to preserve a way of life that they viewed as grounded in the teaching of Moses. The result was a kind of two-tiered religion in which common folk obeyed the will of God, while rabbinic sages did more than that: they *articulated* the will of God, shaping its contents and determining its character as they did so. The Jewish masses strove to approach God by obeying God's commandments, but the rabbis could do better than *approach* God: through the study and teaching of Torah (as they defined it) they could *become like* God, performing miracles and pronouncing the sacred rules that governed Jewish life (see "The Oven of Akhnai").

THE OVEN OF AKHNAI

The idea that by teaching Torah rabbis could become more like God is no mere figure of speech.

Leviticus 11:35 instructs that if an oven becomes defiled it must be dismantled; most ancient ovens were large earthenware chambers, and this procedure involved a lot of work and considerable expense. According to the Mishnah, however (Kelim 5:10), the oven of Akhnai was built out of separate blocks of earthenware and then insulated by putting sand into the seams; since such an oven was always already broken apart, it offered a way to avoid this need. R. Eliezer approved this arrangement and declared that such an oven is immune to defilement, but the sages disagreed.

According to the Talmud (Bava Metzia 59b), once Eliezer had failed to change his colleagues' minds through argument, he turned to performing miracles: he made a tree fly through the air, he made water flow uphill, and he threatened to collapse the study-house on his companions' heads. In every case the answer was the same: "You don't bring a proof from a tree!" R. Joshua, the leader of Eliezer's opponents, actually rebuked the walls: "When sages are arguing over the law, what business is that of yours?" So the walls stopped falling, but out of respect for Eliezer neither did they straighten up; "they still remain leaning over." (Thus, as the story progresses, it tells passers-by how a local curiosity came to be.)

Then Eliezer requested direct support from on high, and a voice came out of Heaven: "Why do you engage with R. Eliezer? The law always agrees with him!" But again Joshua answered, this time quoting scripture back to its presumed author: "It is not in Heaven!" (Deuteronomy 30:12). The Torah is no longer in Heaven; it has been given to us humans – that is, to us the rabbis – to interpret by majority vote (Exodus 23:2). In a later generation, it was told that God, on hearing this interpretation, smiled and said, "My children have defeated me!"

* * *

In this story, a rabbi tells God that interpretation of the Torah is now a human affair. The author is no longer in control of the meaning of his work; the creator can no longer tell his creatures how to live. Thus the rabbis took upon themselves the divine prerogative of defining and clarifying God's will. God had given the Torah, but now the sages would tell the people what it meant; now the sages would tell the people how they might fulfill its commandments.

In a sense, of course, this story merely acknowledges normal human experience; most readers have no access to the author to say what something means. Readers must understand the text on their own, doing the best they can. The Qumran sect (see Chapter 5) avoided this uncomfortable reality through the belief that their constant Torah study was steadily guided by divine inspiration; the rabbis took this responsibility on themselves.

Beneath the surface, however, the story puts forward a radical notion: the community, that is to say its rabbinic leaders, can determine on their own what constitutes fulfilling the will of God. This must be done, of course, with awestruck care, and the will of God, once determined, must be scrupulously fulfilled. This is the ultimate exercise of human free will, and this is the deepest meaning of the covenant: when God entered into a partnership with a human nation, Divine omnipotence had met its limit.

The talmudic story goes on to report that this incident had drastic consequences. The sages excommunicated Eliezer for his obstinacy, and he eventually died under a ban. God smilingly announced, "my children have defeated me," but then the world suffered crop failures and terrible storms: Eliezer himself, who still enjoyed Divine favor, caused wholesale destruction by fire with his angry glance. Gamaliel II, head of the rabbinic conclave, almost drowned in a storm at sea, and finally he died after Eliezer (his brother-in-law!) had prayed for revenge. (See Appendix 2 for further biographical details.)

As always, modern readers are not obliged to read this narrative as straightforward history. The point is more subtle: the rabbis who preserved this story knew that by assuming the right to interpret the Torah and determine sacred law, they had taken on a power once held by God. They knew this was audacious, but they also sensed it could not be helped. Knowing the awesome power of God, they were also aware that the stakes were very high: to misread the will of God would put the very cosmos in danger.

For the rabbis, dedication to Torah thus became a transforming experience, sanctifying those who undertook it and distinguishing them from the mass of Jewry (and, of course, from the mass of humanity). The rabbis of Babylonia developed a strong tendency to interact with one another. They married into other rabbis' families when they could, but even so they spent long months, even years,

THE YESHIVA AND THE FAMILY

At the very beginning of the Torah, God tells Adam and Eve, and then Noah's family after them, to "be fruitful and multiply" (Genesis 1:28; 9:1); early rabbis understood these words as not merely a blessing but a Divine command, and with very few exceptions the ancient rabbis married and fathered children. But the Babylonian Talmud reveals deep ambivalence over the tension between the demands and temptations of family life and the competing demands of dedication to Torah: a lifetime of Torah study necessarily meant withdrawal from family to the all-male atmosphere of the *bet midrash*. The Talmud speaks of men who visited their wives only once a year, and of the consequences when some failed to appear as expected (see Ketubot 62b–63a). These tensions were expressed as a deep fear of the male sexual urge, which was unavoidably repressed for much of their adult lives, and it caused a powerful reluctance to have ordinary dealings with women, who were a constant temptation but fundamentally unsuited for male companionship. Some of these attitudes persist even today in certain parts of the Jewish world.

living in the all-male environment of the rabbinic study-circle or *bet midrash* (see "The Yeshiva and the Family"). There, among their colleagues, they engaged in ever-deeper exploration of the details of Torah law, working out methods for deriving those details from the words of scripture and weaving those details into a single, conceptually integrated body of law.[11]

Driven by this growing preoccupation, Babylonian rabbis began to construct long, elaborate inquiries into the exegetical and logical basis of the teachings they had received. Living in a world of Oral Torah, they shaped these investigations in the form of dialogue: the comments of famous masters were brought to bear on widely diverse questions as though these men had been speaking to one another (some of these were questions that the cited masters had never actually addressed), and these teachings were knitted together by unnamed editors into long, elaborate debates called *sugyot* (sing. *sugya*, from an Aramaic word meaning "proceed"). This process of literary construction gave the Babylonian Talmud its distinctive character and its reputation for engaging in complex debates on obscure subjects. The argumentative, questioning nature of talmudic discussion has left its mark on Jewish culture, Jewish humor, Jewish literature, and Jewish thought into modern times.

* * *

In part, the Talmud's focus on law reflected the rabbis' developing role in society: they were legal experts, and lawyers value precision, consistency, and orderly thinking. Rabbinic teaching acquired a distinctive, lawyer-like character built on cultivation of the mind, prizing clarity rather than profundity, valuing the articulate rather than the eloquent, paying attention to behavior rather than to mood or motive. In part, these preferences reflected the historical circumstances in which the rabbinic movement first arose. Their movement had begun amid the wreckage caused by false messianic hopes, and they were convinced that the Jews could never achieve their own liberation through violent action. Redemption would come from God at a time decided by God: the people could only hope that pious living and submission to God's will might hasten that time. The laws of the Torah, God's rules for daily living, were the Jews' only sure hope for escaping their current terrible condition. A religion that strove for emotional intensity or inexpressible mystical insight above all else could only weaken the tenacious discipline that was necessary to survive exile and subjugation until the Messiah's inevitable arrival.

At the same time, the rabbis were deeply convinced that fulfilling the will of God must not be allowed to shrink into a set of directives to be obeyed without thinking. Of course, the Torah was full of rules and laws, but in the rabbis' view, the Torah was designed to lead men and women toward a holy life: simply following orders could not produce that result. For this reason, they developed the concept of *kavvana* or "intention." Rabbinic law provided detailed instructions as to the proper performance of Jewish rituals, but such rituals needed proper intention as well. The words of the prayer book were established, but prayer without intention was not true prayer. You didn't have to be in the synagogue to hear the New Year *shofar*, but you had to hear it with intention.

Remarkably, the concept of intention seems to have weakened as rabbinic Judaism developed. In several contexts, the Mishnah stipulates *kavvana* as a necessary component in the proper fulfillment of the Torah's requirements. In every case, however, the Talmud interprets this demand in an emphatically minimal way, as though to say that people really cannot be expected to achieve designated mental states on demand.[12] This seems like a conscious attempt to avoid spiritual elitism, but the result was to widen the gap between the rabbis themselves, sanctified by their dedication to Torah and striving for constant awareness of God's presence, and ordinary Jews who could be expected to follow basic rules but perhaps not much more.

With the production of the Babylonian Talmud, rabbinic Judaism reached its mature form. Under rabbinic leadership, Judaism became a religion of text study and behavioral detail. For those who entered the learned elite, Jewish life offered the prospect of personal sanctification; for the nation of Israel at large, Judaism provided a blueprint for building the "kingdom of priests and holy nation" that the Torah had long ago promised they might become.[13]

* * *

The ancient rabbis produced other sorts of books as well, chiefly collections of Bible interpretation that go by the name *midrash*. Rabbinic midrash is interpretation of a particular kind: working from the premise that the Bible is its own best interpreter, rabbis found links between apparently unrelated passages and allowed each such text to shed light on the other. The first citation in "Two Examples of Midrash" comes from the very first paragraph of *Genesis Rabba*, the oldest rabbinic commentary on the first book of the Torah, and provides a fine example of midrash at its best.

Designed as an introduction to the very first words of the Torah ("In the beginning . . . "), the presentation begins by citing Proverbs 8:30, a seemingly unrelated passage. This verse contains a difficult word (*amon*) that is then explained five different ways through association with five different verses containing other forms, themselves difficult, of that word. The last of these translations is set off from the others by a transitional phrase ("another interpretation"), as though to say, "Now comes the real point": this new translation introduces a brief parable about the need for equipment and workmen, architects and plans before anyone, even a king, can build a palace. The parable teaches that the Torah served God in all these roles during the creation of the world, suggests (without quite saying so) that all the previously mentioned translations of *amon* can be applied to the Torah as well,

TWO EXAMPLES OF MIDRASH

These two passages from a fifth-century collection of midrash on the Book of Genesis serve as introductions to chapters 1 and 22, respectively, of the biblical text. All biblical quotations appear in italics for ease of recognition.

I

R. Oshaya opened: "*I was with him as* amon, *a delight every day*" (Proverbs 8:30). *Amon* [can mean] "tutor," *amon* [can mean] "covered," *amon* [can mean] "hidden," *amon* [can mean] "great." *Amon* [can mean] "tutor" as it says "*As an omen carries a suckling child*" (Numbers 11:12). *Amon* [can mean] "covered" as it says "*They that were clothed* [emunim] *in scarlet*" (Lamentations 4:5). *Amon* [can mean] "hidden" as it says "*And he concealed* [omen] *Hadassah*" (Esther 2:7). *Amon* [can mean] "great" as it says "*Are you better than No-Amon*" (Nahum 3:8), which we translate "Are you better than Alexandria the Great, that sits among the rivers?"

Another interpretation: *amon* [can mean] "craftsman" (*uman*). The Torah declares, "I served as the instrument of the Holy One who is Blessed." It is the way of the world that when a human king builds a palace he does not rely on his own judgment but on an architect. Even the architect does not just start building; he has tablets and sketches that show where to put the rooms and the doors. So too the Holy One who is Blessed looked into the Torah and created the world. The Torah says, "*In the beginning God created*" (Genesis 1:1), and "beginning" can only mean *Torah*, as it says "*The Lord created me as the beginning of his way*" (Proverbs 8:22).

(Genesis Rabba 1:1)

II

And it came to pass after these things that God tested (nissah) *Abraham* (Genesis 22:1). It is written, "*You have given those who fear you a banner* (nes) *to display* (l'hitnoses) *on account of the truth*" (Psalm 60:6): [the repetitions of the word *nes* and then of the consonant *s* mean] trial after trial, elevation after elevation, in order to try [those who fear God] in the world, in order to raise them in the world like a ship's banner. And why all this? *On account of the truth*, in order that divine justice be confirmed in the world. If anyone should say "He enriches whom He wishes, He makes

TWO EXAMPLES OF MIDRASH (continued)

poor whom He wishes, He makes kings as He desires. When He wished
He made Abraham rich, when He wished He made him a king," you can
answer: "Can you do what Abraham did? *Abraham was a hundred years
old when his son Isaac was born to him*" (Genesis 21:5); after all this pain
[of waiting for a child] it was said to him, "*Take your son, etc.*" (Genesis
22:2), and he did not delay. "*You have given those who fear you a banner
to display*" – "*God did test/display* (nissah) *Abraham.*"

(Genesis Rabba 55:1)

and then clinches the teaching by quoting another verse from that
original chapter in Proverbs. In the space of three minutes, an ancient
preacher successfully (a) combined five unconnected scriptural passages so that each elucidated the others, (b) solved real interpretive
problems associated with some of these passages, (c) conveyed the
fundamental Jewish teaching that life based on the Torah is mapped
onto the very ground plan of the universe, and (d) subtly rejected
competing Christian claims that the word of God through whom the
world was created had now become flesh in Jesus.[14]

The second example, from the same rabbinic commentary, addresses the question of why God inflicted on Abraham the agonizing "test" (Genesis 22:1) of having to offer his beloved son Isaac as
a sacrifice. Again working through the technique of textual cross-
reference (now to Psalm 60:6), the unnamed preacher diverts attention from the meaning of "test" to the less troubling "display."
Hearers are no longer asked to believe that God cruelly tested the
beloved patriarch: why would a loving, omnipotent God want or
need such a test? In fact, says the preacher, God knew that Abraham
could be trusted and therefore placed his loyalty and piety, as well as
God's own power to reward the righteous, on display for the whole
world to see. Of course, the Torah does seem to speak of a test: did
the preacher really think otherwise, was the preacher really asking his
audience to disregard the straightforward meaning of the holy text
and read against the grain, or was he only suggesting another level
of meaning in an admittedly complex and disturbing narrative? Such
questions have intrigued later scholars ever since this little sermon,
and many others like it, were first set in writing.

THE MAJOR BOOKS OF MIDRASH

During the last centuries of ancient history, rabbinic study-circles compiled several large collections of midrashic material. These were rather diverse in character. Some, often known as *exegetical* midrashim, are organized as verse-by-verse elaborations of the text of scripture. Genesis Rabba, dating from the early fifth century and source of the sample texts in this chapter, is the most famous of these collections. Other collections, known as *homiletical* midrashim, consist of long, sometimes quite rambling explorations of particular passages or themes; these look as though they could be actual extended sermons, though the existing materials are probably artificial literary creations. Leviticus Rabba, dating from the same period and consisting of thirty-seven discourses loosely based on themes found in that book, is the earliest collection of this kind.

Another categorization distinguishes between *halakhic* (legal) midrashim, that seek to derive specifics of Jewish law from details in the Torah, and *aggadic* midrashim concerned with other, nonlegal concerns. Not surprisingly, there is no book of halakhic midrash on Genesis, a book with almost no legal material. On the other books of the Torah, the halakhic midrashim are as follows:

Exodus	Mekhilta of Rabbi Ishmael
	Mekhilta of Rabbi Simeon b. Yohai
Leviticus	Sifra
Numbers	Sifre I
	Sifre Zuta
Deuteronomy	Sifre II

Midrash Rabba, already mentioned, covers the five books of the Torah and also the "Five Scrolls" (see Chapter 1, "What Is in the Bible?"). These ten separate works have been only artificially combined into a single set; they were compiled in different locations over a long period of time, extending well into the Middle Ages.

Another collection of supposed sermons is called *Midrash Tanhuma* after the first sage whose name appears in its pages. This collection exists in two different versions, the traditional version and an alternate version compiled by the great editor Salomon Buber in the late nineteenth century. Similarly, the collection *Psiqta d'Rav Kahana* is so called after the first teacher named there.

THE MAJOR BOOKS OF MIDRASH (continued)

Other books of scripture, chiefly Samuel, Psalms, and Proverbs, have received collections of their own. New books of midrash, increasingly composed of older material but always with some new additions, continued to appear until early modern times.

Genesis Rabba and Leviticus Rabba, among the earliest existing documents of rabbinic literature, are products of the fifth century CE. Fresh collections of midrash, usually mixtures of newer interpretation and older recycled material, continued to emerge well into the Middle Ages, long after the period covered in this book. A brief survey of the major collections of midrash can be found in "The Major Books of Midrash."

Finally, one other literary product of the early rabbis must be recalled as well: the classic Jewish prayer book or *Siddur* ("Order" of prayers). Well before the end of antiquity there were Jewish houses of prayer all over the Mediterranean world, but scholars know very little about what went on in them. It seems unlikely that Jewish worship was standardized throughout the world; more probably, every Jewish community had its own local rules that determined which prayers to say and how to say them, which biblical passages to read and how to read them. The early rabbis, however, quickly began to strive for such regularization, and the classical Jewish prayer book is the fruit of their efforts.[15] The *Siddur* probably contains much pre-rabbinic material (surely much biblical material), but in its classical form it became the most widely circulated rabbinic text in Jewish life. It has remained so, though now in a great variety of regional and denominational editions, to the present day.

10

The End of Ancient History

A FEW CENTURIES AFTER THE RABBIS BEGAN THEIR WORK, THE
Roman Empire adopted Christianity as its official religion. This huge
transformation did not occur overnight, but nevertheless it was
shocking. The Jews had been one ethno-religious group among a great
many, each worshiping its own collection of divinities (of course, the
Jews' "collection" was smaller than the others); now everyone worshiped the same God (in fact, they said it was the *Jewish* God!), and
the Jews alone remained outside the new consensus. Over the fourth
and fifth centuries, the evermore powerful Church put an end to all
other forms of worship, the ancient religions of Greece and of imperial
Rome itself among them: only Judaism remained. A religion claiming to be the very fulfillment of Judaism had swept the world, and
only the Jews themselves refused to acknowledge its claims. The people of Israel had become the only non-Christian minority in a newly
Christian world.

To understand the background of this development, it is necessary
to look back to the beginnings of Christianity. If Christianity began as
a movement among Jewish followers of Jesus, how did it become a
religion in its own right, with a largely non-Jewish membership? This
development, wholly unexpected from the Jews' point of view, was
largely the product of one man's teaching. At its earliest beginning,
the movement was fiercely opposed by a man with the biblical name
Saul, by his own description a dedicated Pharisee who could not
abide the teachings or the practices associated with the followers of
Jesus.[1] On one of his journeys, however, Saul experienced a vision
in which Jesus himself summoned the fierce opponent to become a
follower and bring his message to the world: the persecutor became

179

a missionary, now using the Roman name Paul, and set out to carry the new faith throughout the empire.

In Paul's new understanding, God had offered through Jesus a stunning new religious opportunity to the nations of the world: *non-Jews who believed that Jesus was the Son of God, who had died in atonement for their sins and then risen from the dead, could enter through that belief into a new covenant, equivalent to the ancient covenant of Israel. All of humanity could now worship the Jewish God, and without having to become Jews!*

Why would this message have been attractive? The Jews and their religion were highly visible in the Greco-Roman world. The Jews were numerous (perhaps 20 percent of the population in the Eastern Mediterranean basin), and they were aggressively proud of their distinctive monotheistic faith. Their rituals aroused fascination. The cohesion of their communities and the stability of their families were strongly appealing in a chaotic world. Many people were so deeply attracted by all this that they became Jews themselves, but others held back;[2] moreover, the Jews were also a socially and politically marginal group, usually barred from urban citizenship and often the target of subtle and not-so-subtle hostility. Many Greeks were attracted by the Jews' religion and way of life but had no wish to adopt Jewish identity: now Paul told them that the Jewish God had graciously offered them the best of both worlds.

Paul's message of Christian salvation carried several momentous implications. One has already been mentioned: covenant with God no longer required that one be a Jew. This meant that the Jews' religious uniqueness had been abolished. Of course, this was a terrible blow to the national pride of a people now under oppressive foreign occupation: to most Jews it also made little sense. Most Jews, even those who had been deeply moved by the teachings of Jesus or who had been persuaded of his holiness by the reports of his resurrection, saw no reason why these new convictions should bring about such radical consequences.

In addition, Paul's message involved a transformation of religion from a question of *behavior* to one of *belief*: accepting the truth about Jesus was what mattered, not whether one followed a set of rules. This meant in turn that the Torah, which most Jews believed was first and foremost a collection of commandments (see Chapter 9), could no longer be the chief pathway to religious fulfillment. In Paul's view,

God no longer cared whether those who worshiped him lived by the Torah;
in fact, Paul considered that people who continued to insist on obeying the
Torah's rules in effect rejected the new salvation through Jesus.[3] God no
longer cared whether Christians belonged to the "old covenant"[4] or to the
people who had maintained that covenant for centuries. God cared only that
believers recognize and accept the gift of salvation now offered through the
death and resurrection of Jesus the Messsiah, the Son of God. There were no
other conditions.[5]

Paul's interpretation of Christianity was highly controversial. More
conservative teachers could not accept his nearly complete disregard
for Jewish customs, indeed his fierce hostility toward several.[6] To
them it was unthinkable that fundamental Jewish precepts like circumcision or the Sabbath should have completely lost their religious
significance. Paul may have conceded that Jewish followers of Jesus
might go on following the Torah (modern scholars have not agreed on
this), but he sharply refused to impose Jewish rules on those non-Jews
who accepted his teachings.

Many people, however, were eager to enjoy closeness to the Jewish
God without having to accept the restrictions of Jewish law or the
disadvantages of the Jews' political and social status. Paul's teachings opened the doors of the Church for such religious seekers to
enter, and ultimately the Church came to be dominated by these
people. Diverse Christian communities lived side by side for generations, some combining Christian belief with continued adherence
to the Torah, others rejecting this combination.[7] In the more Torah-
based churches, Jews may have dominated; in other settings, the sheer
weight of non-Jewish numbers eventually carried the day. Once Jews
and others could participate in the new Christian communities on an
equal footing,[8] Jews soon became a minority in the Church: the Jews
were no more than one-fifth of the population of the empire, and the
rapid entry of large numbers of other people soon turned Christianity into a predominantly gentile religion. By the second century, most
Christians were people who had never been Jews, had no interest in
living like Jews, and had no particular interest (except perhaps theological) in the Jewish people and no particular desire to be associated
with them. Christianity was now a gentile religion, its Judaic origin of
no clear relevance. Some Christians inherited the ancestral Greek dislike for Jews; others were simply indifferent. For some, the continued

persistence of Old Testament Judaism was a bothersome puzzle; for others, it was merely a sign of the Jews' own foolishness. Faith and Torah had parted ways.

On the other hand, well into late antiquity, many ordinary Christians remained fascinated with Judaism.[9] Christian laity attended synagogues, celebrated Jewish festivals, and freely socialized with Jews even as Christian leaders strongly disapproved of this conduct: in the leaders' view, continued intimacy with the people of the old covenant could only weaken appreciation of the new. Christian writers of the time complain of a rise in Jewish missionary activity, as though the Jews were belatedly attempting to reverse the Christian tide, but it is hard to tell whether these Christian complaints reflect a real increase in Jewish energy or just express Christian impatience at Jewish resistance to the new faith.

In any case, Christian preaching steadily denounced Judaism as an inadequate (or even Satanic) forerunner of the true faith and steadily attacked Jews for their continued loyalty to their heritage: these attacks often grew intemperate, most famously by accusing the Jews of having engineered the death of Jesus in an attempt to kill God. Once the Church had gained control over the Roman Empire, these hostile attitudes began to find expression in law and in administrative policy.

*   *   *

In the year 313, the Emperor Constantine ended Rome's long persecution of Christians and adopted the new religion himself; after that, the power of the Church over the government of the empire steadily increased, until finally, by the end of the century, pagan temples were closed throughout the empire and all pagan worship was banned. As the Church strengthened its hold on the empire, the conditions of Jewish life began to decline. Unlike polytheism Judaism remained a legal religion, but when Christian clergy encouraged local mobs to seize or destroy local synagogues, the victims could no longer be sure of restitution or even of government protection. In a famous case, the synagogue at Callinicum on the Euphrates River was destroyed, apparently by arson, in the year 388; the Emperor Theodosius I ordered that it be rebuilt and the instigators punished according to law, but under fierce pressure from Ambrose, the bishop of Milan,[10] he was forced to withdraw his directive. Such incidents took place with increasing frequency as the fourth century led into the fifth.

In the Jewish heartland, the patriarchs had steadily grown in prestige after the time of the famous Judah, reaching high noble rank by the late fourth century, but as Church influence rose they fell under increasing rebuke for their "arrogance." Finally, when the Patriarch Gamaliel VI died around the year 425, no successor was appointed and the position was allowed to lapse. Perhaps these developments explain why the Palestinian or Jerusalem Talmud became a closed book at around this time: through loss of morale or material resources, the rabbinic academies of the Land of Israel became unable to nurture their heritage as they had been doing. Their accumulated teachings were preserved but in a choppy, half-edited text, and the center of the rabbinic world shifted east to Babylonia, which was outside the Roman Empire and beyond the reach of Church authorities. The Babylonian schools continued to function, indeed to flourish. In the third century there had been a brief period of persecution in that country as well, at the instigation of the Zoroastrian monk Kartir, and then another a couple of centuries later, possibly triggered when the Exilarch Huna Mari rebelled in 471 and tried to establish his own independent state. Some rabbinic leaders did lose their lives during these episodes, but the long-standing tolerance of the Persian Empire generally prevailed and the growth of rabbinic tradition resumed.[11]

As throughout this book, very little can be said about the inner lives of most Diaspora communities. While laboring under growing disabilities, Jews seem in general to have maintained their customary economic activities. Legal materials from Western Europe in the sixth and seventh centuries continue to speak of Jewish slaveholders and Jews who owned large plantation estates; even emphatic Church laws forbidding Jews to own Christian slaves seem to have been enforced only sporadically and not very efficiently. Jewish commercial activity continued as in centuries past.[12] To be sure, the jurisdiction of Jewish courts was steadily reduced, and in the Byzantine Empire imperial interference in Jewish worship seems to have increased, but overall most Jewish communities seem to have held their own even as their circumstances grew steadily more ominous.

The last centuries of ancient history saw a growth in Jews' use of the Hebrew language in their religious lives. An imperial ruling of 553 CE authorized the use of Greek for Jewish public worship (see later), but religious use of that language appears to have been in decline, perhaps because Greek and Latin had themselves come to be seen as the religious languages of Christianity. Rabbinic commentaries, legal rulings, and the like were increasingly written in Hebrew, the "holy tongue" of the Bible,[13] while the Talmud's reliance on Aramaic (the everyday language of all Jews in Babylonia and most Jews in Galilee, the places where rabbis were active) gave that language a kind of religious quality of its own. The rabbinic liturgy for public worship was almost entirely in Hebrew, though a few brief Aramaic prayers were introduced. Grave inscriptions increasingly used Hebrew, or at least added a few standard Hebrew phrases to epitaphs written in the local vernacular (of course, the evidence is localized and rather sparse). Jews continued to use local languages for their daily lives, but their communal life slowly developed a bilingual character that finally became characteristic of Jewish life everywhere, up to modern times.

The complex religious ambivalence of Christianity toward its Judaic origins may have helped protect the Jews themselves from total disaster. In the Roman Empire the Jews found themselves increasingly hemmed in by the rising power and fixed hostility of the Church. While reduced to the status of a tolerated marginal group, however, the Jews were rescued from total disappearance by the very demands of Christian theology: the final triumph of the Gospel could not be achieved unless the "old Israel" converted en masse, and this conversion had to be sincere or it had no value. Therefore, the beleaguered Jews could not simply be wiped out or obliged by force to join the Church, as the last generations of polytheists had been compelled to do; the scattered remnants of Israel had to be preserved until they willingly joined the "body of Christ." They could be subjugated or humiliated – according to Church teaching, such treatment might legitimately be used to encourage Jews to convert – but the possibility of genuine Jewish conversion had to be maintained. Thus the worsening conditions of Jewish life must be seen not as the incidental result of hostility: these conditions were established as a matter of policy. The sufferings of the Jews could be held up for Christians (and the Jews themselves) to contemplate: what better evidence that the favor of God had been transferred to the new Israel, the true Israel, the authentic vessel of God's gracious love for sinful humanity?

Sometimes, to be sure, the official policy gave way to less patient attitudes. In Spain, now the kingdom of the Visigoths, the first post-Roman rulers adopted a heretical form of Christianity called *Arianism* that was relatively friendly toward Judaism,[14] but in the year 587 King Reccared shifted his loyalty to the Catholic Church, and his successors, beginning with Sisebut in the year 613, embarked on a policy of forced conversion that lasted off and on until the Muslim conquest in 711.[15] In the year 576, in Clermont (now in France), the local bishop arranged for the conversion of all the Jews of the city; similar events took place elsewhere as well, until Pope Gregory I ("the Great," reigned 590–604) had to remind the bishops of Western Europe that in spite of everything Judaism was still a "licit religion." The Western Roman Empire had long since collapsed, but throughout the seventh century rulers of the Eastern Roman (Byzantine) Empire repeatedly decreed the mass conversion of all Jews under their rule.

In Persia too, the kingdom under whose rule the great Babylonian Talmud had been produced, occasional waves of persecution rocked the Jewish settlement (see earlier). However, the last great Persian entry into ancient Jewish history was of a different sort. Rome and Persia had been the dominant powers in the Near East for centuries, and frequent outbreaks of war had not changed the essential stalemate between them. Then, in the year 614, a huge Persian force under King Khosroe II actually overran the Holy Land and put a temporary end to Roman control. The Jews of Palestine were elated. Jerusalem was placed under Jewish control, the Christian community there was violently attacked, and restoration of the Temple under Persian sponsorship (history repeating itself after 1,000 years!) seemed about to begin. However, after only three years, the Persian conquerors reconsidered their policy: they withdrew their support from the Jews and allowed the Christians to resume control. Probably it began to appear that the Jews were less useful as an instrument for harassing the Christians (and thus Rome/Byzantium), and were less reliable as surrogate guardians of order, than the Persians had hoped; it seemed preferable to allow the Christians to feel that Persian sovereignty was not as harmful as they in turn had feared. Thus the last great ancient flowering of the Jewish hope for national restoration came to nothing. A few years later (628) the Byzantine Emperor Heraclius reconquered the area and exacted a terrible revenge on the Jews; a few years after that (636), an Arab Muslim army rapidly overran the Middle East, and the ancient world came to an end.

* * *

Jewish reactions to these developments are largely unrecorded. The rabbis, for their part, displayed a remarkably subdued response to the triumph of Christianity. Rabbinic literature contains many subtle critiques of that religion, but rabbis attacked polytheism as well in pretty much the same fashion.[16] The Talmuds, always eager to explore complexities in Jewish law, never inquire whether the rules pertaining to idols and idol worship could be applied without change to Christianity. It is hard to imagine that this question would never have arisen, unless it was simply obvious to the rabbis that *of course* the rules applied. In their view Christianity was just one more form of gentile idolatry, no different in character from the worship of Zeus or of Caesar: the superficial resemblances to Judaism, the monotheist theology, or the reverence for the Old Testament did not alter this basic reality. A statue of Apollo was surely an idol: what about a crucifix? It seemed unnecessary to ask.

Except in connection with the early rabbis and their followers (see "Archeology and the Study of Ancient Judaism"), almost all information concerning the Jews during the last centuries of ancient history comes from their Christian enemies, and much of it is openly hostile or unwittingly misinformed. Rabbinic activity seems to have been limited to Palestine and Babylonia (Iraq) until the early Middle Ages, and the religious lives of Jews elsewhere in the far-flung Diaspora are virtually undocumented. There were synagogues almost everywhere, but little record survives of what went on in them. An intriguing glimmer of light is shed by the 553 enactment of the Emperor Justinian, already mentioned, in which he confirms the right of Jewish congregations to read the scriptures in Greek (or any other language) if that is their preference and forbids them to read their *deuterosis* (lit. "repetition") together with the holy books.[17] This shows that by the mid-sixth century the Jews' return to using Hebrew as their liturgical language was not yet complete (see earlier); it also appears to suggest that the new literature of Oral Torah had begun to reach the Jews of Constantinople.

During these same centuries of late antiquity, Jews developed two further types of religious literature: the *Targum*, or Aramaic

ARCHEOLOGY AND THE STUDY OF ANCIENT JUDAISM

There are two important sources of information about the inner lives of ordinary ancient Jews outside the world of the rabbis: ancient synagogues and burial chambers. Every Jewish community in the Roman world had a gathering place (Greek *synagogê*); none of these buildings survives intact, but many partially survive. From the size of these structures, historians can gauge the number of people in the community; from their layout, one can gauge what went on in them. Of course, any such conclusions are speculative – too much about ancient Judaism remains unknown – but speculative conclusions are far better than complete ignorance.

Modern investigators are especially fortunate in that the floors of many ancient synagogues were richly decorated with mosaics, and floors of ruined buildings are naturally the most likely to have survived. Some of these mosaics simply offer decorative patterns, but others depict scenes from the Bible or present various combinations of Jewish religious symbols. The sixth-century synagogue from Beth Alpha in northern Israel had a floor with three panels; these depicted, respectively, the Binding of Isaac (Genesis 22), the Zodiac (!), and a jumble of Jewish religious symbols depicted as seen through parted curtains (Figure 6). What does all this mean? Were the pictures merely decorative? Then why decorate a floor with sacred objects that people will dirty with their feet every time they enter the room? Did the mosaics represent a symbolic journey of revelation and salvation, as proposed by the scholar Erwin Goodenough? One might think this farfetched, and other leaders in the field have roundly disputed his proposals, but Goodenough's arguments were weighty and his evidence was impressive. The matter remains unresolved.

The third-century synagogue at Dura-Europus in Syria is nearly unique among ancient synagogues in that its interior survived nearly intact; built right into the city wall, it was filled with rubble when the city came under siege and remained untouched into the twentieth century after the city was conquered and destroyed in 257 CE. When the room was opened up, excavators were astonished to find that every inch of the walls was covered with paintings: some represented biblical scenes (though often with nonbiblical details); some were more enigmatic. The space over the niche where the Torah scrolls were placed during worship, presumably the holiest place in the chamber, was filled as at Beth Alpha with an assortment of Jewish religious symbols in no apparent order (Figure 7).

ARCHEOLOGY AND THE STUDY OF ANCIENT JUDAISM (continued)

These two examples will suffice to illustrate the problem of using archeology for history: ancient objects that are uncovered during excavation are surely of great interest to historians, but they do not explain themselves. Modern scholars must try to figure out what they mean, that is to say, what they meant to the people who made them and placed them where they were found. They must do this without the little index cards that are placed next to such objects in modern museums, and that is not always easy.

6. Mosaic floor from Beth Alpha. The floor of ancient synagogues was often decorated with mosaic pictures. This one was found in the Byzantine-era building at Beth Alpha in Israel. Scholars remain uncertain whether the Zodiac, taken from the world of Hellenistic and Babylonian astrology, had acquired religious meaning for Jews or was used simply for decoration. (Photo courtesy of Todd Bolen/bibleplaces.com)

translation of scripture, and the *piyyut*, or liturgical poem. These eventually were absorbed into the rabbinic way of life, but it is not clear that rabbis initiated or even supervised these developments.

The Targums are not the oldest Jewish translations of the Bible; they were preceded by Greek translations dating back to the Septuagint

7. The Torah shrine at Dura-Europus. In the holiest spot of this ancient synagogue, the designers painted a stunning melange of Jewish symbols. The picture as such seems to carry no message, but it combines almost every visual clue of Jewish piety that can be imagined. A similar mixture of images can be found in one of the floor panels at Beth Alpha. (Photo courtesy of Art Resources, New York)

(ca. 250 BCE for the Torah; see Chapter 3) and perhaps even earlier. It is possible that Aramaic translations arose later because speakers of that language were better able to understand the rather similar Hebrew; it is more likely, however, that Aramaic translations tended to be improvised in the course of worship or study and thus produced no literature.[18] The oldest Aramaic translation of the Torah is attributed to a convert named *Onkelos*, said to have been a disciple of Rabbi Akiva (early second century CE).[19] Eventually several standard Targums gained acceptance: alongside the version of Onkelos on the Torah stood a translation of the prophets ascribed to *Jonathan ben Uzziel*, reputedly another disciple of Akiva. To Jonathan was also attributed a much more elaborate and fanciful translation of the Torah that is almost surely in fact of later date.

The earliest *payyetanim* (authors of *piyyutim*), Yannai, Eleazar Kallir, and Yose ben Yose, are not easy to date but probably flourished during the last generations before the Muslim conquest. The origins of *piyyut* too are almost surely not rabbinic. Early rabbinic prayers, as they appear in talmudic literature, are terse and written in simple though often elegant prose, almost entirely without literary artifice. From their beginnings, however, *piyyutim* were characterized by the use of rare words that appear just once in the whole Bible, very elaborate sentence structure, complicated acrostics, and the like. Such poems trace their ancestry not to the rabbis of the Talmud but to the ecstatic prayers of mystical groups, visionaries who sought to enter heaven and explore the heavenly palaces (*hekhalot*) on no less a vehicle than the chariot (*Merkava*) of God.[20]

Talmudic tradition records that several leading rabbis of the first centuries CE, including Yohanan b. Zakkai and Akiva b. Joseph, took part in the activities of the "riders of the Chariot."[21] Through the intensity of their visions they were said to bring down heavenly fire, so that birds flying over them were in danger of being incinerated. Yet the rabbinic movement overall remained skeptical of such ecstatic tendencies (see Chapter 9), and the rhythmic chants and alphabetical recitations of the Merkava mystics (apparently designed to induce a trance or ecstasy) seem largely to have survived outside rabbinic circles.

Yet, perhaps under the influence of contemporary Byzantine liturgy, *piyyut* found a way into standard rabbinic worship, in connection mostly with the great annual festivals rather than ordinary Sabbaths or weekdays. This development inevitably gave rise to another innovation, the appearance of trained prayer leaders, forerunners of modern cantors, artists who combined mastery of these arcane poems with musical imagination and skill. Originally, any member of the congregation might lead public worship, and within the prescribed structure of themes and *berakhot* the leader could improvise the actual text of the prayers he recited. (Such improvisation was almost unavoidable since written copies of the prayers were exceedingly rare.) As time went on, however, the growing intricacy and diminishing flexibility of the liturgical text excluded many ordinary worshipers from serving in this capacity and reduced their participation to passive listening; this situation persisted until the invention of printing provided copies of the prayer book to the worshiping laity.

* * *

This book will end its story with the explosive arrival of Islam onto the world scene. The Middle Ages provided a very different environment for Jewish life. A religion that had originated in a polytheistic environment, and developed its character through constant resistance to that environment, now found itself in a world divided between two monotheistic colossi, each claiming (in slightly different ways) to be a superior replacement for Judaism itself, each able almost without restriction to determine the conditions, even the very possibility, of Jewish survival.

The early Middle Ages witnessed the spread of rabbinic leadership throughout the Jewish world. This monumental development is almost entirely undocumented. All the great centers of the ancient Diaspora existed and thrived for generations, sometimes for centuries, before the first rabbis arrived. This was true in Babylonia, in Spain, throughout Greece and Asia Minor, across North Africa, in Italy, and in imperial Rome itself. The Talmud gives some information about Babylonia, but when did the first masters of rabbinic tradition arrive in all those other places? Can later legends concerning these founding figures be trusted? To achieve positions of leadership in any location, the first rabbis or their successors had to repeat the achievements of the earliest rabbinic sages: they had to win the trust of both the ruling authorities and the Jews themselves. How did they do this? How long, if at all, did resistance persist, and what happened to the earlier, pre-rabbinic forms of Jewish worship and leadership? In many cases, modern historians can barely guess at the answers to these questions.

The Middle Ages saw the expansion of the European Diaspora into new territories, chiefly Germany and Poland, where rabbinic culture attained unprecedented heights. In Spain and elsewhere, the Jews achieved a second great synthesis with philosophy, only this time the accomplishment escaped Philo's fate and entered into the mainstream of Jewish history. But all that represents a new chapter in Jewish history, and it will be the task of another volume to tell that story.

Three Sample Passages from the Babylonian Talmud

THE FOLLOWING PAGES PRESENT THREE EXTENDED PASSAGES
from the Babylonian Talmud. These extracts were not placed in boxes
within the text because they are too long, but they should be read in
connection with the description of the Talmud to be found in Chapter 9. These texts were chosen because each represents an important
feature of the talmudic enterprise: interpreting older texts, establish-
ing the law, using narrative to explore theology. Each translation is
followed by a brief commentary in italics indicating some characteristic features of the text.

I. BERAKHOT 2A–3A

MISHNAH: From when [may people] recite the evening *Sh'ma*?[1] From
the hour that the priests come in to eat of their *teruma*-offering,[2] until
the end of the first watch;[3] [these are] R. Eliezer's words, but the
sages say, Until midnight. Rabban Gamaliel says, Until the first light
of dawn. . . .

GEMARA: . . . The Master said:[4] "From the hour the priests come in
to eat of their *teruma*-offering." Now when do priests eat *teruma*-
offering? From the hour the stars come out. So let him [straight-
forwardly] teach "from the hour the stars come out"! [By teaching
the law obliquely] he teaches us something extra by the way: Priests
eat *teruma*-offering from the hour the stars come out.

And this teaches us [in turn] that [need for] an expiation-sacrifice[5]
does not disqualify [a priest from eating *teruma*], as it is taught: "And
when the sun sets he shall be clean" (Leviticus 22:7). [Lack of] sunset

disqualifies him from eating *teruma*,[6] but [lack of] expiation does not disqualify him from eating *teruma*.

And from what [evidence can we show] that "and when the sun sets" means sunset and "he shall be clean" means clean [with] the day? Perhaps [the phrase means] the coming of its light[7] and "he shall be clean" means "the man [can] become clean [by bringing his offering]." Rabbah b. R. Shela said, "If so, Scripture should have said, 'he will be clean [later on].' What is 'he shall be clean'? With the day, as people say, 'The sun has turned to evening, and the day is clean.'"

In the West, Rabbah b. R. Shela's teaching had not been heard, so they raised it as a question: Does this "and when the sun comes" mean his sunset and "he shall be clean" mean "clean [with] the day"? Perhaps it refers to the coming of its light, and "he shall be clean" means "the man [can now] become clean." But they answered the question from a *baraita*, as it is taught: "The sign for the matter is when the stars come out."[8] You can conclude that the reference is to sunset and that "he shall be clean" means with the day.

The Master said: "From the hour that the priests come in to eat of their *teruma*-offering." But throw these together:[9] "From when do people recite the evening *Sh'ma*? From when a poor man comes in to eat his bread with salt until the hour he gets up at the end of his meal."

The final part of this text surely contradicts our Mishnah: shall we say the beginning contradicts our Mishnah [too]? No; a poor man and a priest are the same measure [of time].

Then throw these together: From when do people begin to recite the *Sh'ma* in the evening? From the hour that people come in to eat their bread on Sabbath eves: R. Meir's words. But the sages say, From the hour that the priests are allowed to eat their *teruma*-offering. The sign for the matter is when the stars come out, and even though there is no proof of this there is a hint, as it is said, "And we were doing the work, half of them holding spears, from the rising of dawn until the emergence of the stars." And it [also] says, "So we had [the men] as guards by night and workers by day."[10]

(Why "and it says"? If you should say "night" begins when the sun goes down, and they were just extending the workday, come and hear: "So we had [the men] as guards by night and workers by day.")[11]

Now you would think that "a poor man" and "people" are the same measure [of time],[12] but then if you say that "a poor man" and "a priest" are the same measure [of time, as was said earlier], the sages' opinion coincides with R. Meir's![13] So then you must infer that "a poor man" is one measure [of time] and "a priest" is a different measure [of time]. No: "a poor man" and "a priest" are one measure [of time], while "a poor man" and "people" are not one measure [of time].

But then are "a poor man" and "a priest" [really] one measure [of time]? Throw these together:

From when [may] people begin to recite *Sh'ma* evenings? From the hour that the day becomes holy on Sabbath Eves: R. Eliezer's words. R. Joshua says, From the hour that the priests are cleansed to eat their *teruma*-offerings. R. Meir says, From the hour that the priests immerse to eat their *teruma*-offerings. (R. Joshua said to him, But don't the priests immerse while it is yet day?) R. Hanina says, From the hour that a poor man comes in to eat his bread with salt. R. Ahai (some say R. Aha) says, From the hour that most people come in to recline [at dinner].

Now if you say "a poor man" and "a priest" are one measure [of time], then R. Hanina is the same as R. Joshua![14] So must you not conclude that the measure of a poor man and the measure of a priest are different? You must so conclude.

Which of them is later? It is reasonable that "a poor man" is later, for if you say "a poor man" is earlier, then R. Hanina is the same as R. Eliezer! So must you not conclude that "a poor man" is later? You must so conclude.

The Master said: "R. Joshua said to him, But don't the priests immerse while it is yet day?" R. Judah spoke well to R. Meir, but R. Meir could answer him: Do you think I am speaking on the basis of your conception of twilight? I am speaking on the basis of R. Yose's conception of twilight, for R. Yose said, "Twilight is like the blink of an eye; this goes in and this goes out, and it's impossible to stand on it."[15]

R. Meir contradicts himself![16] Two different reporters (*tanna'im*) delivered traditions in R. Meir's name.

R. Eliezer contradicts himself![17] Two different reporters delivered traditions in R. Eliezer's name, or if you like I can say the start [of the Mishnah] is not R. Eliezer's [teaching].[18]

This passage consists of two different inquiries. The first restates the Mishnah's law in terms far more easily applied to everyday life: many people have no opportunity to observe the eating habits of priests, but anybody can watch the heavens to check for the emergence of the stars.[19] This apparent

simplification, however, leads in turn to new complexity. The Talmud intro-
duces a seemingly unrelated law concerning the relation between purity and
"expiation," and that, in turn, demands an elaborate consideration of alter-
native interpretations of Leviticus 22:7. The passage as a whole demonstrates
the Talmud's readiness to digress in the midst of a developing conversation,
its constant search for the biblical roots of the laws it propounds, and its
extreme thoroughness in making sure that it has adopted the most appro-
priate interpretation of scripture. The third sample text that follows will
illustrate these phenomena in a nonlegal context.

The second inquiry examines all known tannaitic opinions with regard
to the question of the Mishnah: when does "evening" begin for purposes of
reciting Sh'ma? The Mishnah offers only one answer to the question – when
newly purified priests eat their teruma*; did other early sages disagree? In*
the end, three baraitas *offer a total of eight other opinions, and the Talmud*
sets out to determine whether (a) some of these may be identical in substance
though different in formulation, and why this redundancy should be present,
(b) whether all the different indications of time can be arranged in sequence
from earliest to latest, and (c) whether the cited authorities can really have
offered all the opinions that are ascribed to them. In the course of this last
inquiry, the Talmud also shows itself ready to accept that incompatible ver-
sions of a sage's teachings may have been handed down. This apparently
shocking possibility seems to arouse no anxiety at all.

This second discussion is more interested in classification than in the
actual law: that has already been determined. The goal now is to identify
every possible legal ruling with a known Master and to make sure that there
is neither redundancy (can two teachers have said the same thing?) nor
contradiction (can one teacher have said two different things?) in the set of
teachings. In this welter of conflicting opinions, no attempt is made to justify
the selection of one ("emergence of the stars") as authoritative; that selection
presumably rests on Nehemiah 4:15–16, verses that are quoted seemingly in
passing.

II. BAVA METZIA 21A–22B

MISHNAH: Which found objects belong to [the finder] and which must
he publicize?[20] These belong to him: [If] he found scattered fruit,
scattered coins, small bundles of grain in a public space, circles of
pressed figs, commercial loaves, strings of fish, slices of meat, sheared

wool from its place of origin, bundles of flax, or tongues of purple[21] –
these belong to him: R. Meir's words.[22] R. Judah says, Anything that
has been altered must be publicized. How so? [If] he found a circle
[of figs] with a potsherd inside it, or a loaf with coins. R. Simeon b.
Eleazar says, Any newly bought object need not be publicized.[23]

GEMARA: . . . Unrealized despair: Abaye says this is not despair, and
Rava says this is despair.[24]

When an object has an identifying mark, everyone agrees that this
is not despair; even if we hear afterward that [the owner] eventually
gave up, there was no despair [when the object was found]; it came
into [the finder's] hand in a forbidden manner. When [the owner]
realizes it has fallen, he says to himself, "I have a marking on it; I'll
identify the marking and take my property." (With a tidal wave or a
flooded river, even if it has a marking the Torah[25] permits it, as we
will observe later.)[26]

Where do they dispute? Over an object without an identifying
mark. Abaye says, This is not despair because he does not know
it has fallen. Rava says, This is despair; when he realizes it has fallen
he will despair, saying, "I have no marking on it!," and he [is deemed]
to have despaired from now.[27]

Come and hear:[28] "Scattered fruit." He doesn't know they have
fallen![29] R. Uqba b. Hama said we are talking about fruit left on the
threshing floor that is intentionally abandoned.[30]

Come and hear: "Scattered coins . . . belong to him." Why? He
doesn't know they have fallen! [We must understand this] according to the teaching of R. Isaac, who said a man checks his money bag
constantly. Here too a man will check his money bag every hour.[31]

Come and hear: "Circles of pressed figs and commercial loaves
belong to him." Why? He doesn't know they have fallen! There too
because they are heavy he will be aware of them.[32]

Come and hear: "Tongues of purple belong to him." Why? He
doesn't know they have fallen [and they are not heavy]! There too,
because they are valuable he feels for them, as according to R. Isaac.

Come and hear:[33] "If someone finds coins in a synagogue or a study
hall or any place where the public gathers, he may keep them because
the owners despair of [recovering] them." But he doesn't know they
have fallen! R. Isaac said, "A man checks his money bag constantly."[34]

Come and hear: "When may any person [enter a field] to glean? When the 'searchers' have gone."[35] (We say:[36] Who are the "searchers"? R. Yohanan said, Old men who walk leaning on a stick. Resh Lakish said, The very last of the gleaners.[37]) And why [may ordinary people glean at all]? Granted, the local poor have despaired [of obtaining any more food from this location], poor people from elsewhere have not despaired [of finding sustenance in this field; why should "ordinary people" be allowed to take anything unless Rava's view is accepted?]. Since there are local poor, outsiders "despair" from the very beginning, saying "The poor people who live there have already taken everything."

Come and hear: "Dates on the road, even beside a date field, and similarly a fig tree that leans over the road and one found figs underneath: they are permitted according to the law of robbery and are exempt from tithes. Olives and carobs are forbidden."[38] Clearly the beginning [of the law, concerning dates] presents no difficulty to Abaye; since [the owner] values them he checks them frequently;[39] similarly he knows that figs will fall [from the tree]. But the latter part, that says olives and carobs are forbidden, presents a difficulty for Rava![40] R. Abbahu said, "[The case of] olives is different, since their appearance serves to identify the field where they grew; even though they fall, people will recognize each man's olives [and not take them]." If so, even the beginning [of the law should prohibit fallen dates and figs] as well. R. Papa said, "When a fig falls it is ruined."[41]

Come and hear: "If a thief or a robber takes from one [person] and gives to another, and so too if the Jordan takes from one and gives to another, what was taken is taken, and what was given is given."[42] Clearly [in the case of] a robber or the Jordan, [the owner] sees [his property taken away] and despairs; [in the case of] a thief, does he see [the theft] that he should despair? R. Papa explained this with reference to an armed bandit. Then he is a robber! [The law refers to] two kinds of robber.[43]

Come and hear: "If a river swept away someone's lumber or trees or boulders and placed them in someone else's field, they belong to [the latter] because the owners have despaired [of recovering them]." So the reason is that the owners have despaired; otherwise [this would] not [be the case].[44] What are we dealing with here? When [the first owner] can retrieve them [afterward].[45] In that case quote the end [of the law]: "If the owners were running after them, [the finder] must return them." If the owners can retrieve them, why go running? Even if they don't run [they can retrieve their property whenever they want].[46] What are we dealing with here? When they can retrieve their property, [but only] with difficulty. If they go running, there is no despair. If they do not go running, they have surely despaired.

Come and hear:[47] When they said that *teruma* unknowingly set aside is valid *teruma*, how did they mean [this]? If someone went down into another person's field and gathered [produce] and set aside *teruma* without permission, if [the owner] considers this [to be] robbery it is not *teruma*; otherwise, it is *teruma*.[48] And how do we know whether or not he considers this robbery? If the owner came along and said to him "Go take the better produce" and there was better produce, then the *teruma* is valid;[49] if not, the *teruma* is not valid.[50] If the owner gathered [more produce] and added it to the pile, it is *teruma* in any case. Then if better produce was to be found the *teruma* is valid![51] Why? At the point the *teruma* was set aside he wasn't aware this was happening![52] Rava [himself] explained this according to Abaye's view: [The owner] had made [the other] his agent.[53] This [explanation] makes sense: if you suppose he had not made [the other] his agent how could his *teruma* be valid? The Torah says, "You also" to authorize agency, but just as your own action must be conscious, so your agent's action must be conscious.[54] What are we dealing with here? [This is the kind of case where the owner] made [the other] his agent and said to him, "Go set aside *teruma*" but did not say, "Take the *teruma* from these [specific heaps of produce]." Now an ordinary householder takes his *teruma* from produce of average value, but [the agent] went and took *teruma* from the best [of the crop] and the owner came, found him doing so, and said, "Go take the better produce." If there was better produce to be found, then the *teruma* is valid; if not, the *teruma* is not valid.[55]

Amemar, Mar Zutra, and R. Ashi[56] happened to be in the orchard of Mari bar Issak. The tenant-farmer brought dates and pomegranates and set these before them; Amemar and R. Ashi ate; Mar Zutra did not eat.[57] Meanwhile Mari bar Issak came along, found them there, and said to his tenant, "Why did you not bring to the rabbis from the best?" Amemar and R. Ashi said to Mar Zutra, "Why won't the

Master eat now? It is taught: 'If better ones were to be found the *teruma* is valid.'"[58] He answered, "Rava said thus: The law of 'Go take the better produce' was only meant to apply to *teruma* because that is a commandment of the Torah and [the owner] is happy [to fulfill the commandment], but here [Mari] only said that because he was embarrassed."[59]

Come and hear: "If the dew was still on [produce] and [the owner] was glad of this, [the produce] falls under the law of 'If [water] be put.'[60] If it dries [before the owner finds out], even if he is happy, they do not fall under the rule." Why so? Because we do not say that since he is happy now we understand he would have been happy even at the time.[61] That case is different because it is written, "If [water] be put"; the law does not come into effect until water is [intentionally] put [on the grain]. If so, the beginning of the law also [should require intentional placement of the water and not refer to dew]. This follows R. Papa, for R. Papa posed a difficulty: It is written "If he puts [water]," but we read "If [water] be put"[62]: how can this be? We require passive "putting" to resemble active "putting": just as active "putting" requires awareness, so too passive "putting" requires awareness.[63]

Come and hear, for R. Yohanan said in the name of R. Ishmael b. Yehozadak:[64] "From where [can we learn][65] that a lost object that was washed away by a river is permitted [to the finder]? As it is written, 'Thus shall you do for his donkey and thus shall you do for his garment and thus shall you do for any lost property of your brother that is lost to him and you find it.'"[66] [The verse speaks of] that which is lost to [its owner] but [may be] found by any man;[67] this excludes that which he loses but may not be found by any man. The forbidden resembles the permitted [since both categories are treated in the one verse]: just as the permitted is permitted whether or not it carries an identifying sign, so the forbidden is forbidden whether or not it carries an identifying sign.

This is a decisive refutation of Rava, and the law follows Abaye![68]

This very long discussion revolves around a simple legal point. The Torah commands that found objects must be returned to their owner, but situations arise where this is impossible. In particular, if the object itself cannot be identified because it has no distinctive features and looks like many others of its kind, then the owner has no way to prove that this particular item was his and so is out of luck (think of losing [or finding!] a ten-dollar bill on a crowded sidewalk). Under these circumstances the owner will abandon all hope of recovering his property, and this abandonment is legally equivalent to renouncing his ownership altogether. The finder is allowed to keep the object because at the moment of his discovery it has no other owner.

*But this scenario depends on the owner's knowing of his misfortune; if he doesn't know the object is lost, he has no reason to relinquish ownership. He surely will despair of recovery once the loss is discovered (or at least we assume this), but this has not yet taken place. At the moment when the finder picks up the lost object, the owner does not yet know it is gone, and presumably he still considers himself its owner: **we** know he will never get it back, but **he** does not. Now what?*

*The dispute between Abaye and Rava concerns this question. Abaye holds that prospective despair is as good as the real thing: since the owner will abandon ownership as soon as he knows of his loss, and since we know of his loss already, we act as though the abandonment has already taken place, and the finder can keep his discovery. Rava, Abaye's great contemporary, rejects this approach; it is not for us to renounce someone's ownership of an object before he himself is ready to do so. **According to Rava, the finder has no legal right to what he has found unless he is sure that the owner is aware of his loss and has despaired of recovering his property.***

The Talmud places this dispute in its current context because tractate Bava Metzia, chapter 2, deals with the matter of lost objects. The Mishnah (as quoted previously) offers a broad distinction between objects that must be returned and those that may be kept by the finder.

Having laid out the dispute, the Talmud looks for some existing law that may help to resolve it. First comes the Mishnah, to which this discussion is attached: phrase by phrase, the mishnaic text is examined to see whether its provisions imply a resolution of the dispute. When the first attempt ("scattered fruit") fails because the rule can be understood according to either Rava or Abaye, the next phrase is examined: perhaps some difference in the logic of the two situations will yield better results there.[69] When the Mishnah is exhausted, the Talmud looks for materials wherever they can be found in the great treasury of Oral Torah, and finally the last case, after more than a dozen failed attempts, decides the argument in favor of Abaye. This final decisive text appears twice in tractate Bava Metzia but nowhere else; the origins of this midrash *and its original context are lost.*

If the editors of the Talmud knew all along that only this last attempt would resolve the dispute between Abaye and Rava, why did they bother to include all the others? This sugya *is an excellent example of the Talmud's growing interest in the logic of legal decision making rather than merely its outcome (see Chapter 9); the main purpose of this very long passage is to demonstrate the painstaking care with which each of the successive proofs is tested and rejected when alternative interpretations are found. The text also suggests that all ancient rabbinic texts were designed not only to convey substantive information but also to aid in the training of rabbinic disciples. Students who have worked through this material know the legal outcome, but they have also seen an object lesson in the need to examine older teachings with scrupulous care and to make sure that all possible interpretations and applications of such teachings have been considered before any can be finally adopted. They have seen the value and the power of detailed textual analysis. They have seen how difficult it can be to prove that a respected colleague's opinions are wrong.*

III. AVODA ZARA 2A–3B

Note: In this section all citations of scripture appear in *italics*. This will help to demonstrate the flexible use of the Bible by ancient rabbinic preachers. In particular, it shows that this extended narrative is grounded in frequent reference to a single verse from Isaiah 43.

Parenthetical insertions in the main story are indicated by indentation.

* * *

R. Hanina b. Papa (some say R. Simlai) interpreted [Isaiah 43:9 as follows]:[70]

In the future the Blessed Holy One will bring a Torah scroll, place it in his lap, and say: "The one who was occupied with this may come and take his reward." At once those who worship the stars[71] gather and enter in a chaotic mass, as it is said, *All the nations gather together,* etc.

The Blessed Holy One said to them, "Don't come before me in a mixed-up crowd; let every nation with its scribes come in [by itself]," as it is said, *And the peoples are assembled.*

"People" can only mean "kingdom," as it is said, *One people will overpower [another] people.*[72]

And could the Blessed Holy One really get confused [by the crowding]? Rather, the purpose was that [the nations themselves] not be confused by [the presence of] one another so that they could hear what he said to them.

At once the kingdom of Rome entered before him first.

What is the reason? Because it was important. How do we know it was important? As it is written, *It will consume the entire land, and stamp on it and crush it.*[73] R. Yohanan said, "This is guilty Rome, whose character is known to the whole world."

And how do we know that the one who is important goes in first? As R. Hisda [taught], for R. Hisda said, "[When] the king and the populace [enter] for judgment the king enters first, as it is said, *To carry out the judgment of his servant*[74] *and the judgment of his people Israel,* etc.[75]

And what is the reason? If you like I can say it is not the way of the world for a king to sit [waiting] outside, and if you like I can say [the king should be judged] before [God] becomes angry [at the sins of all the people].

The Blessed Holy One says to them, "How have you been occupied?" They say to him, "Ruler of the world, we established many markets, we built many bathhouses, we collected much silver and gold, and we did it all so that Israel might occupy itself with the Torah."

The Blessed Holy One said to them, "World-class idiots! Everything you did was for your own benefit: you established markets to have a place for whores and baths to prettify yourselves, and silver and gold are mine, as it is said, *Silver is mine and gold is mine, says the Lord of Hosts.*[76] Is there no one among you who can tell 'this,' as it is said, *Who among you will tell this?*"[77]

And "this" can only mean Torah, as it is said, *And this is the Torah that Moses placed [before the Children of Israel].*[78]

At once they go out dejected; when the kingdom of Rome has gone out, the kingdom of Persia comes in after her.

What is the reason? As it is written, *And behold a second beast, another one like a bear.*[79] And R. Joseph taught, "These are the

Persians, who eat and drink like a bear, and are fleshy like a bear, and grow hair like a bear, and have no rest like a bear."

The Blessed Holy One says to them, "How did you occupy yourselves?" They say to him, "Ruler of the world, we built many bridges, we conquered many cities, we made many wars, and we did it all so that Israel might occupy itself with the Torah."

The Blessed Holy One [will] say to them, "Everything you did was for your own benefit: you built bridges to collect tolls from them, [you conquered] cities to organize forced labor in them, and I make war, as it is said, *The Lord is a man of war.*[80] Is there no one among you who can tell 'this,' as it is said, *Who among you can tell this?*"

And "this" can only mean Torah, as it is said, *And this is the Torah that Moses placed* [before the Children of Israel].

At once they go out dejected.

But once the kingdom of Persia saw that the kingdom of Rome had achieved nothing, why did they go in? They said: They destroyed the Temple and we built it.[81]

So too [will befall] every other nation.

But once they see that the first achieved nothing, why do they go in? They think: Those enslaved Israel and we did not enslave Israel.

And why are these considered "important" and those not considered "important"? Because their kingdoms will endure until the Messiah comes.[82]

* * *

[The translation continues without omission, but a new stage in the "drama" begins at this point. So too later.]

The [nations] say to him, "Ruler of the world, did you offer us [the Torah] and we not accept it?"[83]

And can they say that? Look, it is written, *And [Moses] said, "YHWH came from Sinai and shone forth to them from Seir,"*[84] and it is written, *God will come from Teman, etc.*[85] What did he want at Seir, and what did he want at Paran?[86] R. Yohanan said, "This teaches that the Blessed Holy One brought [the Torah] around to every people and tongue and they did not accept it, until he came to Israel and they accepted it."[87]

Instead, they say [their claim] this way: "Did we accept it and then not fulfill it?"

But there is a refutation to this [as well]: *Why* did you not accept it?

Instead, they say to him as follows: Ruler of the world, did you ever invert the mountain over us like a tub and we not accept it [even so], as you did for Israel, as it is written, *And they stood beneath the mountain* (Exodus 19:17)?

R. Dimi b. Hama said, "This teaches that the Blessed Holy One inverted Mount [Sinai] over Israel like a tub and said to them, 'If you accept the Torah all is well; and if not, there you will be buried!'"[88]

At once the Blessed Holy One says to them, The "first things" will tell us, as it is said, *and inform us of first things*: Where did you fulfill the seven commandments that you did accept?[89]

And how do we know they did not fulfill them? As R. Joseph taught, *[God] stood and measured the land, he saw and released the peoples.*[90] What did he see? He saw the seven commandments that the children of Noah had accepted but not fulfilled. Once he saw they had not fulfilled these he arose and permitted to them [what had once been forbidden].

Then they received a reward [for their disobedience]! Have we found a case of a sinner receiving a reward? Mar b. Ravina said, "This is to say that even though they do [sometimes] fulfill them they receive no reward."[91]

No? But it is taught that R. Meir used to say, "From where [can we show] that even a star-worshiper who is occupied with the Torah is like a High Priest? As the text says [of God's commandments], *which a person can do and live by them.*[92] 'Priests, Levites, and Israelites' is not said but 'a person'; thus you learn that even a star worshiper who is occupied with the Torah is like a High Priest."

Instead [the point must be] to say to you that they receive a reward not as one who is commanded and performs but as one who is not commanded but performs, as R. Hanina said, The one who is commanded and performs is greater than the one who is not commanded and performs.[93]

Instead, the star worshipers say before the Blessed Holy One: "Ruler of the world, Where did Israel, who did accept [the Torah], fulfill it?!"

The Blessed Holy One says to them, "I testify on their behalf that they fulfilled the entire Torah."

They say to him, "Ruler of the world, does a father ever testify on behalf of his son, as it is written, *Israel is my first-born son?*"[94]

The Blessed Holy One says to them, "Heaven and earth will testify for them that they fulfilled the entire Torah."

They say to him, "Ruler of the world, heaven and earth are interested parties, as it is written, *Were it not for my covenant day and night, had I not set the laws of heaven and earth . . .* [95]

> And R. Simeon b. Lakish said, "What is [the meaning of] the scripture, *And it was evening and it was morning the sixth day?*[96] This teaches that the Blessed Holy One entered an agreement with the Creation and said, 'If Israel accepts my Torah all is well, and if not I shall return you to chaos.'" And Hezekiah[97] said, What is [the meaning of] the scripture, *You pronounced judgment from the heavens; the earth heard and grew still?*[98] If it was afraid why did it grow still and if it was still why was it afraid? Rather, at first it was afraid and finally it grew still.[99]

The Blessed Holy One said to them, "People will come from your own number and testify that Israel fulfilled the entire Torah! Let Nimrod come and testify that Abraham did not worship the stars.[100] Let Laban come and testify that Jacob could not be suspected of theft.[101] Let Potiphar's wife come and testify that Joseph could not be suspected of sin.[102] Let Nebuchadnezzar come and testify that Hananiah, Mishael, and Azariah did not bow down to the image.[103] Let Darius come and testify that Daniel never neglected his prayers.[104] Let Bildad the Shuhite and Zophar the Naamatite and Eliphaz the Temanite (and Elihu ben Berachel the Buzite)[105] come and testify that Israel fulfilled the entire Torah, as it is written, *Let them present their witnesses and justify themselves.*[106]

* * *

They said to him, "Ruler of the world, give [the Torah] to us all over again and we shall follow it."[107]

The Blessed Holy One said to them, "World-class idiots! The one who gets busy before the Sabbath can eat over the Sabbath; [as for] the one who did nothing before the Sabbath, how will he eat on the Sabbath?[108] But nevertheless I have an easy commandment called *sukkah*:[109] go and perform it.

> But how can you say that? R. Joshua b. Levi taught the meaning of the verse *Which I command you today*:[110] Do them today, not tomorrow; do them today, but don't expect your reward today.[111]
>
> But the Blessed Holy One doesn't treat his creatures tyranically.[112]
>
> And why does he call it an easy commandment? Because it doesn't cost much money.[113]

At once every person takes [the necessary materials] and builds a *sukkah* on his roof, but the Blessed Holy One has the sun bake them as at midsummer, so every person kicks over the *sukkah* and leaves it, as it is written, *Let us break apart their bonds and cast off their chains.*[114]

> "Bakes them"? But you just said the Blessed Holy One doesn't treat his creatures tyranically!
>
> Sometimes the Jews also experience a long summer that lasts until the festival and they [too] are uncomfortable.
>
> But Rava said someone who is uncomfortable is exempt from [sitting in] a *sukkah*!
>
> Granted they are exempt: do they kick over [the booth]?

At once the Blessed Holy One sits and laughs at [the foolish nations], as it is written, *He that sits in the heavens will laugh.*[115]

> R. Isaac said, "There is no laughter for the Blessed Holy One except on that day."[116]

Readers of this book should take note of two characteristics of rabbinic teaching that appear in the passage just translated, one concerning substance and one concerning style.

Substance: the ancient rabbis did not compose systematic, abstract investigations of important religious questions; instead they addressed those questions through narrative, in this case eschatological fantasy, and through interpretation of scripture. Constructed around a set of comments to a single verse (Isaiah 43:9), and probably designed as a homily for the Festival of Booths, this dramatic presentation of God's final judgment on every nation brings to the fore a set of questions that go to the heart of Israel's covenant:

When will the nations be punished for their mistreatment of the Jews?

Will the nations ever acknowledge that true virtue must be based on the Torah and must be expressed through proper treatment of the Jews?

On the other hand, since the nations never accepted the Torah, is it fair to blame them for not having lived by its rules?

But why did the nations never accept the Torah? Did they never have the chance? (Surely they have the chance now; Jews live everywhere.)

Which would be more satisfying: to see the nations accept the Torah even at this late date (thus confirming Israel's original decision) or to see them punished for having lived without it (and for treating Israel so badly) so long?

And why did the people of Israel accept the Torah? Did they not realize it would bring them inconvenience, persecution, and suffering? Would anyone with a truly free choice in the matter really accept the restrictions of Torah-based living?

And can anyone really live up to its expectations? Once the people of Israel did accept the Torah, did they actually follow it? Can the Jews claim to be more virtuous than anyone else? Did accepting the Torah really make them better than other people, or did accepting the Torah just expose them to God's anger on account of their constant violations of its commands?

These are all questions of fundamental importance in understanding the Jews' claim to a unique bond with the Creator of the world and their boast that the only possible life of virtue and righteousness is a life based on the teachings of Moses. Both of these notions were openly challenged by the growing Christian religion, but the questions were unavoidable in any case. Surely Jews even before Christianity met decent non-Jews in their everyday lives. Surely it was disturbing that not-very-decent non-Jews (that is, the Roman emperors and their armies) controlled the world and could treat the

Jews as they liked. What was all this about, and how would it end? These questions are not all voiced. Some come to open expression ("Ruler of the world, Where did Israel, who did accept [the Torah], fulfill it?!"); others do not. Answers are proposed but then set aside by renewed questioning. These matters, after all, cannot be permanently resolved. In this world humans can never know the whole truth.

Only one thing in this story is certain: in the end, Israel will be vindicated and even God will laugh at the nations' inept attempts to achieve righteousness before it is too late. Of course, this is a rabbi's expression of faith or hope, not an established fact. It provided comfort and encouragement to an audience in need of these, but it proved nothing except on the circular premise that scripture and Jewish tradition are reliable sources of ultimate truth.

Style: rabbinic texts are full of digression and elaboration that brings the main flow to a halt. When the sermon was first delivered, it did not yet contain all the side verses that are now inserted to support ideas that must have seemed obvious to the original hearers: did anyone really need proof that the Roman Empire was important? But rabbis were always looking for scriptural proof-texts to support their ideas, and rabbinic editors sought opportunities to insert such texts into the materials they developed.

On the other hand, editors were never satisfied with the force of such proofs. They interrupted the story to ask how a proof could be reconciled with some other teaching, formulated in some other context, that appeared to say something different. They wondered whether the same proof-text might itself not serve to support some other, not fully compatible idea. In this way, the questions accumulated while the answers were constantly deferred.

It should be noted that in the present instance, style and substance are well suited to one another. The questions raised in this homily do not have definitive answers; they deal with theology and morality, not with law or even with exegesis, and such matters are best treated by acknowledging their ambiguities and finding a way to live with them. This was the great project of the ancient rabbis, and the survival of Judaism is the proof of their success.

Rabbinic Biographies

THE FOLLOWING SKETCHES DO NOT OFFER BIOGRAPHY IN THE usual sense of the term, because they cannot be grounded in careful analysis of available source material. Rabbinic literature cannot easily be used for biography for the same reason that biblical narratives cannot easily be used as sources of history (see Chapter 1). Like biblical narratives, the stories provided in rabbinic literature receive no corroboration from any other body of material. They can be read as distillations of rabbinic memory, that is, as stories about distinguished predecessors that later rabbis preserved and told. But they must be read *as stories*, not archival records of historical incidents. Stories change in the retelling. Stories are preserved because later narrators find them interesting or useful or valuable, but later narrators' interests and values affect the way they are told. Surely there is historical information lurking in these narratives, but that information may less concern the people described in the stories than the later narrators who preserved them, and modern readers will not always be able to trace the path that led from the former to the latter. All this, as noted, can be said about the narratives of scripture as well.

However, with rabbinic narrative a further complication arises as well: very often different rabbinic documents, or even different passages in the same document, contain parallel versions of a single story, versions that may differ in numerous significant details or even in the basic presentation of the episode they appear to describe. When this happens, it is sometimes possible through careful analysis to determine that one version is earlier than the other, but it is rarely possible to assume that the earlier version is necessarily a better witness to a real historical event. The later version may correct previous errors, or both versions may contain imaginative elaborations or insertions that had nothing to do with actual events. Sometimes there is no choice but to recognize that different rabbinic narrators told different versions of their teachers' lives.

For these reasons, the information provided here must be seen as no more than a compilation of ancient rabbis' memories of earlier masters. Among these memories were accurate preservations of actual events, but there is no telling which memories fit that description. Other stories were pure flights of the imagination, just as great heroes in every age have received credit for exploits they never actually performed,[1] and still others were stories that originated in real events but became unrecognizably altered over generations of oral transmission.

The information has been collected here because its historical value lies in its totality rather than in the details. The collection overall reveals that some rabbis were rich and others terribly poor, that some were well connected while others were alienated from the authorities, that some were known as miracle workers while others shunned such powers, and that some were dear friends and others fierce rivals. They all appear to have shared a lifelong commitment to piety and learning, though even this appearance may be the product of later narrators' wish to present these heroes as models of rabbinic dedication. In many cases, no more than a few scraps of information can be provided, but these entries nevertheless create a sense of the diversity to be found among the circles of ancient rabbinic sages.

A note about chronology: Since talmudic narratives almost never refer to events known from other sources, the incidents they describe can almost never be dated, and certain kinds of chronological information (for example, dates of birth and death) can almost never be obtained. It is possible, however, to arrange the talmudic rabbis themselves in rough chronological groupings by generation: who directly encounters whom, who cites whom as an authority from an earlier generation, who names whom as having been his teacher or his student. As a result, the rabbis of the Mishnah and the Talmud are often dated by generation rather than precise years: Yohanan ben Zakkai belonged to the first generation after the Destruction, Abbaye and Rava (see later in this appendix) belonged to the fourth generation of Babylonian Amoraim, and so on. The following entries provide an *approximate* date for each scholar's mature, active years; in most cases, even the length of their lives cannot be known, so it must be understood that a master's career could have extended several decades before or after the indicated time. Dates before 200 are marked BCE or CE; all dates after 200 are CE and are not so marked.

Finally, it should be recalled that the masters listed here represent a very small percentage of all those mentioned in rabbinic literature. They were chosen for the variety of types that they represent and as typical leaders of their respective generations. It should also be remembered that for reasons of style, the stories about these men will be summarized as fact rather than with constant disclaimers like "it is said" or "later narratives report." The actual character of these memories is as described previously.

Before the Destruction of Jerusalem

Simeon b. Shetach (ca. 75 BCE). Brother of Queen Salome Alexandra (see Chapter 5). One of the five "pairs" (*zugot*) of masters said to have led the pre-rabbinic Pharisees before the time of Hillel. In violation of the law, he unconstitutionally executed eighty witches in Ashkelon in a single day "because the hour demanded it" (M. Sanhedrin 6:4, as interpreted in the Jerusalem Talmud).

Hillel (ca. 30 BCE). The earliest great role model of the talmudic sage. Many stories were told in which Hillel displayed the ideal behavior of a rabbinic sage. When he could not afford the entrance fee to the schoolhouse, he listened through a skylight and was buried in an unexpected snowfall (Yoma 38b). When asked to teach the whole Torah while standing on one foot, he calmly responded, "Do not act toward others in a way that would be hateful to you. The rest is commentary: go learn" (Shabbat 31a). Despite his humble origin, he rose to prominence because he could solve a problem concerning the Passover celebration that the greatest authorities of his day could not figure out (Pesachim 66a). The later dynasty of patriarchs traced their ancestry to Hillel.

Shammai (ca. 30 BCE). Contemporary with Hillel; the two formed the last "pair." Shammai and Hillel were associated with two schools

("Houses") that bore their names and flourished during the middle and late first century CE; these two groups differed on a huge number of points of Jewish law, but finally the House of Hillel prevailed when a heavenly voice so ordained (Berachot 51b; Pesachim 114a). In strictly legal contexts, Shammai was respected as an authoritative teacher, but in other sorts of narrative he was sometimes typecast as the inferior alternative to Hillel's admirable behavior. Thus, the individual asking about teaching the whole Torah while standing on one foot went to Shammai before Hillel, but instead of providing an answer, Shammai irritably drove him away.

Gamaliel I (ca. 35 CE). Also known as Gamaliel the Elder. A leader of the Pharisees in Jerusalem before the Destruction. The Mishnah ascribes numerous rulings to him, and he is also mentioned in the New Testament as a leader of the Pharisees (Acts 5:34) and as the former teacher of the Christian Apostle Paul (Acts 22:3; 26:5).

Simeon b. Gamaliel I (ca. 65 CE). Son of the preceding. A younger Pharisaic leader, he is identified by Josephus (*Life* 190–191) as a participant in the council that guided the early stages of the great rebellion against Rome. He is not mentioned in any post-Destruction context, and was probably murdered by the radicals during their violent seizure of power in Jerusalem.

The Dynasty of Patriarchs

Gamaliel II (ca. 90 CE). Son of the preceding; apparently successor to Yohanan b. Zakkai (see later in this appendix) as leader of the rabbinic gathering at Yavneh, perhaps as a result of negotiations with the Roman governor of Syria (see Chapter 8). He exercised his leadership in a high-handed fashion, humiliating learned colleagues and insisting on having his way; he was finally removed from his position of authority, and was restored only after he had apologized to the others and made amends (J. Berakhot 4:1 7cd; B. Berakhot 27b–28a).

Simeon b. Gamaliel II (ca. 150 CE). Son of the preceding; also victim of a failed attempt to remove him from his position of leadership. The rebellion of Bar Kokhba took place during Simeon's early adulthood, and his restoration to authority when peace was restored marks the beginning of the continuous patriarchal dynasty associated with Hillel. It remains uncertain, however, whether the office had much power in those early days.

Judah I "the Patriarch" (ca. 180–200 CE). Son of the preceding, known as "Judah the Prince" and often simply as "Rabbi," as though he were the ultimate exemplar of Torah-based leadership. Famous as compiler of the Mishnah, though his exact role in that accomplishment is uncertain, and also as a personal friend of the emperor. He was exceedingly wealthy and chief Torah authority of his time. It was said of him that from the time of Moses untill that of Judah the Prince, "Torah and greatness had not been in one place" (Gittin 59a; Sanhedrin 36a).

Hillel II (ca. 360 CE). Patriarch, son of Judah III or IV. In a letter of the Emperor Julian (ruled 361–363), the ruler refers to a Jewish patriarch named Hillel as his "brother"; the reference was presumably to this Hillel, though it may have been to some unknown local official. In the Middle Ages, Hillel II was credited with having established the Jewish calendar on a firm mathematical basis, thus eliminating the need for live testimony that the new moon had been sighted, but there is no contemporary reference to such a development (see Chapter 8, "Early Rabbinic *Taqqanot* and *Gezerot*"). The patriarchate remained in this family into the following century, but it was abolished with the death of *Gamaliel VI* in 425.

Other *Tanna'im*[2]

Yohanan b. Zakkai (ca. 75 CE). Founder of the rabbinic gathering at Yavneh after a heroic escape from the besieged Jerusalem (see Chapter 8) and author of several important enactments that began the process of adjusting to loss of the Temple (see Chapter 8, "Early Rabbinic *Taqqanot* and *Gezerot*").

Hanina b. Dosa (60?–80? CE). A famous early wonder-worker. Hanina could pray for the sick and know at once whether they would recover; a snake once bit him, but the snake died. Later rabbinic narrators could not help being impressed by such powers, but continued (as in the case of Eliezer b. Hyrcanus) to honor Torah learning more than the ability to perform such miracles.

Eliezer b. Hyrcanus (ca. 90 CE). One of the leading sages at Yavneh, from a wealthy family, who gave up his patrimony for a life of Torah. Associated with the minority House of Shammai, he often failed to convince his colleagues of his views and eventually died under excommunication on account of his obstinacy over the Oven of Akhnai (Bava Metzia 59b; Sanhedrin 68a). Even when he performed miracles to demonstrate that God favored his rulings, the others responded, "You can't bring proof from a miracle."

Eleazar b. Azariah (ca. 90 CE). When Gamaliel II was temporarily removed from his position of leadership (see earlier), Eleazar b. Azariah was appointed to replace him on account of his wealth and distinguished priestly lineage. He was very young when promoted, but to give him the appearance of venerable age, his hair miraculously turned gray overnight.

Joshua b. Hananiah (ca. 90 CE). The great contemporary and adversary of Eliezer b. Hyrcanus, said to have been very poor. The disputes between Eliezer and Joshua constitute the largest body of rabbinic opinion that survives from the first generation after the Destruction. The arrogance of Gamaliel II (see earlier) was more often aimed at Joshua than at any other individual (see sources cited previously; also see Mishnah Rosh Hashanah 2:8–9; B. Bekhorot 36a).

Elisha b. Abuya (ca. 130 CE). The most famous renegade rabbi of ancient history, he abandoned his Jewish heritage after seeing a child die while obeying his father as the Torah instructs (see Exodus 20:12; and Deuteronomy 22:6–7). He concluded that "there is no justice and no Judge" and adopted a Greek way of life. He is said to have encouraged the Roman persecution of Judaism, though this may be a later rabbinic fantasy about the dangers that face those who become attracted to pagan customs. His most famous student was Meir (see later in this appendix), who remained loyal to his teacher even after Elisha deserted Judaism.

Ishmael (ca. 130 CE). Akiva's major contemporary. The modern writer A. J. Heschel has developed an elaborate analysis of the differences between Ishmael's approach to the Torah and Akiva's; unlike Akiva, Ishmael held that "the Torah speaks in human language" and often discounted textual details in favor of the main point of a passage.

Simeon b. Zoma, Simeon b. Azzai (ca. 130 CE). Both men are usually called only by their fathers' names, and usually without the title "rabbi." Together with Akiva and Elisha b. Abuya (see earlier), these two sages "entered the orchard," that is, they engaged in mystical contemplation of the Divine chariot (see Chapter 10) and the heavenly palaces. Ben Zoma lost his mind as a result of these speculations, and Ben Azzai died. Elisha b. Abuya was notorious for having abandoned Judaism (also as a result of illicit speculations?), and only Akiva "departed whole (lit., in peace)," yet another mark of his greatness. Ben Azzai was also exceptional among the rabbis in that he never married. "What can I do," he said, "my soul desired the Torah [more than a wife]! The world will be sustained by others."[3]

Tarfon (ca. 130 CE). A leading sage of Akiva's generation, from a wealthy family of priestly extraction. His Greek name (properly *Tryphon*) suggests that his family had absorbed a significant measure of Greco-Roman culture. During a famine he married 300 women so that they could share in his priestly entitlements.[4]

Judah b. Ilai (ca. 150 CE). Another student of Akiva; more teachings in the Mishnah are attributed to him than to any other rabbinic sage.

Akiva b. Joseph (died ca. 135 CE). Another great culture hero of the rabbinic tradition. A poor man, he married a wealthy heiress who became famous for her loyalty to him when he went off to study Torah (starting at the age of forty!) for fourteen years. Akiva was famous for his ability to find meaning in every letter and every grammatical peculiarity of the Torah; Moses himself was once allowed to sit in on Akiva's lessons and could not understand him (Menachot 29b). The main teacher of a whole generation, Akiva died a cruel martyr's death during the persecutions that followed Bar Kokhba's uprising.

Meir (ca. 150 CE). One of the leading students of Akiva (see earlier). His wife, *Beruriah*, was famous for her wisdom and learning, but she died of shame after being seduced by one of her husband's students. All anonymous teachings in the Mishnah are held by some authorities to stem from Meir. His father is never identified, which gave rise to a tradition that he was a convert, perhaps even a descendant of the Emperor Nero.

Simeon b. Yohai (ca. 150 CE). Another in the circle of Meir and Judah b. Ilai. Famous for his resentment of the Roman occupation, he spent thirteen years hiding from the authorities in a cave and almost destroyed the world with his angry "evil eye" when he emerged. In the Middle Ages, Simeon was believed to have written the *Book of Splendor* (*Zohar*), the greatest of the kabbalistic texts; his reputed grave in Meron, Israel, remains a goal of pilgrims to this day.

Amora'im[5] of the Land of Israel

Simeon b. Lakish (ca. 280), often called *Resh Lakish*. Contemporary and brother-in-law of Yohanan. A former brigand and gladiator, he turned to a life of Torah-study and became a distinguished teacher, but the two masters had a falling out when Yohanan reminded Simeon of his disreputable background. Simeon died of shame, and Yohanan died of regret (Bava Metzia 84a).

Yohanan (ca. 280). The leading rabbinic sage of his generation. Famous for his handsome appearance, he buried ten of his sons (Berakhot 5b).

Abbahu (ca. 300). Unlike most of his colleagues, Abbahu lived in a large city (Caesarea) and became famous for his ability to engage in argument with polytheists and Christians.

Babylonian *Amora'im*

Rav (ca. 225). Born into one of the first Babylonian families to engage in rabbinic Torah-study, he went to the Land of Israel to learn from Rabbi Judah the Patriarch and then returned home and in *Sura* organized the first Babylonian center of rabbinic teaching. His name was Abba, and he is often called Abba Arika ("long") on account of his height and to distinguish him from others with the same personal name. In preparation for his return to Babylonia he was given reduced rabbinic authority (Sanhedrin 5a), and this was indicated by the abbreviated title *rav* rather than the fuller Palestinian title *rabbi*; since he was the first to bear this title, it was also used as his normal designation, just as Judah the Patriarch came to be called *rabbi* (see above). Sages trained in Babylonia are usually designated *rav*, and differences between their formal authority and that of sages in the Land of Israel remained an issue for quite some time (see Bava Kama 84b).

Samuel (ca. 225). Most important contemporary of Rav; he probably never studied in the Land of Israel but founded an independent rabbinic study-circle in *Nehardea*. The Talmud contains hundreds of disputes between Rav and Samuel over the law or over interpretation of the Mishnah; many of these are possibly literary constructions and not records of actual face-to-face disagreements between the two men. Samuel was famous for his astronomical knowledge: "I know the pathways of heaven as clearly as the pathways of Nehardea" (Berachot 58b). The city of Nehardea was destroyed shortly after Samuel's death, and the center of rabbinic teaching shifted to Pumbeditha (see following entry).

Judah b. Ezekiel (ca. 275). Founder of a new study-circle in *Pumbeditha*. Major leader of the second generation of Babylonian *Amora'im*, along with *Huna* and *Hisda* at Sura. The group at Pumbeditha tended to be less tied to the Mishnah in their legal rulings than those at Sura. The academies of Sura and Pumbeditha remained the most distinguished institutions of rabbinic learning for nearly a thousand years: in the Middle Ages both moved to the new capital city of Baghdad.

Rabbah, Joseph, Abayye (ca. 320–340). Successors to Judah b. Ezekiel at Pumbeditha. Abayye and Rava (see following entry) are the most famous pair of masters in the Babylonian Talmud.

Rava (ca. 340). Head of his own study-circle at *Mahoza*; the center seems not to have outlived its distinguished master. Much of the Talmud is constructed as a series of debates and arguments between Abayye and Rava; see Appendix 1 for an extended example.

Papa (ca. 360). Head of his own short-lived study-circle at *Nersh*. He is said to have had ten sons who were rabbinic masters in their own right.

Dimi (ca. 380). Briefly head of the Pumbeditha academy. Dimi belonged to a group of sages (the "sages who go down") who frequently traveled back and forth between Babylonia and the Land of Israel and served as important conduits of rabbinic teaching from one country to the other.

Ashi (ca. 425). The last of the great Babylonian *Amora'im*. Said to have compiled the first complete Babylonian Talmud, though the text did not achieve its final form for another several generations.

APPENDIX 3

The Sabbath

ONE OF THE MOST IMPORTANT INSTITUTIONS OF JEWISH LIFE throughout the ages, the Sabbath and the seven-day week have appeared in almost every chapter of this book. In order to give a focused picture of one aspect of ancient Judaism in its historical development, this appendix gathers those discussions into a single portrait. Similar portraits could have been offered of other important features of the tradition – the use of scripture, for example, or prayer, or family life and community structure – but this one case will serve as a model for those others as well.

Biblical Evidence

Modern writers have linked the seven-day week to certain features of the ancient Babylonian calendar, but these links are not convincing. At a later time, astrologers developed a seven-day cycle of days corresponding to the seven "planets" (the Moon, Mercury, Venus, Sun, Mars, Jupiter, and Saturn, in that order), and this cycle can still be detected in the names that some modern European languages use for the days of the week. But the Israelite Sabbath cannot be connected to any of those developments, and the Bible simply takes the seven-day cycle for granted.

The Bible does provide two explanations for the seven-day week, but only one can be called historical: that is the connection established in the second Decalogue between the Israelite's *obligation* to allow his servants and animals to rest and the Israelite's own *opportunity* to rest thanks to God's having rescued the nation from bondage in Egypt (Deuteronomy 5:15). If it was a religious duty to let others rest out of gratitude to God, how could the Israelites themselves not rest as well?

The other explanation is not remotely historical: that is the connection between God's having rested after six days' labor in creating the world and the Israelite's obligation to recognize God's creative power by resting every seventh day as well. The idea that God created the world in six days and then "rested"[1] appears not only in the famous beginning chapter of the Bible but also in the first version of the Decalogue (Exodus 20:8) and elsewhere in scripture (Exodus 31:17); of course, it seems more plausible that the story of a six-day creation should have arisen to explain the seven-day week than the reverse, but this must stand for now as conjecture.

The Torah presents the Sabbath as reflecting the nature of the cosmos itself. When the manna fell in the desert, it fell only six days a week, with a double portion every sixth day so that people could eat on the seventh.[2] When the desert sanctuary, itself an image of the universe, was constructed, the instructions to Moses emphasized that no labor was to be performed on the Sabbath.[3] The septimal nature of time was reflected on a larger scale as well: every seventh year the land was to rest fallow, and no agricultural work was to be done.[4] Perhaps on account of its cosmic significance, violation of the Sabbath was deemed a capital crime – literally for individuals and figuratively for the nation. As the people wandered through the desert, a man who violated the Sabbath was brought to Moses and at God's direct instruction was stoned to death,[5] and failure to have allowed the land to rest was one of the causes of the exile.[6] At the same time, the Sabbath became one of the prime symbols of God's covenant with Israel.[7]

There is little indication of the manner in which the Sabbath was observed. The Torah repeatedly stresses the need to avoid labor on that day, but in general does not state which acts constitute forbidden work.[8] The list of annual holidays in Leviticus 23 begins with a reminder to observe the weekly Sabbath, but again without any instructions as to how this was to be done. A special public sacrifice every Sabbath is prescribed in Numbers 28:9–10, but the Torah gives no hint at all of the Sabbath's role in the lives of private individuals.

The later books of scripture hardly change this picture. Isaiah 66:23 indicates that Sabbaths and new moons were a time for appearing before God in worship, and 2 Kings 4:23 suggests that those same days were occasions for visiting holy "men of God," that is, prophets. Isaiah 56:4–6 names Sabbath observance as a sure way to strengthen individuals' covenantal bond with God.

On the other hand, the prophetic books are also full of anger at the people for trying to ignore the Sabbath rest or find a way to reduce its inconvenience. Jeremiah 17:21–27 pleads with the people to stop carrying burdens on the Sabbath day. Amos 8:5 berates the people's impatience for the Sabbath to end so that they can resume their dishonest trade practices. Ezekiel 20 describes the Sabbath as a sign of God's wish to sanctify Israel but then denounces the people for their repeated disdain for this gift. Nehemiah in his memoirs reports that he placed troops at the gates of Jerusalem to prevent merchants from bringing their wares into the city on the Sabbath, and then had to chase them away to prevent them from camping outside the city gates before the Sabbath was over.[9]

Later (Pre-Rabbinic) Evidence

As the Maccabees' rebellion against Antiochus IV gathered steam, the king's forces quickly realized that pious Jews would not lift arms on the Sabbath, even in self-defense. It was Mattathias, father of Judah the Maccabee and the elderly leader of the uprising, who declared that even the most pious Jews had to be willing to defend themselves on the holy day, or their piety would itself become their death sentence.[10] This attitude later became normative in rabbinic law, but it is hard to know whether it was resisted in the Maccabees' own time. Josephus reports that a Babylonian Jew named Asineus chose to defend himself on the Sabbath rather than let his enemies capture him too easily, but he reports this decision as Asineus's own choice, as though no previous Jews had ever reached the same conclusion.[11] The Qumran *pesher* to Habakkuk reports that the Wicked Priest attacked the desert community while they were celebrating the Day of Atonement, but that is also a fast day when people are weak, so the priest may not have worried that his enemies would try to defend themselves.

Greek writers of the time repeatedly claim that Jewish Sabbath observance made it easy for foreign armies to conquer Jerusalem and offer specific historical examples of such conquests.[12] In general, Jewish inactivity on the Sabbath captured the attention of Greek and Roman authors. Some Greeks admired this feature as a sign of the Jews' philosophical bent,[13] but most writers, including almost all Romans, condemned the Jews' laziness, as they saw it, and found confirmation of their general view of Judaism as barbaric and unenlightened.[14]

These same writers make frequent reference, often hostile, to particular Jewish Sabbath customs. The philosopher Seneca mocked Jewish Sabbath lamps: the soot was annoying, and surely God didn't need the light (*Epistle* 95). The poet Persius refers to the Jewish use of wine on the Sabbath (*Satire* 5.183), and Plutarch apparently thought that Jews routinely got drunk on that day (*Convivial Questions* 4.6.2). On the other hand, some writers speak of the Sabbath as a fast: the Emperor Augustus himself, in complaining that he was too busy to stop for meals, once compared himself in his hunger to a Jew observing the Sabbath.[15] It is hard to know what to make of this. Was it simply an error, a piece of misinformation that non-Jews routinely passed on? Was it drawn from the observation that Jews, or at least many Jews, did no cooking on the Sabbath (see later in this appendix), or an overgeneralization from the Day of Atonement, when Jews really did fast, and which the Torah itself calls a "Sabbath of Sabbaths"?[16] Is it even possible that many Jews in Rome did fast on the Sabbath, a practice that died out as rabbinic teachings opposing the custom continued to spread? Various recent scholars have preferred one or another of these explanations, but in this matter (as in so many others) certainty is impossible.

Returning to the Jewish sources, Philo and Josephus treat the Sabbath from their respective customary viewpoints. Philo says little about the specific activities prohibited on the Sabbath[17] but goes on at length about the mystical properties of the number seven;[18] he also stresses that the Sabbath affords an opportunity even for ordinary people to engage in relaxed philosophical contemplation, an opportunity (he implies) that no other religious-cultural system can match.[19] In the Decalogue and elsewhere,[20] he writes, the Torah says that the Sabbath belongs to God because Sabbath bliss is the closest approach to God's own experience that is available in this world.[21]

Josephus, for his part, mentions that Jews keep the Sabbath in recognition of God's having created the world in six days,[22] and includes at several points the information that Jerusalem was captured because its inhabitants would not fight on the Sabbath.[23] He is inconsistent on the question of defensive warfare on the Sabbath, sometimes implying that it is allowed, elsewhere that it is wrong.[24] In *Against Apion* Josephus defends Sabbath observance against its critics and refutes hostile Greek accounts of the practice;[25] he also provides a long list of Roman enactments and interventions that recognized the Jews' right to keep the Sabbath and protected them from interference by others (mostly Greeks).[26]

In the Dead Sea Scrolls an entire section of the *Damascus Covenant* contains rules of Sabbath observance,[27] and a separate collection of mystical hymns assigns each poem to one of the Sabbaths of the year.[28]

The Rabbinic Evidence

In keeping with their general approach to Jewish religious life, the early rabbis set out to bring uniformity to Jewish Sabbath observance in two important respects. They developed a standard set of ceremonies to mark off the holy day, and they sought to bring some coherence to the basic concept of forbidden Sabbath labor.

Despite the absence of scriptural information concerning the prohibition of labor on the Sabbath, the Mishnah provides a succinct list of such activities:

> The main categories of labor are forty less one: sowing, ploughing, reaping, binding sheaves, threshing, winnowing, cleansing crops, grinding, sifting, kneading, baking; shearing wool, washing or beating or dyeing it, spinning, weaving, making two loops, weaving two threads, separating two threads, tying, loosening, sewing two stitches, tearing in order to sew two stitches; hunting a deer, slaughtering or skinning or salting it or curing its hide, scraping it or cutting it up, writing two letters, erasing in order to write two letters; building, pulling down, putting out a fire, lighting a fire, striking with a hammer; or taking anything from one domain into another.[29]

Examination of this list reveals that the listed activities are not a random set, but provide a detailed breakdown of the basic activities of civilized life: preparing bread and clothing, writing (!), and building shelter. The last item suggests that dividing space into multiple private "domains," that is, the idea of personal property, is similarly a fundamental element in civilized life. Every American child learns in grade school that "food, clothing, and shelter" are the basic human needs; it is striking that the rabbinic list adds writing, in other words the Torah, to this set.

The list also carries out a detailed analysis of the nature of human action, taking broad goals ("food") and breaking them down into the irreducible steps they entail. This collection of details thus amounts to a systematic inquiry into the nature of significant action; it also implies an abstract definition of forbidden labor: an action is forbidden if its performance produces a concrete, meaningful outcome. The rabbinic discussions of this matter go on for over 100 pages.

As for ceremony, the rabbis ordained that every Sabbath must begin and end with a set of blessings[30] recited over a cup of wine, preferably in connection with a meal. The initial set is called *Qiddush* or "sanctification"; declaring the holiness of the Sabbath day, this blessing connects the Sabbath with both the creation of the world and the departure from Egypt, thus affirming both of the biblical justifications for this ancient practice. The final set, called *Havdala* or "separation," combines wine with fragrant spices and a burning flame and affirms God as having established the basic distinctions that give shape to the world: holy/profane, light/darkness, Israel/the nations, Sabbath/workweek. The use of wine in these rituals is noteworthy because it has no biblical roots at all: the Torah ordains that every sacrifice be accompanied by a libation of wine onto the altar, and it knows that Nazirites might abstain from wine in their quest for holiness,[31] but it never suggests that people should regularly consume wine in connection with a religious observance. Yet, many important Jewish ceremonies in addition to those just mentioned[32] came to be marked by the ceremonial blessing of a cup of wine. This custom is presumably pre-rabbinic in origin, but its earliest development can no longer be traced.

The rabbis also laid great stress on the Sabbath as a day of joy and spiritual nourishment. They ordained that Sabbath meals should be larger and more elaborate than ordinary weekday food. They developed a standard liturgy for synagogue worship, based on the ordinary weekday services but more elaborate. They regularized the public reading from the Torah, in Babylonia completing the entire Pentateuch every year.[33] In a bold pronouncement they said that proper observance of the Sabbath gives one a foretaste of the joys of the world to come.[34]

About 100 years ago, the famous Zionist writer Ahad Ha-am (Asher Ginzberg, 1856–1927) wrote that the Sabbath has preserved the Jews more than the Jews have observed the Sabbath.

Glossary

Note: Certain biblical personalities are included in this glossary along with historical figures from the Second Temple period, but no rabbis. Short biographies of selected ancient rabbis can be found in Appendix 2. The numbers following many headings indicate the chapters in which significant discussion of particular items or persons can be found; the entries *A1* and *A3* designate Appendix 1 and Appendix 3.

Aaron (1, 3). Brother of **Moses**, spokesman for his brother before Pharaoh and the people (Exodus 4:15–16), and first high priest (Exodus 28). Since the Jewish priesthood was hereditary, every later *kohen* **(priest)** was deemed to be Aaron's descendant. In the **Torah**, Aaron's character is ambiguous: he builds the Golden Calf (Exodus 32), he slanders Moses (Numbers 12), and he somehow violates God's trust and is barred from the Holy Land (Numbers 20). Nevertheless, rabbinic tradition remembered him as distinguished for his love of peace (M. Avot 1:12).

Abraham (1). Father of the Jewish nation. Settled in Canaan at God's direct behest, he received a promise that his descendants would inherit the land (Genesis 12). He inaugurated the practice of circumcision, performing the act on himself when he was ninety-nine years old (Genesis 17:24). God's choice of Abraham for this vital historical role is never clearly explained.

Alexandria (6, 7). Founded by Alexander the Great (331 BCE), the royal capital of Egypt under the **Ptolemies**, and the largest city and cultural capital of the Hellenistic world. **Septuagint** translation of the **Torah** prepared ca. 250 BCE. Remained an important center after the Roman conquest (31 BCE), home to the largest Jewish community of the **Diaspora**. **Philo** claims (*Flaccus* 43) that there were 1 million Jews in Egypt, but he can be suspected of exaggerating; Josephus writes that 50,000 Jews in Alexandria were slaughtered when the great rebellion broke out in Judaea (66 CE). The entire community was destroyed during the Diaspora rebellion of 115–117 CE.

allegory (6). Any text that seems to be talking about one thing but really means something else. According to **Philo**, the entire **Torah** – its stories and its laws – must be read as an allegory. The real lessons of the Torah have to do with the nature of religious experience and the contemplative path to knowledge of God. The characters in biblical narrative, as well as the details of Jewish ritual law, are coded embodiments of deeper truths.

Antiochus III (4). **Seleucid** monarch (223–187 BCE); conquered Judaea from Ptolemy V in 198. Josephus (*Antiquities* 12.138–146) records documents in which the conqueror promised to leave the Jews unhindered in their observance of ancestral law.

Antiochus IV (4). *Seleucid* monarch (175–163 BCE), younger son of **Antiochus III**. During his reign, violence broke out in Judaea among rival contenders for the high priesthood and over the issue of **Hellenism**. Trying to restore order, the king attempted to suppress traditional Jewish customs. The struggle against this attempt brought the **Maccabees** to power.

Apocrypha (4). Grk., "items hidden away." The Greek-speaking Jews of **Alexandria** included a greater number of books in their collection of holy scriptures than the Hebrew-speaking Jews of the Land of Israel, and the Christian Church adopted this larger collection as the Old Testament. By the time of the Protestant Reformation, Jews had abandoned the use of religious texts in Greek, and the reformers thought it wrong for the Church to revere books that the Jews themselves had set aside; about a dozen books (see Chapter 4, "The Apocrypha") were accordingly removed ("hidden away") from the official scriptures of the Protestant churches. However, they were not simply discarded: in view of their long history, they were preserved in a separate collection of books deemed inferior to canonical scripture but worthy of study nonetheless.

Assyria (1). Leading power in the Near East during the late eighth century BCE, centered in northern Mesopotamia (modern Iraq). In 722 an Assyrian army under Shalmaneser V conquered the northern Kingdom of Israel and carried its inhabitants (the so-called ten lost tribes) into exile (2 Kings 17). In 701 a similar attempt under *Sennacherib* to capture Jerusalem and the Kingdom of Judah failed (2 Kings 19:35).

Babylon (1, 9, 10). Ancient city in central Mesopotamia, capital of a powerful empire that captured Jerusalem under Nebuchadnezzar II (586 BCE) and put an end to the Kingdom of Judah (see **Assyria**). Judaeans exiled to Babylon formed the core of a community that flourished for centuries and much later (from the third century CE) became the first major center of rabbinic teaching in the **Diaspora**. The main body of the Babylonian **Talmud** was compiled in the fifth century CE, though revisions continued into the sixth.

Babylonian Exile (1, 2, 3). Destruction of the First **Temple** and eviction of the nation from its land caused a religious crisis: how could the God of the **covenant** have allowed his chosen people and his own holy sanctuary to be destroyed in such a manner? Was **YHWH**'s promise not to be trusted? Many surely despaired and abandoned the covenant, but overall the exiled community preserved its identity and survived to return home. For those people the exile confirmed the Deuteronomic idea that national suffering is punishment for disloyalty to God; those in **Babylon** who did not abandon the God of Israel became more fiercely loyal than ever. (Among those who remained in Judah, matters were different: see Chapter 3.)

Baraita (A1). Aram., "outside." An item of rabbinic teaching similar to the teachings in the **Mishnah** but not found in that collection.

blessing (8). Heb., *berakha*. The characteristic unit of rabbinic prayer, containing an initial fixed formula ("Blessed are you, Lord, our God, king of the world") and a conclusion that reflects the occasion for reciting it. This can be the performance of a **mitzva**, or recitation of a liturgical text, or experience of bodily pleasure through taste or sight or smell.

canon (1, 4). The official list of books deemed holy scripture; actually, the concept is Christian. Over the first centuries of its existence, leaders of the Church worked out an authoritative list of such writings. Judaism never had an equivalent, though a consensus slowly grew, not firm until the third century CE, as to which books "defile the hands" (that is, are holy; see M. Yadaim 3:4–5).

covenant (1, 2, 3, 4). A contract or a pact: the fundamental concept of biblical religious thought. The god **YHWH** repeatedly enters into covenants with important biblical heroes, those with Noah, **Abraham**, and **Moses** being of greatest consequence. As with any contract each side undertook commitments to the other, but these were not always clear, and the human participants often failed to satisfy their obligations. Were God's promises conditional? Could the people lose their land? Did the covenant with YHWH forbid the worship of other deities in any form whatever? The **prophets'** uncompromising answers to these questions were a minority view in their own time, but ultimately they became the core concepts of Judaism.

Cyrus (3). King of **Persia**; conquered **Babylon** (539 BCE). The Hebrew Bible ends with his proclamation that the exiled people of Judah could return home and rebuild their Temple (2 Chronicles 36:23); he was therefore acclaimed in prophetic circles as **YHWH**'s own **Messiah**, that is, anointed one (Isaiah 45:1).

David (1). First really successful king of Israel (mid-tenth century BCE), founder of a dynasty that reigned until the **Babylonian Exile**. In scripture a heroic figure – successful conqueror and great poet – though also a person of sometimes ignoble deeds. Received God's promise that his family would reign forever (2 Samuel 7:16); therefore, when the kingdom was overthrown, the Jews developed a permanent expectation that it would be restored. This expectation eventually took the form of waiting for the **Messiah**.

Day of Atonement (Yom Kippur) (1). Holiest day of the Jewish calendar; marked (at least in later times) by a twenty-five-hour abstention from food, drink, and other physical comforts. The day began (Leviticus 16) as an annual cleansing of the public Sanctuary from any accidental defilement that might have occurred, but over time it became a day of personal repentance and renewal (Leviticus 23:26–32).

Decalogue (Ten Commandments) (1, A3). A list of ten religious rules that appears twice in the **Torah** (Exodus 20:2–17; Deuteronomy 5:6–21) and pur- ports to give the actual words spoken by the voice of God at Mount **Sinai**. In later times, this list was often taken to provide the basic foundation of true religion, and has remained of central importance to this day in some varieties of Judaism and Christianity. The actual division of the text into ten "commandments" varies in Jewish, Catholic, and Protestant versions. The Torah refers to this list as "the ten words" ("decalogue": Deuteronomy 4:13; 10:4), never "the ten commandments."

Diaspora (3, 6, 10). Grk., "dispersion, scattering." The word refers to the scat- tered Jewish communities outside the **Eretz Yisra'el** that spread and devel- oped, especially under the Roman Empire. The Diaspora began with the **Babylonian Exile**, and by the start of the Common Era a majority of the world's Jews lived outside their ancient national homeland.

Egypt (1, 3, 6). According to scripture, the Israelites emerged into history as former slaves escaping from Egyptian bondage. In Deuteronomy 28:68, returning to Egypt is the ultimate punishment that could be inflicted on a sinful nation. Nevertheless, in later times the Jews flourished in Egypt: an early military colony at Elephantine lasted for generations, and in **Hellenistic** and early Roman times the Jewish community in **Alexandria** was the largest in the world. After the war of 115–117 this community virtually disappeared.

Elijah (2). An early **prophet** and miracle worker, fierce opponent of wor- shiping gods other than **YHWH**. He organized a contest (1 Kings 18) between himself and the priests of Baal in which YHWH's miraculous intervention led to the (temporary) eradication of Baal worship. At the end of his life (2 Kings 2) Elijah was carried bodily into Heaven on a fiery chariot, and is expected to return at the end of time to announce the **Messiah**'s arrival. His chief disciple was *Elisha*. Neither left any writings; both were remembered for their strong personalities and their many wondrous acts.

Eretz Yisra'el Heb., "Land of Israel." The standard name in rabbinic literature for the Jews' native homeland, divided into three districts: Judaea, Galilee, and Transjordan. In rabbinic law, certain provisions of the **Torah**, chiefly having to do with the Sabbatical year (Leviticus 25), tithes, and other priestly entitlements, apply only in *Eretz Yisra'el*. The precise boundaries of the Land of Israel vary from one text to another; in seeking to determine these, the **rabbis** seem to have relied on biblical evidence and on the actual distribution of Jewish populations in their own time.

eschatology. From the Greek word for "last": the word designates any conception of "last things," or how the world will end. Judaic eschatology revolves around a number of powerful images: coming of the **Messiah**, rebuilding of the **Temple**, ingathering of the **exile,** resurrection of the dead and the last judgment. However, these images were never woven into a single, authoritative scenario describing the expected unfolding of actual events. See Appendix 1 for a sample eschatological narrative.

exile (2). Initially the **Babylonian Exile**, but eventually a more general attempt to give religious meaning to the fact that the bulk of the Jewish people no longer lived in their ancestral homeland. Modern writers often prefer to allude to this fact with the more neutral term **Diaspora**.

Exodus (1). Grk., "departure." Word used to describe the Israelites' escape from Egyptian bondage. In Jewish memory the Exodus became the prototype of the redeeming power of God.

Ezekiel (1). Major **prophet** of the **Babylonian Exile**. Of priestly descent, he seems to have been taken to **Babylon** in the earlier exile of 597 BCE. The early chapters of his book contain a detailed (though vague) description of the chariot (Heb., *merkava*) in which God rides to visit the Earth; this vision heavily influenced Jewish mystics of the early centuries CE. The last section of the Book of Ezekiel contains a detailed though utopian description of the future restored Jewish commonwealth.

Ezra (3). Priest and scribe in the Persian Empire. Brought a copy of the Book of the Teaching (**Torah**) of Moses from **Babylon** to the restored community in **Jerusalem**; presided over the early attempts to establish that book as the lawbook of *Yehud*.

Hanukkah (4). Heb., for "dedication." The name of an annual eight-day celebration of the **Maccabees'** restoration of traditional rites at the **Temple** in **Jerusalem**.

Hasmonaeans (4). The family of the **Maccabees**, high priests (154–35 BCE) and kings (ca. 104–63 BCE) of Judaea.

Hellenism (4). The Greek way of living. Under **Seleucid** rule in Judaea, a dispute broke out among groups of Jews over the question of whether the people would be wise to adopt Greek ways in place of the traditional customs ascribed to **Moses**. For a while Hellenistic reforms were imposed on the people by force, but the **Maccabees** successfully led a rebellion against this program and established a traditionalist regime under their own leadership. Nevertheless, Judaism continued to be affected by the Greco-Roman environment in which it existed; large sections of the **Diaspora** carried out their Jewish lives in Greek.

Isaac (1). Son of **Abraham**, father of **Jacob**, the second of Israel's three patriarchs. Most famously connected with the *'Akeda* (binding), the test of his father's willingness to sacrifice Isaac at God's command. When Isaac was old and blind, his younger son Jacob obtained by trickery the blessing that his older twin Esau had expected for himself.

Isaiah (1). The earliest of the major Israelite prophets, ca. 700 BCE. Modern scholars see the Book of Isaiah as a composite: the first thirty-nine chapters are generally the work of the historical **prophet**, but the remainder seem to have been produced generations later, by one or more prophets at the time of the **Babylonian Exile**.

Jacob (1). Third of *Israel*'s patriarchs, also called Israel. Father of twelve sons, after whom the twelve tribes of historical Israel were named.

Jeremiah (1, 2). **Prophet** during the last years of the Kingdom of Judah, carried to **Egypt** against his will after the fall of Jerusalem. His teachings and literary style are very similar to those of the Book of Deuteronomy: national disaster is a punishment from God because the nation has abandoned the covenant and worshiped false gods.

Jerusalem (1, 3, 4, 5, 7, 10). Capital of Israel and Judah from the time of King **David**. Site of the **Temple**. Destroyed by invading armies in 586 BCE (**Babylon**) and 70 CE (**Rome**).

Joseph (1). Son of **Jacob**. Unwisely favored by their father, he earned his brothers' hatred, so they faked his death; sold to **Egypt** as a slave but favored by God in all things, he rose to great power and became an effective ruler of the land. Later, during a terrible famine, he was reconciled with his brothers and arranged for the family to come to Egypt, where there was food. This is how the ancestors of Israel came to be living in the country where they were enslaved.

Joshua (1). Disciple and successor of **Moses**. The Book of Joshua describes Israel's conquest of the Promised Land, though archeological discoveries have cast doubt on its historical value.

Josiah (2, 3). King of Judah (died 609 BCE). During his reign, a previously unknown book of the teachings of **Moses** was found in the **Temple**. In conformity with that book, Josiah closed all shrines of **YHWH** except for the central Temple in **Jerusalem**.

Julius Caesar (5, 7, 10). Ruler of the Roman Empire (died 44 BCE). Favorable to the Jews, probably because they had supported his drive for power. Confirmed the Jews' right to live according to their own traditions; provided exemptions from the demands of Roman law when those demands conflicted with Jewish tradition. Since Caesar's great-nephew became the first Roman emperor (Augustus), these became the established policies of the empire.

kavvana (9). Heb., "intention." The **Mishnah** repeatedly demands that religious actions be performed with intention, that is, with conscious awareness; it is not entirely clear whether the reference is to awareness of religious obligation or awareness of what one is doing. The concept is variously applied to ceremonial acts (e.g., blowing the ram's horn on the New Year or eating unleavened bread on **Passover**) and to more inward activities such as reciting *Sh'ma*. The Babylonian **Talmud** characteristically minimizes this requirement, interpreting intention in the narrowest possible way; for example, one must not mistake the sound of the ram's horn for a donkey's bray.

kohen (priest) (1, 3, 4, 7). The ancient Jewish priesthood was drawn from a hereditary branch of the tribe of Levi, tracing its line back to **Aaron**, the brother of **Moses**. Only priests could offer sacrifices in the **Temple**. As long as the Second Temple stood, the high priest was effectively the head of the Jewish polity in the Land of Israel, and the leading priestly families constituted the aristocracy of Judaea. The crisis under **Antiochus IV** began when the king broke with precedent and dismissed a living high priest. Under the later **Hasmonaeans**, the high priests from that family were also kings of Judaea. Once the Romans took power in Judaea the high priesthood became a political office, to be filled at the discretion of the sovereign. When the Temple was destroyed the priesthood lost its political power almost at once, but the emerging rabbinic leadership left certain priestly entitlements in place.

Levite (1, 3, 5). At an unknown but early time, the tribe of Levi withdrew from the ordinary structure of Israelite society and took on the special role of ritual assistants at the sacred center. In late Second **Temple** times, which are better documented, the Levites served as musicians (instrumental and vocal) to accompany the rites and also as Temple gatekeepers and night watchmen. According to tradition, the priests were a family from this tribe; under the

Hasmonaeans, tithes that were the Levites' entitlement (Numbers 18:21) were diverted to the priests alone (M. Ma'aser Sheni 5:15).

Maccabees (4). When rebellion against **Antiochus IV** broke out in 168 BCE, the leader, Judah, was known by the nickname Maccabee (1 Maccabees 2:4); modern explanations of this epithet are varied and uncertain. By extension, ancient and modern writers have applied the term collectively to Judah and his four brothers or even to the **Hasmonaean** dynasty that was descended from Simon, the last brother to survive. Of the four so-called Books of the Maccabees, two are normally included in the **Apocrypha** and two in the larger collection of ancient Jewish **pseudepigrapha**.

Merkava (10). Heb., "chariot." In the years following the Roman destruction of **Jerusalem** (and perhaps earlier), a mystical movement flourished in Judaea that sprang from the **prophet Ezekiel**'s vision (Ezekiel 1–3, 10) of the chariot of God. Through ecstatic meditation, practitioners would ride this chariot through the heavenly palaces (*hekhalot*) and gain access to heavenly secrets. Certain early leading masters (e.g., Yohanan b. Zakkai, Akiva b. Joseph; see Appendix 2) were associated with this movement. It seems to have reached its peak by the fourth century CE, though certain modern writers prefer a later date.

Messiah (5, 10). Heb., "anointed one." In scripture the word can be applied to anyone chosen by God for a sacred role – priests (Leviticus 4:3), kings (1 Samuel 10:1, 16:13; 1 Kings 19:15–16; 2 Kings 9:3), and **prophets** (1 Kings 19:16) – and reflects the practice of designating such people by ceremonially pouring oil on their heads. Later the word came to be applied to the "anointed king" of the House of **David** whom God would send as redeemer at the end of days to gather in the exiles, rebuild the **Temple**, and restore Jewish nationhood. Christian messianism, which lost interest in Jewish national restoration, developed the concept in different directions, emphasizing the forgiveness of sins and entry into eternal life.

midrash (9). Heb., lit. "inquiry." The characteristic style of rabbinic Bible interpretation, aimed at uncovering new layers of meaning through either the combination of seemingly unrelated texts or the painstaking examination of minute textual details. By extension, *midrash* can also mean the result of such interpretation, therefore (in its most common modern usage) nonbiblical narratives or legends. But *midrash* can equally be applied to the clarification of law or of any obscure passage in scripture. A list of major ancient collections of *midrash* can be found in Chapter 9.

Mishnah (9). A compilation of rabbinic teachings, mostly legal, dating from around 200 CE, edited under the supervision of R. Judah the Patriarch (Nasi). The oldest surviving rabbinic book, though fragments of older materials may survive in other places. The Mishnah takes the form of a law code, but it contains numerous unresolved disagreements and nonlegal passages: it was probably designed as a training curriculum for rabbinic disciples rather than as an actual guide to Jewish law. Consists of six Orders subdivided into a total of sixty-three **tractates**, each loosely organized around a specific topic, usually of Jewish law. A list of these topics can be found in Chapter 9.

Mitzvah (sing.), *mitzvot* (plur.). Heb., "commandment(s)." The technical term in rabbinic language for ceremonial or ethical actions required by the **Torah**. A widespread overall description of the rabbis' conception of a pious life was "study of Torah and fulfillment of its *mitzvot*."

Moses (1, 3, 9). The founder of the Jewish religion and agent (through the power of God) of Israel's liberation from Egyptian bondage. After leaving **Egypt**, he twice spent forty days in private communion with God on Mount **Sinai** and brought down the "teaching" (**Torah**) that would form the eternal basis of Jewish life. All subsequent forms of Judaism claimed to be in keeping with the teachings of Moses; even the rabbis' Oral Torah was traced back to him. The official written version of the teaching of Moses was found in the book that **Ezra** brought back from **Babylon**.

Nehemiah (3). Governor of *Yehud* under the **Persian** Empire (ca. 444 BCE). Supported **Ezra** in the effort to establish the **Torah** as law of the land. A forceful, combative individual; his memoirs form the background of the book in scripture that bears his name.

Passover (1). Probably the oldest Israelite/Jewish festival, combining elements of a celebration of spring with historical commemoration of the **Exodus** from **Egypt**. The festival was marked by the ritual consumption of a roasted lamb and abstention for a week from all leavened foods. After the **Temple** was destroyed the lamb sacrifice became impossible, but the Passover feast (Seder) remained an important annual observance.

Pentateuch (1, 3). Grk., "five books." The Written **Torah**, the five books of Moses.

Persia (3). For two centuries the dominant power in the ancient Near East; ruled the Land of Israel from 539 to 333 BCE. The **Torah** officially became the law of the law of *Yehud* by decree of the Persian King Artaxerxes. The Persian Empire was finally conquered (333–331 BCE) by Alexander the Great, and the **Hellenistic** era began. The Land of Israel was again briefly conquered by Persians in the seventh century CE; see Chapter 10.

Pharisees (5). Members of a religious movement in late Second Temple times; famous as teachers on account of their knowledge of tradition and characterized by careful attention to **purity**. Had a wide following but enjoyed significant political authority only during the reign of Queen Salome Alexandra (76–69 BCE). Early **rabbis** saw themselves as successors to the Pharisees; early Christians saw the Pharisees as their chief rivals, so they are depicted with great hostility in the New Testament Gospels.

Philo (6). Jewish philosopher and community leader in **Alexandria** (early first century CE). Led a delegation to the Emperor Nero (40? CE). Most famous for his **allegorical** interpretation of the **Torah**, in which every story and every law carries an important encoded lesson concerning religious experience, the good life, or the nature of God. Forgotten by the Jews, he was honored by the Christian Church as a forerunner of Christianity.

piyyut (10). Poetry, often elaborate and full of artifice, that is designed for use in synagogue services.

Pompey (5). Roman general who put an end to the **Seleucid** Empire and brought Judaea under the rule of **Rome** (63 BCE). His great rival was **Julius Caesar**, and the Jews supported Caesar out of hatred for Pompey; Caesar responded with a set of enactments favorable to the Jews.

prophets (1, 2, 3). Intermediary messengers between Israel and **YHWH**. There were different viewpoints among the ancient prophets, but their most characteristic affirmations were that God would not tolerate either social injustice or the worship of other deities: each of these was a violation of the **covenant** that would bring terrible consequences. Before the **Babylonian Exile** most people resisted the prophets' message, but in the end this message became the foundation of postbiblical Judaism. Most of the Jewish Bible consists of the prophets' orations or writings or stories about incidents in their lives.

pseudepigrapha (4) Gk., "falsely attributed writings." In late antiquity, many writings circulated under the names of biblical heroes that had not in fact been written by those personalities; the oldest surviving such text is the Book of Daniel. Some of these were ascribed to known biblical writers, others to people (going back as far as Adam and Eve!) who had not actually written any extant materials. Probably this practice arose out of authors' wish to gain a readier audience for their message. None of these books (except for the Bible itself) was preserved by Jews; they exist today in copies prepared in many languages and preserved through the Middle Ages in Christian monasteries.

Ptolemies (4). A royal dynasty descended from Ptolemy Lagos, a general of Alexander the Great, whom he appointed governor of **Egypt**. After Alexander suddenly died young, Ptolemy declared himself king of Egypt, and his descendants ruled that country for 300 years, with their capital at **Alexandria**, until the Roman Octavian defeated Cleopatra VII and took the country for himself. Under the Ptolemies a flourishing Jewish community developed in Alexandria and elsewhere, though its relations with the dominant Greeks were sometimes tense. The **Septuagint** translation of the **Torah** was prepared in Alexandria around 250 BCE.

purity (5). The **Torah**, especially in Leviticus, contains numerous detailed rules for the preservation of purity (Heb., *tohorah*) and the avoidance of defilement (Heb. *tum'ah*). Defilement was normally the result of contact with dead bodies or certain bodily (mostly sexual) fluids, and by extension through an unidentified skin condition usually translated as "leprosy." Childbirth also left the mother temporarily unclean, though it is important to emphasize that "unclean" never meant "dirty." The main practical consequence of defilement was that unclean persons were barred from the **Temple** and from any contact with sacred objects or sacred foods, but the **Pharisees** were known for their commitment to maintain purity even in everyday life.

rabbi (8, 9, 10). "Master." Title of the sages, member of a religious movement that strove to achieve leadership of the Jewish community in *Eretz Yisra'el* and Babylonia in the generations following the destruction of *Jerusalem*. Their claim to authority was based on their mastery of *Torah*, and their restoration of Judaism after the Temple was lost survived into modern times. The **Mishnah**, the **Talmuds**, and various books of *midrash* provide compilations of rabbinic teaching and stories about ancient rabbinic masters. See also **Torah**.

Rome (5, 6, 7). City in Italy that achieved domination of the Mediterranean world over the last centuries BCE. Rome conquered Judaea in 63 BCE and **Egypt** with its large Jewish population in 31 BCE. A Roman army destroyed the **Jerusalem Temple** in 70 CE. Of the great centers of Jewish population, only Babylonia remained outside Roman control. In the Land of Israel, the **rabbis** achieved positions of leadership by reaching an accommodation with Rome. When the family of the Emperor Constantine adopted Christianity, the entire empire began a process of Christianization that eventually left only the Jews outside the new religious consensus.

Rosh ha-Shanah. The New Year's celebration; also the name of a tractate in the **Mishnah**.

Sabbath (1, 6, 8, A3). The Jewish day of rest, occurring once every seven days. This observance affirmed God's creation of the world (Genesis 1–2), as well as the covenant with **Moses** as reflected in the **Decalogue** (Exodus 20:8), even the **Exodus** from **Egypt** (Deuteronomy 5:15). In Greco-Roman times, Sabbath observance was one of the most widely noted features of Jewish life: Jews disappeared from the marketplace and gathered in their synagogues and homes to perform mysterious but fascinating rituals. From the time of **Julius Caesar** on, Roman administrative practice acknowledged the Jews' right to observe the Sabbath without disturbance. The early **rabbis** worked to standardize both the rules for avoiding labor on the Sabbath and the ceremonies that marked the day's holiness.

Seleucids (4). A royal dynasty descended from Seleucus, another general of Alexander the Great, whom he appointed governor of **Babylon**. Over the decades following Alexander's death, Seleucus built a large kingdom extending from Mesopotamia into Asia Minor. The Seleucid **Antiochus III** conquered Judaea from the **Ptolemies** in 198 BCE, and his son **Antiochus IV** lost the province to the **Maccabees** after a failed attempt to impose **Hellenism** on the resistant Jewish population.

Septuagint (3, 6). Grk., "seventy." The Greek translation of the **Torah**, prepared in **Alexandria** around 250 BCE; the name reflects the story that thirty-five (or thiry-six) separate pairs of translators all produced exactly the same rendition of the original. Made possible the spread of Greek-speaking Judaism throughout the Greco-Roman world, and therefore also the spread of Christianity. The name is sometimes used for the Greek translation of the entire Bible, but the various books were actually translated separately over a period of several generations.

Sh'ma (8). Heb., "Hear," first word of Deuteronomy 6:4. The first word of a twice-daily three-paragraph (Deuteronomy 6:4–9, 11:13–21; Numbers 15:37–41) liturgical recitation that has been a core element in Jewish worship since the beginning of the Common Era. In rabbinic interpretation, the three paragraphs represent acceptance of the "Yoke of Heaven," acceptance of the "Yoke of the Commandments," and remembrance of the **Exodus** from **Egypt**.

shofar. The ram's horn that is blown on the New Year (see Leviticus 23:24; Numbers 29:1).

Sinai (Mount) (1, 8). The location of God's revealing the **Torah** to **Moses** (Exodus 19–24). After the ancient **rabbis** developed the concept of Oral Torah, all Jewish tradition was deemed to have come from this revelation, except that much had been excluded from the Written Torah of the **Pentateuch**.

Solomon (1). King of Israel, son of **David** (late tenth century BCE). Credited with great wisdom; reputed author of several books of the Bible (see Chapter 1, "What Is in the Bible?"); built the first **Jerusalem Temple** (1 Kings 6–7).

sugya (9, A1). An extended discussion in the **Talmud**.

Sukkah (1, 5, A1). Heb., "tabernacle, booth." During the autumn Festival of Tabernacles, people would build and dwell in temporary huts, reminiscent of

Israel's days in the desert. The incident of the high priest and the water libation (see Chapter 5) took place during this festival, as did the **eschatological** drama found in Appendix 1.

Talmud (9, 10, A1, A2). Heb., "study"; Aram. *gemara* is a synonym. Ancient compilations of rabbinic teaching, in the form of loose commentary on selected Mishnaic tractates, thousands of pages long. The Jerusalem Talmud was compiled in the academies of *Eretz Yisra'el*, probably around 400 CE; the larger and more authoritative Babylonian Talmud was compiled in that country, largely during the sixth century.

Tanakh (1). Heb. acronym: **Torah**, Nevi'im (prophets), Ketuvim (writings). In modern times, a widely used designation for the twenty-four books of holy scripture; the term was not used until the Middle Ages. See Chapter 1 for a list of the twenty-four.

Targum (10). Aramaic translation of scripture.

Tefilla (8). Heb., "prayer." The word can designate any prayer, but in rabbinic discourse it particularly means the sequence of eighteen (later nineteen) blessings that form the central petitionary prayer of the service. Also called *'amida*, the "standing" prayer, on account of the worshiper's posture when reciting it.

Temple (1, 4, 7, 8). The central shrine of Jewish worship until the first century CE. First built in **Jerusalem** by King **Solomon** and destroyed by the Babylonians, then rebuilt under the Persians, only to be destroyed for good by **Rome** in 70 CE. Much of the **Torah** contains detailed instructions for performance of the Temple sacrifices and preservation of the Temple's **purity**. Local Jewish temples also existed in **Egypt**, first at Elephantine under the Persians, then at Heliopolis under the **Ptolemies** and the Romans, but these never achieved worldwide significance. Several attempts to restore the Temple under the later Roman Empire came to nothing, but the expectation that the Temple and its ceremonies will be restored at the end of days remained an important part of Jewish religious hope into modern times.

Teruma (A1), "heave-offering." A gift of produce that farmers were obliged to supply to the priests. Priests who consumed this food had to be ritually clean, a requirement that supplied the background to the first paragraph of the **Mishnah** and the **Talmud**.

Titus (7). Roman general and emperor; son of **Vespasian**. The Second **Temple** was destroyed by an army under his command. A triumphal arch in **Rome** built in honor of Titus depicts Roman soldiers carrying the spoils of the Temple.

Torah (1, 3, 9). Heb., "teaching." The official name of the **Pentateuch** from the time of **Ezra**. In rabbinic discourse, the term designates the entirety of Jewish religion, not least the Oral Torah containing the teachings of the **rabbis** themselves. Rabbis claimed that mastery of Torah imparted the power to work miracles (including using the "evil eye") and enjoy long life, and that mastery of Torah was the only true basis for Jewish leadership. In rabbinic eyes, a fulfilled life was one dedicated to learning and teaching Torah; such a life transformed ordinary individuals into holy men. Torah learning was sporadically available to women, but no important rabbi was a female.

tractate (9). One of the sixty-three subdivisions of the **Mishnah**. See Chapter 9.

Vespasian (7). Roman general and emperor; appointed by Nero to put down the Jewish rebellion of 66. He left during the campaign to take power as emperor and entrusted the Jewish war to his son **Titus**.

YHWH (1, 2). The name of the God of Israel. In postbiblical times, this name was supposedly no longer spoken out loud except by the high priest on the Day of Atonement, and it was replaced by substitutes, most familiarly "the Lord"; modern scholars are in fact unsure of its correct pronunciation. However, later magical scrolls contain apparent invocations of the Jewish God by his name, so it appears that some private individuals (perhaps only gentile sorcerers) continued to use the name into later times.

Chronology

Note: The earlier dates, printed in *italics*, are conjectural, based on the narratives of the Bible. They are not corroborated by other literary or archeological evidence. Later dates without markers are all CE.

ca. 1100 BCE	*Israelites settle in Canaan.*
ca. 980 BCE	*David founds a royal dynasty with the capital in Jerusalem.*
ca. 930 BCE	*David's son Solomon builds the First Temple in Jerusalem.*
ca. 900 BCE	*Death of Solomon; the Kingdom of Israel splits.*
722 BCE	The Assyrians conquer the Kingdom of Israel and carry off the "ten lost tribes."
596, 586 BCE	The two Babylonian conquests of Jerusalem; at the second, the city and kingdom are destroyed and the leadership is taken to Babylon.
539 BCE	Cyrus, king of Persia, conquers Babylon. The exiles are permitted to return to *Yehud*, but many remain in their new homes.
410 BCE	Final destruction of the Jewish temple at Elephantine.
333–331 BCE	Alexander the Great conquers the Persian Empire; start of the Hellenistic period.
301–201 BCE	Judaea under the rule of the Ptolemies in Egypt; thereafter under the rule of the Seleucid dynasty.
ca. 250 BCE	The Torah is translated into Greek (Septuagint) at Alexandria.
ca. 175 BCE	Seleucus IV attempts to raid the Temple in Jerusalem.

ca. 168 BCE	Antiochus IV interferes with the high-priestly succession; declares Jerusalem to be a *polis*; initiates persecution of traditional Jewish ways. Start of the Maccabean rebellion.
165 BCE	Judah the Maccabee rededicates the Temple.
152 BCE (?)	Jonathan the Maccabee becomes high priest; inaugurates the Hasmonean dynasty.
ca. 103 BCE	Hasmonean high priests begin using the title "king."
63 BCE	Pompey conquers Judaea; ends the Hasmonaean monarchy.
ca. 20 BCE–ca. 45 CE	Philo of Alexandria.
37–34 BCE	Reign of Herod the Great.
26–36 CE	Pontius Pilate governor of Judaea; execution of Jesus of Nazareth.
66 CE	Outbreak of Judaean rebellion against Rome (70: destruction of Jerusalem Temple; 73–4: capture of Masada).
after 70	According to tradition, first gathering of sages at Yavneh.
115–117	Jewish rebellion against Rome in North Africa, Babylonia, etc.: Jews virtually wiped out in Alexandria, Cyprus, Cyrene.
132–135	Rebellion of Bar Kokhba, followed (135–138) by persecution of Judaism in Judaea.
ca. 200	Compilation of Mishnah under Judah the *Nasi*.
ca. 225	Rav (Abba Arika) organizes first rabbinic instruction in Babylonia.
313	Emperor Constantine ends persecution of Christianity.
ca. 400	Jerusalem Talmud.
ca. 425	First volumes of *Midrash Rabba*.
425 (?)	Abolition of patriarchate.
ca. 550	Babylonian Talmud.

614–629	Persian occupation of the Land of Israel.
622	*Hegira*: beginnings of Islam.
630s–640s	Rapid spread of Islam in the Middle East, including centers of Jewish life.

Notes

A Note of Introduction

1. 2 Kings 18, late eighth century BCE.
2. Even in the Bible, portions of the Books of Daniel and Ezra are written in Aramaic, as are one verse in the Book of Jeremiah (10:11) and two words in Genesis 31:47.
3. The word first appears in a slightly earlier context, the reign of Hezekiah's father, at 2 Kings 16:6.
4. An important early exception is the author of the Second Book of Maccabees in the Apocrypha (see "The Apocrypha" in Chapter 4), who repeatedly (2:21; 8:1; 14:38) uses the word to designate the traditional Jewish way of life, now under threat by a rival way of life called *Hellenismos*, "the way Greeks live." This is the earliest recorded appearance of *Ioudaismos*, and the word may have been invented by this author.
5. This is how the word is used in the New Testament by the Apostle Paul: see Galatians 1:14.
6. A brief chronology of important dates is supplied near the end of the volume.

1. The Prehistory of Judaism

1. Throughout this book, the word *God* will be capitalized only when it refers to the One God of the Bible, the God of mature Judaism. Obviously, this excludes all references to the deities of polytheistic nations; less obviously, it also excludes biblical references to Israel's god in contexts that seem to recognize the existence of other (possibly inferior) gods. This distinction will be elaborated on later in this chapter and in subsequent chapters of this book.

   In the early chapters of this book, when describing historical periods in which people still pronounced the four-letter personal name of God, that name will be transcribed according to its Hebrew consonants as *YHWH*. On account of the extreme holiness of this name and the immense power it embodied, in later times people ceased to pronounce this name in everyday life and its actual sound was forgotten. For later periods, when this name was no longer spoken but was replaced by a circumlocution such as *the Lord*, a similar practice will be adopted here.

2. In this book, *Bible* will always mean the Jewish Bible, often called the *Old Testament* in Christian usage. A complete listing of the books of the Jewish Bible can be found in the box "What Is in the Bible?"

3. Archeology can confirm that a certain account is *plausible* or *realistic*, but without documentary corroboration of some kind (and archeologists often do find documents!) it cannot determine whether an account is *accurate* or *true*.

4. Readers familiar with scripture will note that the following summary omits many famous characters and stories. It concentrates on those themes that remained important in the religious worldview of later generations.

5. The punishment for this horror was concentrated on *Ham*, one of Noah's sons and the ancestor of the Canaanites whom Israel would eventually displace from the Promised Land. Genesis 10 also identifies Ham as the ancestor of the Africans, a fact that has been cited in later racial theories to support views that the biblical writers would have considered alien and fantastic.

6. The themes of this story foreshadow later Jewish experience: the guest nation renders great service to its host, only to suffer the terrible effects of a poisonous combination: the host's ingratitude and the guests' own vulnerability. The idea that "the stories of the fathers foreshadow those of the sons" became a standard theme in later Jewish readings of the Bible.

7. At several points (Exodus 12:37; Numbers 1:46, 26:51, etc.), scripture reports that the children of Israel leaving Egypt numbered over 600,000 adult males.

8. As a symbol of the nation's inconstancy, the holy ark contained not only the Tablets of the Law, but also the fragments of an earlier set; these first tablets had been shattered by Moses when he discovered the people worshiping a golden calf (Exodus 32). They had built this forbidden object while he was still on the mountain receiving God's word, while the sound of God's own voice must still have echoed in their ears.

9. See A Note of Introduction for more discussion of the name *Jews*, *Judah*, and *Israel*.

10. The law codes in the Torah make some provision for life in towns, mostly concerning the ownership of houses, but almost no reference at all to the economic life of towns: commerce, crafts, manufacturing, and the like.

11. Two of the three patriarchs had multiple wives, as did several of the kings of Israel, most notably David and Solomon. The father of Samuel had two wives as well. It appears that these men were all rich.

12. This arrangement possibly applied to full wives only. *Concubines,* or wives of lower status, may have existed in more of a social limbo.

13. A childless widow or divorcee might return to her father's house: see Genesis 38:11 (narrative) or Leviticus 22:13 (priestly law).

14. Most notably of all, the royal family of David was descended in one line from the Moabite woman Ruth, even though Deuteronomy 23:9 seems to ban marriage with Moabites. (This rule may come from a later time; in order to avoid the appearance of illegality, rabbinic interpreters limited the ban to marriage between Israelite women and Moabite men.) After the exile, Ezra and Nehemiah forced men of Judah who had married foreign women to send them away; see Chapter 3.

15. An important exception is the annual household sacrifice of the paschal lamb; see discussion on page 15.

16. At a slightly later time, Babylonian astrologers began to think in terms of a seven-day cycle corresponding to the seven "planets" (including the sun and moon) of their day. Centuries later, this idea spread throughout the Greek and Roman worlds.

17. In the days of the kings and later, the Sabbath was apparently deemed a suitable occasion for visiting a holy man or shrine; see 2 Kings 4:23; Isaiah 66:23.

18. Later rabbinic texts derive thirty-nine basic categories of forbidden labor from the building of the Tabernacle in the desert. See Appendix 3.

19. See Amos 7:10–17; Jeremiah 26:8–11.

20. Zechariah 14:2–6; here too, one might ask whether this was a prediction or a warning.

21. In the days of the Maccabees, filled with religious enthusiasm, people thought that a revival of prophecy might be in the offing, but this did not occur. See Chapter 4, with reference to 1 Maccabees 4:46 and 14:41.

2. The Beginnings of Monotheism

1. Readers of this book need not master the diplomatic negotiations in detail, but they can be reconstructed from a combination of Numbers 20:14–21, Joshua 13:25, and the story here in Judges.

2. A brief but typical list of such national gods (there under the prophets' influence called *detestations*) appears in 2 Kings 23:13. The list in Kings identifies Kemosh as the deity of the Moabites, not of the Ammonites as here. Archeological discoveries suggest that the identification in Kings is the correct one.

3. The Torah often describes YHWH as "jealous"; see Exodus 20:5 and Deuteronomy 5:9 (see Chapter 1, "'The Ten Commandments,' Two Versions"); also see Exodus 34:14, Deuteronomy 4:24, 6:15.

4. The prophet's opponents in Jeremiah 44, the chapter just examined, represent the main departure from this viewpoint.

5. 1 Kings 18. Was God's fire the lightning that preceded this storm?

6. See, for example, Jeremiah 3:8–9; Hosea 4:13–14.

7. 2 Kings 18:4. The name is a play on the Hebrew word *nehoshet*, meaning "bronze" or "copper."

8. Jeremiah 5:19. See also Deuteronomy 32:17; Joshua 24:20; Psalm 81:10.

9. See, for example, Daniel 9:13; 12:1.

10. Until very recent times, Jewish folk belief paid careful attention to the presence of angels, demons, etc., in the world. It never occurred to most people that such a concept was incompatible with Judaic monotheism, and it never occurred to most rabbinic leaders (there were exceptions) to denounce such beliefs as superstition or the like. In general, the concept of *superstition* is elusive and is not very useful in the study of religion; a superstition is a belief held by others, or a practice based on such a belief, of which one disapproves, but there is no impartial criterion for deciding which beliefs or practices should be put into that category.

3. The Book and the People

1. The reference to heart and soul and might also appears in Deuteronomy 6:5, where it describes the religious goal of every follower of YHWH. This verse is included in the twice-daily recitation known as *Sh'ma* ("Hear O Israel, YHWH our God is One"), and it has been fundamental to the religious experience of Jews for 2,000 years. See the box "The *Sh'ma*" in Chapter 8 for the complete text of this recitation. This similarity and others have led scholars to conclude that the book Hilkiah found may have been (an early version of) Deuteronomy.

2. Hezekiah was appointed coruler (or designated heir) in 729 BCE; in 714 his father, Ahaz, died and he became sole monarch. On the praise of Hezekiah see 2 Kings 18:1–7.

3. See "The Origin of a Prophetic Book."

4. See 2 Chronicles 36:22–23 (the last paragraph of the Jewish Bible), repeated in Ezra 1:2–4. In gratitude, Isaiah 45:1 addresses Cyrus as YHWH's "anointed" or "messiah."

5. Ezra 7:1. There were three Persian kings named Artaxerxes, and modern scholars have not been able to agree on which one is meant here.

6. See "Scribes" for more on scribes.

7. Presumably this really means the relevant officials in the royal bureaucracy.

8. Ezra's great collaborator, Nehemiah, was just such a well-placed Judahite.

9. See Nehemiah 9.

10. For a review of the biblical festivals, see Chapter 1, "The Biblical Calendar."

11. See 2 Kings 24:14–16; 25:11–12.

12. The Torah itself, of course, stresses the gravity of Sabbath violation, and there are references to the Sabbath in earlier prophets' writings as well (Amos 8; Jeremiah 17). But the practice appears to have been more

rigorously enforced from the time of Ezra and Nehemiah on. See Nehemiah 13:15–18, and see Appendix 3.

13. See "The Origin of a Prophetic Book." The Bible refers to other ancient writings, presumably similar in character to the biblical books themselves, that were already lost; see Numbers 21:14 ("The Book of the Wars of YHWH") and 2 Samuel 1:18 ("The Book of Yashar"), as well as the constant references in the Book of Kings to the "Chronicles of the Kings of Judah and Israel." After 722 BCE, refugees from the destroyed nothern kingdom brought many documents and much oral tradition into Judah. In essence, therefore, the exiled Judahite leaders were assembling the national heritage of all Israel, that is, all that had survived the double catastrophe.

14. See Chapter 4.

15. See "The Torah Comes to *Yehud*."

16. At around the same time (late fifth century BCE), an exchange of letters between Jews in Egypt and the authorities in Jerusalem touches on religious matters (sacrifices, the Passover celebration) but never cites a sacred text. See the later account of the Jewish settlement at Elephantine in the Upper Nile Valley. In general, very little can be said of Jewish life in the early Diaspora; see Chapter Six.

17. Interpretations surely changed over time. The story in Nehemiah 8 reflects an understanding of Leviticus 23 that differs from the one eventually codified in rabbinic law. Ezra's contemporaries used the "olive leaves and oilwood and myrtle and palms and thickwood to make booths as it is written" (Nehemiah 8:15), while in later times (up to today) the collected branches were used for other ceremonial purposes, not to construct the booths (the species are different as well!). See "Interpretation within the Bible" for other examples of interpretation within the Bible itself.

18. The dramatic story of Ezra reading the scroll to the people actually is found in the Book of Nehemiah.

19. All this is found in Nehemiah 13, the last chapter of the book. For the exclusion of Ammonites and Moabites, see Deuteronomy 23:3–5, which Nehemiah's text all but reproduces.

20. See the last chapters of the Book of Ezra.

21. See Chapter 2, "A Debate on the Meaning of Disaster."

22. See Nehemiah 13:4–9; also see 13:28–29. It appears that these texts are drawn from Nehemiah's own memoirs; his contemporaries might have described things differently.

23. See Haggai 2:11–13.

24. The story appears most famously in the *Letter of Aristeas*, supposedly written by a Greek eyewitness to these events but probably the work of an Alexandrian Jew. See also Josephus, *Antiquities*, the beginning of Book 12. (The historian Josephus is introduced in "Josephus" in Chapter 5.)

25. See Philo's *Life of Moses*, 2.41. (Philo is introduced in Chapter 6.)

26. These developments are known from fragments of the official correspondence that have been preserved. See B. Porten, *Archives from Elephantine: The Life of an Ancient Jewish Military Colony* (Berkeley: University of California Press, 1968).

27. This phrase recurs over and over again in Deuteronomy. According to tradition it meant Jerusalem, and it was understood to bar sacrificial worship anywhere else: a key feature of King Josiah's reform was the destruction of all shrines to YHWH outside Jerusalem. However, Deuteronomy is set in the time of Moses, so the capital of David's future kingdom could not be identified by name. This ambiguity gave rise to a dispute with the Samaritans that lasted for centuries. See "The Samaritans" for more on this group.

28. It was a recurrent theme of ancient Jewish history that religious disputes broke out over conflicting interpretations of the holy text. See the following chapters for more on this theme.

4. Crisis and a New Beginning

1. The English word *barbarian* is derived from a Greek word meaning "anyone who is not a Greek."

2. On Josephus see Chapter 5, "Josephus."

3. See Josephus, *Antiquities*, Book Twelve.

4. Ancient temples were widely used for safe deposit, in the belief that thieves would hesitate to steal from such holy locations, and it was widely suspected that ill-gotten funds were often mixed into these deposits. Kings routinely sent search parties into temples to recover funds that presumably did not belong there. The Seleucids, in particular, were always short of cash after a catastrophic defeat in 190 BCE by Rome. The Romans had levied an indemnity on the defeated Antiochus III that amounted to nearly 1 million pounds of gold.

5. See 2 Maccabees, chapter 3. Daniel 11:20 may contain an oblique reference to the same event, perhaps on the basis of Zechariah 9:8. The Books of the Maccabees belong to a collection called the *Apocrypha*. See "The Apocrypha."

6. It is possible that every high priest of the Second Temple technically served by royal appointment and at the king's pleasure, just as Ezra and Nehemiah had technically served at the pleasure of the king of Persia. If this was the case, the king routinely granted automatic ratification to the candidate the Jews expected him to nominate; this was usually the son of the previous holder of the office. By withdrawing his support from one brother and appointing the other, Antiochus actually used the power that his predecessors had forgone.

7. In the days of the Hellenistic kingdoms, new cities were often named after their founders. In his brief life, Alexander the Great founded more

than a dozen Alexandrias all over Asia, as well as the more famous one in Africa.

8. See 2 Maccabees 4:14. The gymnasium was the cultural center of every ancient Greek city. The word comes from the Greek *gymnos*, meaning "naked," because men exercised in the nude. This, of course, caused further offense to the more conservative people of Jerusalem.

9. The author of Daniel refers twice (11:31; 12:11) to a "stupefying abomination" being installed in the Temple. The same phrase appears (though now in Greek) at 1 Maccabees 1:54. No author spells out the reference.

10. See Daniel 12:2.

11. These ancient *Hasidim* have no connection to the Jewish revival movement with the same name that began in Europe a little over 200 years ago.

12. See 1 Maccabees, chapter 2.

13. These enemies included Greeks and Syrians along with Jews who were ready to abandon the teachings of Moses.

14. 1 Maccabees 2:40–41 (translation of J. Goldstein in the *Anchor Bible*).

15. See Chapter 8.

16. 1 Maccabees 2:46.

17. 1 Maccabees 4:46.

18. See 1 Maccabees 8 on Rome and 1 Maccabees 12:6–23 on Sparta. The treaty with Rome was a brilliant diplomatic harassment of the Seleucids, but the treaty with Sparta, now a powerless small town, seems only to have been a sentimental gesture. There may have been an obscure link between Sparta and the Jews: 2 Maccabees 5:9 reports that Jason, the would-be high priest, fled to Sparta after his quest for power failed.

19. 1 Maccabees 1:11–15 (translation by J. Goldstein in the *Anchor Bible*, slightly modified).

5. The First Kingdom of Judaea

1. See Chapter 4, "The People Appoint Simon Head Priest," and see 1 Maccabees 5 for even earlier examples of actions carried out by Judah himself.

2. Romans and the Jews had been friends by treaty for 100 years, since the days of Judah the Maccabee (1 Maccabees 8).

3. The full Hebrew title of the document is *Miqsat Ma'aseh Torah*, "Some Matters Concerning the Torah." The *4Q* at the beginning of the abbreviation indicates that the text was discovered in Qumran Cave Four. "The Dead Sea Scrolls (I)" provides more information about the Scrolls.

4. Scholarly opinions differ as to the identity of these authorities. Some place the document very early in the period and identify the priest as the transitional Alcimus. Others, presuming that a little more time needed to pass before such a letter could be written, identify one of the early Hasmonaeans.

5. King David had lived a long time earlier, but the prophet Ezekiel used the phrase "children of Zadok" as a general name for the priests of his own generation, and this way of speaking may have persisted into the time of the Second Temple.

6. This can be assumed for purposes of discussion, but it is always possible that his hand merely slipped. The importance of the story is that few people at the time seem to have believed that his action was innocent.

7. Josephus, *Antiquities*, 13.297; compare 18.16.

8. Deuteronomy 17:8–11.

9. On Philo, see Chapter 6.

10. Ordinary sexual activity conveys impurity (see Leviticus 15:18), so this may explain Essenes' avoidance of marriage. More information about the rules of purity can be found later in this chapter.

11. According to Josephus (*War* 2.567), one of the leaders of the rebellion against Rome was known as John the Essene. If Essenes were pacifists, how could one of their number have become a leader in war? Perhaps John thought that this was the apocalyptic war at the end of the world, an event that some (perhaps most) Essenes thought was imminent, or perhaps he was a former Essene called by that name to distinguish him from the many others named *Yohanan*.

12. *War*, 2.143.

13. See Chapter 4.

14. The later rabbis eventually provided a number of symbolic recognitions of the priests' continuing holiness. When the Torah is read in synagogues, the first portion should be allocated to a priest. At public banquets, a priest should preside over grace. Among observant modern Jews, the specific rules in the Torah that govern priests' marriage or their participation in funerals (see Leviticus 21:1–10) remain in effect. However, the early rabbis were also careful to ensure that the priests would retain none of their previous power or authority. The Mishnah (Nega'im 3:1) provides an amusing example of priestly prestige without authority: in a case of suspected leprosy, the priest had to make the official declaration of "clean" or "unclean" as provided in the Torah (Leviticus 13), but a rabbinic sage stood over him and told him what to say.

15. The New Testament mentions many Jewish groups that were active during the time of Jesus, but it never mentions the Essenes. Early Christianity also displayed certain Essene-like features: collective living (Acts 4:32), messianic expectation, eager anticipation of the end of the world. For these reasons, some have conjectured that after Qumran was destroyed, the surviving Essenes melted into the Christian groups that were developing in their area.

16. Josephus, *Life*, 191.

17. The name Pharisee can thus convey admiration or resentment, depending on whether the separation is seen to involve avoidance of defilement or

avoidance of other people. The sources do not indicate whether the group chose this name for itself or lived with a nickname ("Separatists") that other people flung at them until they simply accepted it for themselves. Other religious groups (for example, the Quakers or the Methodists) have received their names in a similar fashion.

18. Most of these rules can be found in a compact section of the Torah, Leviticus 13–15.

19. See Leviticus 16.

20. Christian writers after the destruction of Jerusalem were probably also aware of the rabbis who claimed to be the Pharisees' heirs and competed with the developing Church for the "hearts and minds" of the Jewish masses. This competition would have intensified Christians' tendency to think ill of the Pharisees in Jesus' own time.

21. This description reflects Josephus's portrayal in his later book, the *Jewish Antiquities*; in his earlier book, *The Jewish War*, Josephus offers a much more guarded portrayal of the Pharisees' influence. Scholars have differed as to whether the variation reflects a change in the historian's attitude, changes in the later political situation that he was trying to reflect (or guide), or a simple accident of style.

6. Diaspora and Homeland

1. The origins of the Elephantine settlement in Egypt cannot be determined, but that community may have predated the Exile. See Chapter 4.

2. See 2 Kings 17:1–6; 18:9–11.

3. In recent centuries, many fanciful theories have been proposed identifying far-flung peoples as descendants of the "ten lost tribes." In the nineteenth century, people in England toyed with the idea that their country had been settled by refugees from the Assyrian exile; others suggested the same about Japan. Most remarkably, an American scholar some years ago suggested that Israelite remnants were the ancestors of the native peoples of Tennessee!

4. The prophet Ezekiel (or more precisely his father) belonged to this group, and the prophet's writings are full of communications between the exiles in Babylon and their friends and former colleagues in Jerusalem.

5. This was in keeping with the instruction of the prophet Jeremiah, still in Jerusalem (see Jeremiah 29:4–7); in a letter to the exiles he wrote that Jews would be in Babylon a long time, and he urged them to establish a stable, prosperous community.

6. The Bible (1 Chronicles 3) contains a list of David's descendants down to around 400 BCE, nearly 200 years after the kingdom fell and the royal family was taken to Babylon.

7. Ezra 9–10; Nehemiah 13:23–27. Nehemiah 13:28–29 reports that even a high priest's grandson had married such a woman.

8. Nehemiah 5; compare Exodus 22:25; Leviticus 25:35–37; Deuteronomy 23:19–20.
9. See Nehemiah 13. The prophets worked for centuries to increase respect for the Sabbath; see Amos 8:5; Jeremiah 17:21–27; Isaiah 56:2–6.
10. See Chapter 4.
11. See Chapter 3. This is not to say that the record was historically authentic, only that priestly ancestry remained a valued distinction among the exiled Jews in Babylon.
12. The office lasted until the eleventh century CE. See Chapters 9 and 10 for further discussion of the exilarch in talmudic times.
13. See Chapter 9.
14. See Deuteronomy 17:16; 28:68.
15. See Jeremiah 44:1.
16. See Chapter 3.
17. According to the *Letter of Aristeas*, probably written around 200–170 BCE, these captives were freed en masse by King Ptolemy II, son of the monarch who had first brought them there.
18. This is the (unverifiable) claim of the Jewish philosopher Philo writing toward the middle of the first century CE (*Against Flaccus* 55), and means that there were perhaps 1 million Jews in Egypt at around that time.
19. Modern English-speaking Jews have done the same thing, though with a slightly different set of words. Thanks to the Christian Bible, *Sabbath* was already an English word, but *kosher* was not until the mid-1800s.
20. Only fragments of this writer survive, embedded as quotations in the works of other ancient writers.
21. Scenes such as the ten plagues that could not be performed with decorum were apparently kept off stage and merely described by the characters. This was a standard convention of Greek drama, to be seen as well, for example, in the off-stage self-mutilation of King Oedipus.
22. See Philo, *On the Migration of Abraham*, 89–92.
23. Philo most famously led a delegation to Rome to meet the Emperor Caligula and induce him to show greater tolerance of the Jews' religious needs. In his mature years, he and his even wealthier brother Alexander must constantly have been involved in the civic affairs of their city; Alexander seems to have served as *alabarch* (head? tax collector?) of the Alexandrian Jewish community.
24. Josephus twice puts this very question into the mouth of the Jews' political enemies. See *Against Apion* 2.65–67 (Apion of Alexandria) and *Antiquities* 12.125–126 (unnamed opponents in Ionia).
25. This accusation and others like it can be found in many Greek and Latin texts. Jews train their children to hate outsiders. Jews never give correct travel directions to non-Jews. Most shockingly, every year Jews capture a Greek, fatten him up, and then sacrifice (and eat?) him. The frequency of these charges suggests that they were widely believed.

26. *Antiquities* 14.190–264; 16.162–170. Many of these extracts show clear signs of miscopying and other sorts of inaccuracy; such errors can be signs of forgery, but most recent scholars have been willing to accept the documents as fundamentally authentic.

27. Philo provides eyewitness descriptions of these events in two of his works, *Against Flaccus* and *The Embassy to Gaius*. The latter work is a memoir of his trip to Rome to meet the emperor.

28. This was the Greek perception; the Jews of Alexandria had in fact not prospered under Roman rule, and their status remained deeply uncertain.

29. The motive was partly political, to give all such people a stake in the empire's well-being, and partly economic, to force all such people to accept civic office (and the costs of civic office) along with earlier citizen groups.

30. This point needs emphasis, because the English verb *proselytize* sometimes implies an active effort to attract people to a religious community. There is no clear evidence that ancient Jews engaged in such efforts; many, perhaps most, perhaps even all of the proselytes seem to have approached the local Jews on their own initiative. There are many stories in the Talmud of rabbis discussing religious matters with non-Jews, but there is not a single story of a rabbi starting such a conversation.

31. See Yevamot 47a–b.

32. See Chapter 7 on these wars and Chapter 10 on the Christianization of the empire.

33. In Latin *metuentes Deum*; in Greek *phoboumenoi* (or *sebomenoi*) *ton theon*.

7. A Century of Disasters

1. The *Parthians*, related to the Persians, had built a large kingdom to the east of the Roman domains. Heirs to the ancient rivalry between the Persians and the Greeks, they frequently warred against the Romans, most famously destroying a Roman army led by the triumvir Crassus in 53 BCE. In 225 CE, the Parthian kingdom was overthrown by the Persian Sassanian dynasty, but the Roman–Persian rivalry continued until the end of ancient history. On the Persian conquest of Judaea in 614 CE, see Chapter 10.

2. This humiliating act disqualified Hyrcanus from the office of high priest; men with bodily defects could enjoy priestly entitlements but could not take part in the Temple rituals (see Leviticus 21:16–23).

3. Most of the western wall of the Temple enclosure, though not the Temple structure itself, and some of the southern wall remain as sites for pilgrimage or tourism in Jerusalem today.

4. The Emperor Augustus, referring to the Jews' famous refusal to slaughter and eat pork, once remarked that he would rather be one of Herod's pigs than one of Herod's sons.

5. Almost all of our information about the origins of Christianity is provided by later Christian writers; people of deep religious faith, they naturally reflected their beliefs in their writings. Thus surviving depictions of Jesus and his associates – who they were, how they acted, what they themselves believed – are all imbued with later writers' conceptions. Later conceptions of Jesus were diverse, and so are descriptions of his actions and teachings. It is nearly impossible to determine whether Jesus saw himself as the Messiah or the Son of God; later informants (most of them missionaries eager to spread a particular message) took for granted that their Lord had seen himself as they saw him, and so they attributed their own views to him.

6. *Moral* purity, not the Levitical purity discussed elsewhere in this book.

7. Josephus, *War*, 2.169–174; *Antiquities*, 18.55–59.

8. *War*, 2.224–227; *Antiquities*, 20.105–111.

9. Josephus, *War*, 2.228–231; *Antiquities*, 20.113–117. Josephus reports this and the previous incident in consecutive passages, but it is not clear that they occurred at the same time.

10. The next year Agrippa passed through Alexandria on the way to his new realm, and was greeted with wild enthusiasm by the Jews of that city. This incident seems to have been an important factor in the terrible outbreak of anti-Jewish violence that followed soon after. See Chapter 6, especially "The Emperor Claudius and the Jews of Alexandria."

11. Outside Judaea, the king was generally willing to violate Jewish norms through the sponsorship of gladiator contests, the issuance of coins with human images, and the like. In this he repeated the policies of his grandfather, Herod. The expanded kingdom, though named Judaea, housed many and diverse non-Jewish people, and the king wanted to satisfy the wishes of all his subjects when he could. Nevertheless, Agrippa's non-Jewish subjects resented their king's unexpected piety, and they happily celebrated his early death.

12. Agrippa II was soon given a kingdom well to the north, but Judaea now remained under direct Roman rule, with King Agrippa supervising the Temple and appointing (or dismissing) the high priests. When open rebellion broke out in the year 66, the king showed his loyalty to Rome by supporting the empire against the rebels. He seems to have lived almost to the end of the century and to have died without heirs. Other branches of the Herodian family also continued to rule small, far-flung kingdoms, but the Judaean monarchy was now abolished forever.

13. T. A. Burkill, writing in Schürer (see Suggestions for Further Reading), 1.455.

14. The *sicarii* mingled in crowds and killed random people with hidden daggers, hence their name. This early form of urban terrorism was designed to unnerve the governing Romans and reduce other Jews' confidence that their rulers could maintain public safety. It worked.

15. The following narrative is based almost entirely on the writings of Josephus.

16. Josephus (*War* 6.420) speaks of 1,100,000 deaths during the siege of Jerusalem alone, but in ancient historical writing such numbers are often exaggerated.

17. When the Jews of Alexandria were rounded up during the riots of 38, their Greek opponents seemed to know where to find them. In general, it seems that the Jews could be identified in the cities of the Roman Empire.

18. Sometimes, of course, religious behavior can be concealed; this is especially important in times of persecution or oppression. At first, Roman courts looking for secret Jews forced men to disrobe before a magistrate to see whether they were circumcised, but this insulting procedure was soon abandoned, and citizens were forbidden to bring accusations against others of practicing Judaism in secret. The Emperor Nerva (reigned 96–98) actually issued a coin celebrating the ban on such accusations.

19. In later years, even a Jew who washed up on Cyprus after a shipwreck was immediately put to death. In Babylonia, newly conquered by the Romans, another outbreak led to enormous Jewish losses as well.

20. The empire's persistent refusal to reopen the Temple naturally served to justify and nourish this hatred. Obscure reports, mostly by unsympathetic Christian writers, suggest that the Emperor Trajan (ruled 98–117) did authorize the rebuilding of the Jerusalem Temple. The project was soon abandoned: surviving records suggest arson or earthquake (in which Christians naturally saw the hand of God) as the most plausible explanations.

21. The emperor's full name was *Publius Aelius Hadrianus*, and Jupiter's most famous temple was on the Capitoline hill in Rome. This was the temple that now received the *fiscus judaicus*.

22. Enforcement of the rule with respect to converts was often sporadic and not always very effective. The ban on circumcision took on new meaning after the empire adopted Christianity as its official religion: any Jew who participated in the circumcision of a Christian might now be put to death.

8. The Rebirth of Judaism

1. Short biographies of selected early rabbis can be found in Appendix 2.

2. Jewish law did not permit overnight storage of the dead in Jerusalem.

3. See Gittin 56a–b.

4. On Gamaliel's father, Simeon, see Josephus, *Life* 190–191; on Simeon's father, also named Gamaliel, see the Acts of the Apostles 5:34. Both of these men are also frequently mentioned in the rabbinic literature of later centuries. Subsequent generations traced the family back to the great Hillel, a leading teacher at the turn of the eras, but this may have been a later claim designed to increase the family's prestige.

5. Eduyyot 7:7.

6. The jurisdiction of these Jewish courts may have been limited to small civil cases (property disputes, damage suits, etc.) and matters of personal status (marriage, divorce, inheritance, and the like). Whole tractates of the Talmud are devoted to rabbinic discussion of these themes, while the rabbis' treatments of other topics such as capital punishment or issues of political legitimacy seem more theoretical and unrelated to contemporary reality.

7. See Chapter 5, citing Josephus, *Life* 191.

8. The Talmuds report that both Gamaliel and his son (another Simeon) were the targets of conspiracies aimed at removing them from authority. On Gamaliel see B. Berachot 27b–28a and the parallel at J. Berachot 4:1 7cd; on his son Simeon see B. Horayot 13b–14a. To be sure, the stories in their present form contain legendary elements and should not be taken as simple reports of historical incidents.

9. J. Sanhedrin 1:3 19a.

10. See C. Hezser, *The Social Structure of the Rabbinic Movement in Roman Palestine* (Tübingen: J. C. B. Mohr [Paul Siebeck], 1997).

11. A survey of rabbinic literature, including a description of the character and contents of the major rabbinic texts, can be found in Chapter 9. A certain amount of information concerning the ancient rabbis can also be found in the works of Christian writers and the legislation of later Roman emperors.

12. For example, to "decree a fast" in times of drought: Mishnah Ta'anit 3:6.

13. B. Bava Batra 60b; Avoda Zara 36a; Horayot 3b; Bava Qama 79b.

14. Certain distant corners of the Jewish world, most notably Ethiopia and parts of India, were so isolated from the Jewish mainstream that rabbinic authority never became established there at all, or at least not until modern times.

15. The reports of this friendship may well be exaggerated, reflections more of Jewish pride than of historical reality. Modern scholars have not been able to determine which emperor would have been Judah's friend, but Judah's honored position in an important minority group probably did bring him to several emperors' attention: one of these may have developed warm personal ties to the Jewish leader. As for Judah's combination of wealth and learning, see Gittin 59a; Sanhedrin 36a.

16. It appears that a patriarchal tribunal took over this function; later rabbis claimed that the matter had been in their hands from the days of Yavneh on (see "Early Rabbinic *Tagganot* and *Gezerot*"). Writers in the Middle Ages report that the Patriarch Hillel II (mid-fourth century) did away with the need for witnesses by publishing mathematical formulae for determining the calendar, but there is no contemporary confirmation of this report. The authorities at an unknown time finally dispensed with eyewitness testimony, but there is no way to determine the age or source of the

formulae or the time they came into use; religious rituals tend to persist, and it is entirely possible that decisions concerning the calendar were quietly grounded in rules of this kind long before the formal interrogation of witnesses was actually ended.

17. See Baruch M. Bokser, *The Origins of the Seder* (Berkeley: University of California Press, 1984).

18. On first fruits, see Deuteronomy 26:1–11. Exodus 19 reports that the revelation at Sinai took place in the third month after the Exodus, but it provides no date. Unlike the link in the Torah between the theme of freedom and the celebration of Passover, the association of the Feast of Weeks with the revelation at Sinai requires an imaginative leap.

19. It must be remembered that most synagogues in the ancient world were not under rabbinic control, and rabbinic norms initially prevailed only in those locations where rabbinic leadership was voluntarily accepted. The rabbinic prayer book did not achieve widespread distribution until the Middle Ages. By the third century at the latest, however, the rabbinic order of worship was established and ready for adoption as rabbinic influence spread.

20. Even today the traditional prayer book varies from one Jewish subculture to another: Eastern Europe, Middle East, etc.

21. Deuteronomy 6:7 and 11:19, both verses included in the *Sh'ma* recitation, require that God's word be studied "when you lie down and when you rise up." The rabbis took this instruction to heart and directed that the *Sh'ma* be recited every evening and every morning.

22. See Numbers 28:1–8.

23. For a while this third prayer remained controversial, since it had no parallel in the sacrificial system; see B. Berakhot 28b; J. Berakhot 4:1.

24. See B. Yoma 86b.

25. Medieval synagogues, like Orthodox synagogues today, expected that women would remain separate from men during services. For centuries the standard arrangement was that the sexes used separate entrances and women climbed directly to a balcony from which they could watch the proceedings but not be seen. Since ancient synagogues are all ruins, it cannot be determined whether they had such balconies or where the women's place was located if they did not. It is generally taken for granted that the sexes were separated, as they had been in the Temple, even if the arrangement cannot be precisely described.

26. The formula is found in a long and a short version, as indicated by the parentheses.

27. "From the way a man recites benedictions it can be seen whether he is a sage or an ignoramus" (Tosefta Berakhot 1:8). This two-level conception of Jewish community is basic to early rabbinic Judaism. See Chapter 9.

28. Further additions and modifications have been continually inserted. In recent times, the issue of revising or "updating" the liturgy in response

to science, feminism, and other important cultural features of modernity
has been one of the great points of division among the major religious
movements (Reform, Orthodox, etc.).

29. The first-century Roman poet Persius (*Satire* 5.183) and the slightly later
Greek writer Plutarch (*Quaestiones conviviales* 4.6.2) both know that Jews
drink wine on the Sabbath, though their knowledge of Jews surely came
from nonrabbinic sources. The *Community Rule* in the Dead Sea Scrolls
also seems to presume that all communal meals will involve the blessing
of wine (1QS 6:2–6; 4QSd end).

30. See Michael Satlow, *Jewish Marriage in Antiquity* (Princeton, NJ: Princeton
University Press, 2001).

9. The Rabbis and Their Torah

1. Archeologists have discovered that the title *rabbi* was widely used outside
the movement of the sages. Rabbinic Judaism and rabbinic literature were
formed by a particular group of people using the titles *hakham* and *rav*;
others apparently used these as well, however, and have left no sign
of what the titles meant to them. Possibly they conveyed nothing more
than general respect; not everyone who is addressed as "sir" has been
knighted by the queen of England.

2. The rabbis' Christian contemporaries renounced their Judaic roots most
crucially on this very point. At the urging of the Apostle Paul, the Church
moved toward the idea that scripture chiefly embodied not instruction
but *Gospel*, the "good news" that God had arranged through Jesus to
bring salvation to humanity. This salvation was available through *faith*,
not through behavioral adherence to the Torah. To most Jews, a religion
that did not require obedience to the Torah but claimed to be grounded
in scripture made no sense at all. See Chapter 10 for further discussion
of this point.

3. See Mishnah Rosh Hashanah 2:9.

4. See Plato, *Phaedrus* 274e–276c.

5. In practice there were some limits to this openness. Certain rabbis, on
the strength of their greater piety or learning, became known as the
luminaries of their generation and generally enjoyed the deference of
their colleagues. More fundamentally, some women were educated but
none became rabbis, because rabbinic society was rigorously patriarchal.
Even men, moreover, required leisure (Greek *scholê*) to learn what a rabbi
needed to know, so those who needed to work without letup in the fields
or at some craft must have found it hard to find time to gain the necessary knowledge. Finally, access to a teacher was essential but *hakhamim*
could not be found everywhere, especially in the early days when the
movement was small. For these reasons, certain families supplied rabbis

for several generations: nothing was more helpful than to have a rabbinic teacher in one's own home!

6. This Abba is almost always called simply *Rav*, as though he were the role model for all later Babylonian rabbis; by convention, rabbis trained in the Holy Land were called by the full title *rabbi*, while Babylonians carried the shorter title *rav*. The latter title implies a somewhat more narrow range of legal authority (see B. Bava Qama 84b), though the actual legal powers of all ancient rabbis remain unclear.

7. A third-century rabbi named Geniva subjected the Exilarch Mar Uqba to endless criticism and harassment, until finally the exilarch turned him over to the Persian authorities for execution (B. Gittin 7a). This was recognized even at the time as an extreme case, but Babylonian rabbis' persistent refusal to pay taxes and other fees to the exilarch (see B. Nedarim 62b, Bava Batra 7b–8a) reflects the same tensions. Other talmudic passages (e.g., Sanhedrin 27ab; Yevamot 17a) depict rabbis who did pay their taxes, their objections notwithstanding.

8. The *Tosefta* ("supplement") is another text that grew up alongside the Mishnah. Organized very similarly into tractates and chapters, and probably dating from a generation or two later, the Tosefta seems to contain material that could have been incorporated into the Mishnah but for some reason was not. Sometimes the Tosefta appears to comment on the Mishnah text or to expand it, and sometimes it simply copies out large extracts without adding much at all, but there is also much material in the later collection that shows no relationship to the earlier one. Modern scholars remain uncertain as to the origins and the purpose of this later document.

9. Three extended sample passages from the Talmud, with extensive annotation, can be found in Appendix 1.

10. In the Land of Israel, rabbis seem to have been less detached from the larger Jewish community than in Babylonia, and seem to have aimed at a way of life they could share with that community. It is difficult, however, to measure the degree of this difference.

11. The Hebrew term for *tractate*, designating one of the subdivisions of the Mishnah, is *massekhet*, literally "webbing." A similar link connects the English words *text* and *texture* and *textile*.

12. For example, Mishnah Berakhot 2:1 requires that the *Sh'ma* be recited with *kavvanah*, but the Babylonian Talmud (13a) says this means that the reader of a Torah scroll (that is, someone who happened to come upon the *Sh'ma* by accident, as it were) must be reading for content and not merely proofreading. Similarly, Mishnah Rosh Hashana 3:6 demands that on the New Year the ram's horn (*shofar*) be heard with *kavvanah*, but again, the Talmud (28b) says this means only that the hearer must not mistake the sound for a donkey's bray.

13. See Exodus 19:6, the prelude to God's appearance at Mount Sinai when the Torah was given. ·

14. See the beginning of the New Testament Gospel of John. Of course, this last element of religious contention would have been lost on people who were not aware of, or had no interest in, Christian teachings.

15. See Chapter 8 for further discussion. The Mishnah (200 CE) already seems to know of a fixed order of worship and even a fixed text for much of it, though it does not actually provide that text.

10. The End of Ancient History

1. Biographical information about Saul/Paul is exceedingly scanty; a few details can be found in the New Testament itself. See in particular Philippians 3:5 (the only biographical report presented as written by Paul himself); also see Acts 22:3; 26:5. These texts are not very specific about Saul's objections to the new movement.

2. See Chapter 6.

3. See Galatians 2:21 ("If justification is through the Torah, then Christ died for nothing.")

4. The word *testament* is an old synonym for *covenant*.

5. Actually, some further requirements did remain. God did care, in Paul's view, that people should live morally, that is, with sexual restraint. Throughout his tumultuous career, Paul worked hard, and not always successfully, to clarify which demands of the Torah remained in effect after others had so emphatically been abolished. See in particular 1 Corinthians 5:1–3, where Paul expresses astonishment that his followers have set the laws of morality aside (even though so much else has lapsed), or Romans 1:24–27, where he reveals his abhorrence of sexual behavior he deems unnatural.

6. See Galatians 4:8–10 and (most shockingly) 5:12; also see Romans 14:5–6 and Colossians 2:16 (the latter possibly not by Paul).

7. The Gospels' fierce hostility to the Pharisees is a by-product of this diversity. In the first three Gospels (called *synoptic* because they are alike and so can be viewed together), Jesus seems not to reject the Torah but to offer his own radical interpretation of its teachings (Matthew 5:17: "I have not come to abolish the Torah but to complete it.") This conception put the new movement in direct competition with the Pharisees, already famous as teachers and interpreters, for the "hearts and minds" of the Jewish masses.

8. See Galatians 3:28; 1 Corinthians 12:13.

9. It is very difficult to determine whether Jews actively encouraged this attraction or simply welcomed Christian visitors who came around on their own. See Chapter 6.

10. Ambrose was the teacher of the famous Christian theologian Augustine.

11. On internal developments in the Babylonian rabbis' approach to Torah, see Chapter 9.
12. Large-scale moneylending, a famous Jewish activity during the Middle Ages, seems to have arisen only later.
13. The Mishnah had been composed in Hebrew at a time when almost no one was left who actually spoke that language.
14. The monk Arius (died 336 CE) had taught that Jesus Christ, the Son of God, was in some way subordinate to the Creator, God the Father. In the end this position was condemned as heretical and was driven out of the Church, but the authorities needed several generations before they could put an end to it. Meanwhile, the Arian denial that Jesus was fully divine led to a Christian theology that was less fiercely hostile to Judaism, in fact potentially compatible with it; in addition, Arian rulers tended to develop friendly relations with Jews as a way of expressing their independence of the official Catholic Church. In return, orthodox Christians tended to attack Arianism as hardly better than Judaism itself.
15. When the Muslims conquered Spain the Jews welcomed them as liberators, but that story goes beyond the frame of this book. Much of the Byzantine Empire as well soon came under Muslim rule.
16. Some of the subtlety may have been imposed by later Christian censors, who did not always tolerate open denial or mockery of their faith. Rabbinic attacks on ancient polytheism were not always subtle at all, and this makes the modern reader curious to know what may have been lost from rabbinic critiques of the early Church. In general, the ancient rabbis were not very interested in religious dialogue: their literature is full of stories about rabbis in conversation with non-Jews but offers not a single case of a rabbi initiating such an exchange.
17. Most scholars have understood that the term refers to the Mishnah (lit., "repetition") and that the emperor sought to bar the use of rabbinic teaching in the synagogue, but this has not been firmly established.
18. The word *meturgeman*, from the same root as *Targum*, can be used for anyone who repeats out loud the words of a public teacher. It was considered beneath a sage's dignity to have to shout, so a less distinguished member of the study-circle was appointed to perform that task. These individuals often expanded on the teacher's brief remarks, so they too might be called translators.
19. A more or less contemporary translation into Greek is attributed to an otherwise unknown *Aquila*, whose name bears an intriguing resemblance to *Onkelos*. Both of these persons may be legendary. In his order of 553, Justinian permitted Greek-speaking Jews to use the Septuagint or the Greek translation of Aquila, but no other.
20. This religious movement arose out of fascination with the prophet Ezekiel's bizarre vision of the chariot of God in the first, third, and tenth chapters of his book.

21. See in particular the cycle of stories in the Babylonian Talmud, Hagiga 13a–16a, and the corresponding section of the Jerusalem Talmud, Hagiga 2:1 77a–d.

Appendix 1. Three Sample Passages from the Babylonian Talmud

1. On the *Sh'ma* see Chapter 8 and especially "The *Sh'ma*."
2. *Teruma*, or "heave-offering," is one of the gifts of produce that farmers were obliged to supply to the priests (Numbers 18:11–12). This food must have provided an important share of the diet in priestly households, but persons in a state of defilement were barred from partaking of it. Therefore, a priest who was unclean would normally immerse himself in a proper "gathering of water" (*mikveh*) as close to sunset as possible, and then proceed to his dinner as soon as the new day had begun, before some accident left him unclean once more. The regularity of this procedure provides the basis for the Mishnah's answer here: it was as though you could set your clock by the behavior of the priests in your vicinity.
3. According to another section of this discussion, the night is divided into either three or four watches. In either case, the end of the first watch will come significantly before midnight.
4. This phrase is used to bring back a previously quoted phrase for further discussion.
5. After recovering from certain kinds of especially serious impurity (leprosy, childbirth, etc.), one had not only to engage in the usual ritual bath but also to offer a special "expiation" sacrifice (Leviticus 12, 14, 15). One could not eat *teruma* while in a state of impurity, but the Talmud's point here is that priests could resume eating their holy food as soon as the impurity itself was removed, even if the expiation sacrifice had not yet been offered.
6. That is, the newly purified priest must wait until sunset before he can eat holy foods.
7. The Hebrew for *sunset* literally means "the coming of the sun"; presumably the original reference of the phrase was to the sun's "coming home" after a long day's work giving light to the world. But perhaps the phrase should be understood in terms of the more common perception of the sun as referring to the sun's appearance in the morning sky, "coming back" into the world after the dark night.
8. A *baraita* (lit., "outside") is a Mishnah-like teaching that was omitted from the Mishnah. This particular *baraita* will return later in the discussion.
9. This is a standard talmudic term for introducing a text that appears to contradict another, just-cited passage. By "throwing them together," the Talmud attempts to confront and resolve the contradiction.

10. Nehemiah 4:15–16. The reference is to the rebuilding of Jerusalem's walls under Nehemiah's leadership. The armed guards were needed because Nehemiah's enemies were trying to obstruct or even sabotage the project.

11. By itself the first verse doesn't prove when night begins, only when Nehemiah's workers quit for the day. The second verse demonstrates that they quit when they did because night had begun. On the other hand, the second verse by itself says nothing about the emergence of the stars. Therefore, both texts are needed to show that night begins with the emergence of the stars.

12. That is, most people are poor.

13. Why would the same opinion be presented in one place as the consensus view and in another as the view of a single sage?

14. That is, their opinions coincide. Why are they listed as though they are distinct? So too in the next paragraph.

15. That is, it is impossible to determine with confidence when the moment of twilight has arrived. R. Judah, in contrast, holds that twilight is a measurable interval of time, so that the priests, who bathe *before* twilight, must then wait for night to eat the *teruma*.

16. That is, two incompatible opinions are attributed to R. Meir, namely, that the *Sh'ma* can be recited (a) when people begin to eat their Sabbath meal and (b) when priests bathe to restore their purity before eating *teruma*. The second opinion designates a considerably earlier time than the first.

17. The Mishnah, at a point where R. Eliezer seems to be speaking (see note 18), rules that the *Sh'ma* may be recited when the priests go in to eat their *teruma*, while the last *baraita* reports a different opinion (again providing an earlier hour) in Eliezer's name.

18. The Mishnah begins by asking *from when* the *Sh'ma* can be recited, a question that receives a single unattributed answer. It then provides three answers, each attributed to an identified authority, to the unasked question *until when* the *Sh'ma* must be recited. R. Eliezer provides the first of these three answers, and on superficial reading the anonymous answer to the initial question can be attributed to him as well, but the Mishnah does not actually indicate whether that answer also stems from Eliezer. The whole first question and answer could possibly represent the view of some other unnamed authority.

19. Of course, matters are not really that simple. Will any stars do, or must they be of average brightness, and how bright is that? Also, what if the night is cloudy? Still, there is no denying that the Mishnah's rule of thumb demands access to a rather exotic phenomenon, in fact one that was entirely unavailable in the Diaspora (including Babylonia itself), where the rules concerning priestly entitlements did not apply at all.

20. That is, when must the finder try to locate the owner?

21. That is, strips of wool or textile dyed purple.

22. All the listed objects are generic commercial products or other sorts of random objects that presumably have no identifying mark. The finder could not describe them adequately, nor could anyone claiming to have lost them. The next Mishnah, not quoted here, provides a mirror-image list of found objects ("bundles of fruit, bundles of coins," ...) that the finder must try to return because they display identifying characteristics.

23. Again, it is presumed that anything straight from the market is likely to look exactly like other objects of its kind.

24. According to the Torah (Deuteronomy 22:1–3), one is obliged to return any found object to its owner. However, in rabbinic law, if the owner has abandoned all hope of recovering his lost property, his ownership is deemed to have lapsed, and anyone who finds the now ownerless object is allowed to keep it. The Talmud here asks about someone who does not realize that he has lost something. If he knew, he would immediately despair of recovering it and any finder could keep it; however, he does not know of his loss and so has not relinquished his ownership. Can the finder keep it anyway, on the ground that the owner will relinquish his ownership sooner or later? Abaye and Rava were Babylonian sages of the early fourth century CE; their names appear in the Talmud more than any other from the period. The "debates of Abaye and Rava" are twice mentioned in the Talmud (Sukka 28a; Bava Batra 134a) as the quintessential talmudic arguments.

25. Lit., the "Merciful One."

26. A parenthetical phrase already found in the talmudic text itself.

27. That is, from the moment the object was actually lost. At this point, the text inserts a mnemonic consisting of three meaningless words, the fifteen letters of which help the student remember the long series of proofs that will now unfold. All this material was memorized, not written down, and mnemonics like these were frequently developed to make sure that all items in a long sequence were preserved.

28. This is a standard talmudic phrase used to introduce a text that is cited in the hope of resolving a standing dispute. The first four attempts in the present *sugya* are based on phrases taken from the Mishnah itself.

29. Yet, the finder can keep them! Doesn't that answer the question in favor of Rava?

30. The case is therefore irrelevant to our question. The owner's motive in abandoning the fruit has no bearing on the case.

31. Thus, again, the owner will quickly have discovered his loss and despaired of recovering it before the finder discovers the coins.

32. That is, a man carrying such articles will quickly know he has dropped them and despair at once of getting them back.

33. Having exhausted the clauses of the Mishnah, the Talmud now tries to resolve the dispute with materials drawn from elsewhere, starting with a *baraita* of unknown provenance.

34. From the flow of the discussion, it appears that R. Isaac's observation was originally attached to the *baraita* just quoted, and not to our Mishnah at all. The Talmud first cites Isaac's comment in connection with the Mishnah because the larger structure of the discussion requires beginning from there, and only gets around to citing Isaac's comment in its original context after the Mishnah has been exhausted.

35. Gleaning is a privilege of the needy (see Leviticus 23:22), but when the needy have taken everything they want, ordinary people can take anything that remains. The "searchers" are the poor, who search for every possible grain of fallen produce because their need is so great. The text is cited from M. Peah 8:1.

36. This awkward introductory phrase implies that the definitions of *searchers* have been imported from some other original context.

37. R. Yohanan and Resh Lakish (R. Simon b. Lakish) were leading Palestinian rabbis of the late third century CE.

38. M. Maaserot 3:4, slightly modified.

39. Thus, the owner's "despair" at seeing the fallen fruit is conscious and occurs before any passers-by have taken anything.

40. If the owner is destined to renounce ownership of the fallen olives, Rava should allow the finder to take them at once, in keeping with his opinion that "unrealized despair counts as despair."

41. This distinction between olives and figs allows both Abaye and Rava to interpret the various parts of the law in accordance with their respective views.

42. That is, the initial owners have no hope of recovering their possessions, and the new owner can legally keep the transferred objects.

43. That is, the word *thief* does not have its usual meaning, and Abaye's position can be maintained.

44. Thus, the law appears to support Abaye.

45. In that case there is no despair at all, and the law only concerns a special case.

46. Thus, the law appears to support Abaye.

47. A similar question, though not this particular text, appears at Tosefta Terumot 1:4.

48. The *teruma* now belongs to priests. The owner was going to have to donate *teruma* in any case, but does he object to having lost property in this way without his consent?

49. The owner's generous remark conveys his consent.

50. The remark was presumably sarcastic.

51. This rule suggests that the owner's right to the produce has been terminated even though he did not know his property had been taken.

52. Does this not support Rava's position that unrealized despair can be recognized at law?

53. Thus, the other had the legal right to consecrate the owner's property, even though the owner was not aware of the precise moment when the consecration took place.

54. Numbers 18:21–24 instructs that the Levites must receive a tithe of all produce, but then 18:26–32 instructs the Levites themselves to give a tithe of this tithe to the priests. Verse 28 contains an odd detail: "You also must give YHWH's *teruma* from all your tithes. . . ." Who else is being addressed here ("you *also*")? No one but the Levites receive tithes! Rabbinic interpreters took the "also" to refer to agents or representatives: I can appoint someone else to discharge my obligation for me. The Talmud here provides an important clarification of this procedure, namely, that the agent is subject to all the same regulations as the person who appointed him. Thus, the agent's action must have been conscious, and the question of unrealized or unconscious despair cannot arise at all.

55. The point of this long, elaborate discussion is to *avoid* deciding between Rava's and Abaye's opinions concerning unrealized despair. The law of *teruma* allows an agent to set *teruma* aside without the owner's knowing he has done so, but the rule is interpreted very narrowly: the owner did know that the agent was going to set aside his *teruma* but would himself have done so in a slightly different manner. The owner can nullify the agent's action through sarcasm but can also validate that action and accept it retroactively. This would indeed suggest that one's property rights can be terminated even while one is unaware of the circumstances that cause that termination (as Rava suggests in general), but by limiting the question of *teruma* to a special case in the law of agency, it has been made irrelevant to the larger question at hand.

56. Leading Babylonian rabbis of the early fifth century CE. This story serves as a case in point concerning the preceding legal discussion but sheds no new light on the dispute between Rava and Abaye.

57. Since the owner did not know his property had been taken, he had not relinquished his right to it. To eat the fruit now would be to steal it. This appears to refute Rava's idea that we can impute relinquishment to the owner before he knows of his loss.

58. There were better fruits; thus, Mari bar Issak was expressing his consent to what had been done.

59. Thus, the tenant had no legal right to offer the fruit, and his guests had no legal right to accept it, even though the owner now turned out to have consented to the offer.

60. According to Leviticus 11:38, newly harvested grain does not become susceptible to defilement until it has been moistened. Such newly susceptible grain is said to fall under the rule of "If [water] be put." Tosefta Makhshirin, chapter 3, deals with a variety of cases where grain is moistened without the owner's consent or even his knowledge, but the particular rule cited here does not appear in that chapter.

61. And this seems to refute Rava's opinion.

62. The verb for *put* in the biblical text can be read as either active or passive: we could understand either that only active watering makes the grain susceptible or that any moistening has this effect. R. Papa offers a compromise reading: the moistening can be accidental, but it must have the owner's knowledge and consent.

63. Thus, once again, the cited law avoids the question of unconscious consent and cannot be used to resolve our dispute.

64. On page 27a this *midrash* is attributed to R. Simeon b. Yohai.

65. That is, which biblical passage implies the following law?

66. Deuteronomy 22:3. The verse commands that any such object be returned to its owner.

67. This *midrash* is based on the apparently unnecessary "to him" in the verse; this is taken to mean that the object must be lost specifically to its owner while remaining available to people in general. A wandering donkey or a mislaid garment are examples of such an object, but an object swept away by a river is not.

68. At the end of this very long discussion, the final resolution is astoundingly brief; the Talmud does not even bother to spell out the logic of the final "come and hear." The point is this: if the owner learns that his property is missing but does not know that a river in flood has carried it off, he will not despair of recovering it, since he assumes that any finder will trace the identification and return the object to him. When he finds out that the object was lost in a flood he will then abandon hope, but he has not yet discovered this crucial piece of information. Nevertheless, one who finds such an object and *knows it was carried off by a river* may keep it; this must mean that we ascribe despair to the owner, even though he has not yet abandoned hope of recovering his object, in anticipation of the despair that he will eventually acknowledge. This has been Abaye's position all along, in opposition to Rava's. The discussion concludes with a second mnemonic, not translated in the text; this one lists the six cases in the Talmud where Abaye's opinion prevails over Rava's. In general, the opposite is the case.

69. Note the assumption that each example given in the Mishnah must represent a situation that is logically different from that reflected in the other examples; otherwise, the Mishnah itself would be unnecessarily redundant, an unacceptable state of affairs.

70. This verse provides the link between the preceding discussion in the Talmud (not quoted here) and the extended narrative now presented. The entire verse reads as follows: *All the nations gather together and the peoples are assembled. Who among them will tell this and inform us of first things? Let them present their witnesses and be justified, let them hear and say, "It is true."* Quotations of this verse in the following narrative will not be referenced.

71. This is a standard rabbinic euphemism for idolaters or gentiles. The phrase is ancient, but in the course of the Middle Ages it was inserted by Church censors in many places where the simpler *gentiles* had once appeared; the purpose was to avoid the suggestion that the text was talking about Christians.

72. Genesis 25:23.

73. Daniel 7:23. The chapter contains a vision of four "beasts," symbols of four great ancient empires, that will arise to dominate the earth. It is remarkable that rabbis living at the time of the Roman Empire had to prove that Rome was important by quoting the Bible.

74. That is, the king.

75. 1 Kings 8:59.

76. Haggai 2:8. It is not clear whether the narrator means that even God quotes the Bible to make points; the narrator, or a later editor, may have added the quotation on his own.

77. These words are introduced by the standard term for citing scripture, but they do not actually appear in the Bible. The text in Isaiah 43 reads: "*Who among* them *will tell this.*" A similar phrase ("*Who among you will hear this?*"), referring to reports of God's power, appears in Isaiah 42:23, and the pseudoverse in our story combines features of each.

78. Deuteronomy 4:44.

79. Daniel 7:5.

80. Exodus 15:3. Note the structural similarity between this response and the previous response to the Romans: two refutations of the nation's claim followed by an assertion of God's own prerogative.

81. The reference is to King Cyrus's permission to rebuild the Temple after the Babylonian Exile (Ezra 1:2–3; 2 Chronicles 36:23); see Chapter 3. That same Temple was destroyed by the Romans under Titus in 70 CE; see Chapter 7.

82. The ancient rabbis did not imagine that history would simply continue for thousands of years more after their own time.

83. The terms of the discussion now shift. It cannot be denied that the gentile nations have failed to live up to the Torah's demands, but they never agreed to live up to those demands! Is it fair now to hold that against them? This counterclaim gives rise to an extended attempt by the rabbinic editors, building on the story line of the original narrative, to figure out the best possible justification for the nations' claim that God's benevolence toward the people of Israel is basically unjust. This turns out to be difficult: various legends and *midrashim* quoted from other contexts keep undermining these formulations of the nations' claim. All these legends and *midrashim*, of course, are of Jewish, probably rabbinic, origin; the discussion is driven by rabbinic dialectic, not by any real conversation with non-Jews, and it reflects the rabbis' own anxiety over Israel's claim to a special relationship with God.

84. Deuteronomy 33:2.

85. Habakkuk 3:3.

86. That is, why do the prophets describe God as having visited all those places? The continuation of Deuteronomy 33:2 mentions Mount Paran as well.

87. Thus, the nations cannot claim that they never had a chance to accept the Torah!

88. This remarkable *midrash*, which appears several times in rabbinic literature, expresses the rabbis' awareness that Israel's acceptance of the Torah was an astonishing act and raises the question of whether they had done so under some kind of duress. One can also sense the insight that Jews of their own time really did accept the Torah under a kind of duress: Jewish children were raised to believe that they had no choice but to continue the chain of Jewish tradition into another generation. By adulthood, they felt the weight of their upbringing hanging over them "like an inverted tub."

89. Working on the basis of Genesis 9, the rabbis developed the concept that all humanity received seven commandments after the flood in the time of Noah. These were: (1) to avoid idolatry, (2) to avoid violent bloodshed, (3) to avoid incest and adultery, (4) to avoid eating the flesh of a limb ripped from a live animal, (5) to avoid blasphemy, (6) to avoid robbery, and (7) to establish systems of justice.

90. Habakkuk 3:6. This nonliteral translation renders the verse in the light of R. Joseph's teaching. A more literal rendering of the second phrase might be *"he looks and the nations tremble."*

91. Releasing the nations from their obligation was not a reward for their defiance; on the contrary, it deprived them of any possible reward for future compliance.

92. Leviticus 18:5.

93. This is a fundamental principle of rabbinic ethics, entirely unlike the modern idea that people who act virtuously because they have been so instructed are somehow morally inferior to those who act rightly on their own. This principle is often cited to justify the rabbis' tendency to exclude women from certain roles of religious performance, such as wearing *tefillin* or leading public worship. The rabbis taught that men are commanded to take on such roles but women are not (see M. Kiddushin 1:7), and it was preferable to assign such roles to the commanded, whose reward would be greater, than to those who merely wished to assume them on their own.

94. Exodus 4:22. It is hard to know whether the narrator means to say that the gentiles tacitly recognize Israel's close link to God; possibly this is only another round of textual dialectic.

95. Jeremiah 33:25. This is an obscure point, but the verse is taken to say that the very existence ("the laws") of heaven and earth depend on the covenant, that is, the Torah. Thus, heaven and earth are not disinterested witnesses as to the Torah or its covenant with Israel.

96. Genesis 1:31.
97. A rabbinic master of the third century CE, not the king of Judah who reigned a thousand years earlier (2 Kings 18–20).
98. Psalm 76:9.
99. That is, once heaven and earth saw that Israel had indeed accepted the Torah, their fear of annihilation subsided and they "grew still."
100. Nimrod, a great-grandson of Noah, is mentioned in Genesis 10:8–10 as a "mighty hunter" and king; a much later rabbinic legend narrates that he threatened to kill Abraham in a fiery furnace unless he worshiped an idol, but Abraham was saved by a miracle (see Pesahim 118a; Genesis Rabba 38:13). There is no hint of such an encounter in scripture. See later.
101. For twenty years the ancestor Jacob worked as a shepherd for his uncle Laban (Genesis 29–31), and in all that time he never took for his own purposes an animal from his uncle's flock (31:36–39).
102. That is, sexual sin. Joseph, the son of Jacob, was hated by his brothers, who sold him into slavery in Egypt. While Joseph was working for Potiphar, an officer of Pharaoh, his master's wife tried to seduce him but failed (Genesis 39). The talmudic text here reads "Potiphera," but that person appears later in Joseph's story as his father-in-law (Genesis 41:45). The two names differ in Hebrew by only a single letter.
103. Daniel 3. This story supplied the idea for the legend about Abraham and Nimrod mentioned in note 100.
104. See Daniel 6, especially verse 11. King Darius had ordered that all prayers and petitions in the kingdom be addressed to him rather than to any god, but Daniel kept on praying, three times a day as required, to the God of Israel.
105. These were the so-called friends of Job, who came and gave him false comfort as he suffered. The great commentator Rashi (1040–1105), citing Bava Batra 15b, says that the fourth name, in parentheses, should be removed because Elihu himself was an Israelite.
106. In context, the prophet challenges the other nations to present witnesses in their own behalf, but here the rabbinic homilist reverses the sense: witnesses will come forth from the nations of the world and justify *the people of Israel*. The reference is not just to the last-named friends of Job, but to the entire list of foreign witnesses that precedes this quotation.
107. Again a change of subject: never mind the past; Divine mercy requires that the nations receive a second chance.
108. Cooking is forbidden on the Sabbath (see Appendix 3). If you don't prepare your Sabbath food in advance, how will you eat once the holy day has begun? The point is clear: it is too late to request a second chance once the Last Judgment has begun.
109. The booth that is built for the autumn Festival of Booths. See the Glossary.

110. Deuteronomy 7:11. This verse appears in the twice-daily recitation of *Sh'ma*.
111. That is, the nations can't expect to pick up the Torah at the last possible minute, having delayed throughout history, and then also expect to receive an immediate reward for doing so!
112. If they're willing to try, he's willing to let them.
113. The festival booth can be constructed out of greenery that can be found at no cost in nature.
114. Psalm 2:3.
115. Psalm 2:4.
116. Another long narrative on the same theme of the nations' futile attempt to become virtuous at the end of time now follows, this time based on verses from Psalm 2.

Appendix 2. Rabbinic Biographies

1. Perhaps the most famous such imagined exploit in American history concerns the young George Washington and the cherry tree.
2. Rabbis who worked prior to the appearance of the Mishnah are designated *Tanna'im*.
3. JT Yevamot 4:12 6b.
4. Yevamot 69b; at Sotah 4b it is suggested that Ben Azzai was briefly married but sent his wife away, but the suggestion seems to arise from the logic of the discussion, not from any solid biographical information.
5. The *Amora'im* were rabbis who taught after the appearance of the Mishnah, teachers whose names appear only in the Talmuds or in later collections of Midrash. Rav, the first Babylonian master mentioned later, was considered a transitional figure, and his teachings were occasionally granted the higher level of authority that was assigned to traditions of the Tanna'im ('Eruvin 50b; Ketubot 8a; etc.).

Appendix 3. The Sabbath

1. The word that is normally translated as "rest" (*sh-b-t*) actually means "cease": after six days' creative activity, God stopped working.
2. Exodus 16:6, 22–30. Since the revelation at Sinai had not yet occurred, this was the people's first encounter with the phenomenon of Sabbath rest.
3. Exodus 31:12–17; 35:2–3.
4. Exodus 23:10–13; Leviticus 25:2–7.
5. Numbers 15:32–36.
6. Leviticus 26:34–35. This point is repeated, as though for summary emphasis, in the very last chapter of the Bible; see 2 Chronicles 36:21.
7. Exodus 31:12–17 combines all these themes: covenant with God, six days' creation, violation to be punished by death.

8. There are a few details. The lighting of fire is forbidden in Exodus 35:3. A story in Numbers 15 tells of a man put to death for "gathering sticks" on the Sabbath, but the word translated as "gathering sticks" is otherwise very rare, and its meaning is therefore unclear. Later rabbinic interpreters tried to identify forbidden labors with the activities needed to build the desert sanctuary; see later.

9. Nehemiah 13:14–23.

10. 1 Maccabees 2:40–41. The pre-Maccabean *Book of Jubilees* indeed prohibits all war-making on the Sabbath (50:12).

11. *Antiquities* 18.323.

12. See Plutarch, *On Superstition* 8. The historian Cassius Dio lists three separate occasions on which Jewish Sabbath observance allowed Jerusalem to be taken. Josephus reports such incidents as well; see later.

13. Philo attempted to stress this connection: see *On the Special Laws* 2.60–61.

14. The late Roman writer Rutilius Numantianus spoke of "every seventh day condemned to a shameful inactivity" (*On His Journey* 1.391).

15. Suetonius, *Augustus* 76.

16. Leviticus 16:31; 23:32.

17. He does mention the ban on lighting fires (Exodus 35:3): see *On the Special Laws* 2.65.

18. *On the Creation of the World* 13–14; *On Abraham* 28–30; *On the Decalogue* 102–103.

19. *On the Special Laws* 2.60–61; *On the Life of Moses* 2.216.

20. See Exodus 20:10.

21. *On the Cherubim* 86–87. In a similar vein, later rabbinic masters claimed that the Sabbath is the closest approach in this world to the joy of the next; see later.

22. *Antiquities* 1.33.

23. So, Pompey was able to capture Jerusalem in 63 BCE (*War* 1.146) and Ptolemy I several centuries earlier (*Antiquities* 12.4). The latter case is ambiguous, because Ptolemy had not entered as a conqueror but peacefully and by guile, as though he desired to offer sacrifice in the Temple.

24. Compare *Life* 161 (never allowed) with *Antiquities* 14.63 (permitted when attacked).

25. *Ag. Ap.*, 1.209–2.27.

26. *Antiquities* 14.185–264. These citations deal with many topics, the Sabbath sporadically among them. See also *Antiquities* 16.162–173.

27. *CD* 10.15–11.18.

28. The so-called *Song of the Sabbath Sacrifice*. It is unknown whether these hymns were really recited in the Sabbath services of the group.

29. M. Shabbat 7:2.

30. See Chapter 8 on the significance of the *berakha* or blessing.

31. See Numbers, chapter 6.

32. Also marriage and the circumcision of baby boys.
33. The custom in Palestinian synagogues was to read less each week and complete the Torah in three years or a bit more. Eventually the Babylonian custom prevailed.
34. Genesis Rabba 17:5, 44.17; B. Berachot 57b.

Suggestions for Further Reading

Editions of Primary Texts

Many recent editions of the Bible include the *Apocrypha*. Separate translations of the books in that collection can be found as well. There is no need to list those here.

James H. Charlesworth, ed. *The Old Testament Pseudepigrapha*. Garden City, NY: Doubleday, 1983–1985.

A near-complete assembly of all ancient Jewish literature outside the Bible; only the other well-known materials (Dead Sea Scrolls, the works of Philo and Josephus, the rabbinic documents) are omitted. Each text is introduced and translated; the introductions pay particular attention to the significance of each text for Jewish (and Christian) religious developments.

Amnon Linder, *The Jews in Roman Imperial Legislation*. Detroit: Wayne State University Press and Jerusalem: Israel Academy of Sciences and Humanities, 1987.

This work provides the text of every reference to the Jews in legal materials from the Roman Empire (mostly from the fourth century and later), along with a translation, introduction, and commentary.

Menahem Stern, *Greek and Latin Authors on Jews and Judaism*. Jerusalem: Israel Academy of Sciences and Humanities, 1974–1984.

A collection of all known references to Jews in ancient Greek and Latin literature; Christian authors, however, are excluded. Each text is accompanied by a translation along with a detailed introduction and commentary.

On the *Dead Sea Scrolls*, see later in this section.

The works of *Philo* and *Josephus* can be found in numerous modern editions, complete and otherwise. The best-known complete translations can be found in the multivolume *Loeb Classical Library* edition.

Nearly all of the ancient rabbinic literature has been translated into English, in most cases in numerous versions. These too will not be listed here.

Secondary Works

NOTE: For the convenience of readers, these suggestions are limited to complete books published in English. Foreign-language works, or articles from periodicals, can be traced through the more complete bibliographies found in some of these works. The sections of this list follow the sequence of chapters in this book, but of course, many of these works cover a broad range of subjects and could have appeared in several of the sections. Needless to say, the selections reflect the prejudices and preferences of the present author; again, the bibliographies in these volumes will point readers to others with different points of view.

BIBLICAL RELIGION, BIBLICAL HISTORY

John Bright, *A History of Israel*, 4th ed. Louisville, KY: Westminster John Knox Press, 2000.
A survey of Israelite history through and beyond the period reflected in biblical narratives. The approach accepts the fundamental reliability of the biblical narrative, though not its details.

John Bright, *Early Israel in Recent History Writing*. Chicago: A. R. Allenson, 1956.
Although not recent, this book compares two different historical approaches to biblical narrative: the critical approach of two major German Bible scholars, Albrecht Alt and Martin Noth, and the far more conservative stance of the Israeli Yehezkel Kaufmann. Even though the examples are dated, the book offers beginning students an excellent introduction to the problem of method in the study of biblical history.

Roland de Vaux, *Ancient Israel: Its Life and Institutions*. New York: McGraw-Hill, 1961.
A two-volume set that examines in turn the social and religious institutions of preexilic Israel.

Yehezkel Kaufmann, *The Religion of Israel*. Chicago: University of Chicago Press, 1960.
A historical survey of Israelite religion through the time of the Babylonian Exile. Kaufmann asserts that Israelite religion was fully monotheistic from its earliest times.

Morton Smith, *Palestinian Parties and Politics That Shaped the Old Testament*. New York: Columbia University Press, 1971.

A systematic presentation of the view that the Hebrew Bible reflects a monotheistic view that was held by only a minority during most of the biblical period and became dominant only at the time of the Maccabees.

ELEPHANTINE

Bezalel Porten, *Archives from Elephantine: The Life of an Ancient Jewish Military Colony*. Berkely: University of Chicago Press, 1968.

JEWS AND GREEKS; THE MACCABEES

Elias Bickerman, *The Jews in the Greek Age*. Cambridge, MA: Harvard University Press, 1988.

A series of essays by one of the groundbreaking historians of the topic.

Victor Tcherikover, *Hellenistic Civilization and the Jews*. Philadelphia: Jewish Publication Society of America, 1959.

One-half of this book surveys the background and the aftermath of the Maccabean rebellion up to the Roman conquest. The other half examines the political and cultural encounter between Jews and Greeks in the Diaspora, especially in Alexandria.

JEWS AND THE ROMAN EMPIRE

Michael Grant, *The Jews in the Roman World*. New York: Scribner, 1973.

Emil Schürer, *The History of the Jewish People in the Age of Jesus Christ*, 4 vols., revised and edited by Geza Vermes et al. Edinburgh, T & T Clark, 1979.

This is actually a thoroughly revised version of a classic history written over 100 years ago. Schürer's name was kept as a way of honoring his contribution, but the book (a four-volume set) is entirely new. The work provides a detailed history of the Jews from the Maccabees to Bar Kokhba, as well as a detailed survey of the important features of Jewish religious life (school, synagogue, etc.).

E. Mary Smallwood, *The Jews under Roman Rule*. Leiden: Brill, 1976.

DEAD SEA SCROLLS

There are many editions of the scrolls and many introductions to their contents and their significance. It will suffice here to mention one reliable survey:

Geza Vermes, *The Complete Dead Sea Scrolls in English*, rev. ed. London: Penguin, 2004.

THE JEWISH DIASPORA

John M. G. Barclay, *Jews in the Mediterranean Diaspora*. Edinburgh: T & T Clark, 1996.

This volume concentrates on those locations where evidence is relatively abundant (chiefly Egypt, Rome, and Syria) and examines the Jewish cultural integration and political status in such areas. The book concludes with a useful inquiry into the nature of Jewish identity in the ancient world.

John J. Collins, *Between Athens and Jerusalem*, 2nd ed. Grand Rapids, MI: William B. Eerdmans, 2000.

A survey of different conceptions of Jewish identity that are found in the wide range of ancient Jewish literature.

Erwin Goodenough, *An Introduction to Philo Judaeus*, 2nd ed. Oxford: Basil Blackwell, 1962.

In this short work, Goodenough presents Philo as the greatest ancient exponent of the form of Judaism laid out in his Jewish Symbols in the Greco-Roman period *(see later under* "Ancient Jewish Mysticism"*).*

Erich Gruen, *Diaspora: Jews amidst Greeks and Romans*. Cambridge, MA: Harvard University Press, 2002.

Unlike other writers who have focused on the tensions between Jews and others, this prolific author stresses the Jews' successful integration into Greco-Roman culture and society.

Peter Schäfer, *Judeophobia*. Cambridge, MA: Harvard University Press, 1997.

A study of the emergence and early history of Jew hatred (later called anti-Semitism*) in the ancient world.*

Harry A. Wolfson, *Philo*, rev. ed. Cambridge, MA: Harvard University Press, 1968.

A dramatically different presentation of Philo, in which Philo's view of Judaism greatly resembles the rabbis', though with an overlay of Greek philosophical language and conceptions.

THE TRANSITION TO CHRISTIANITY

The literature on the origins of Christianity is understandably enormous. The following books are suggested for the particular light that they shed on the Jewish background out of which Christianity emerged.

John J. Collins, *The Apocalyptic Imagination*, 2nd ed. Grand Rapids, MI: William B. Eerdmans, 1998.

David. S. Russell, *The Method and Message of Jewish Apocalyptic*. Philadelphia: Westminster, 1964.

THE ANCIENT SYNAGOGUE

Steven Fine, *This Holy Place*. Notre Dame, IN: University of Notre Dame Press, 1998.

Joseph Gutmann, *The Synagogue*. New York: Ktav, 1975.

Lee I. Levine, *The Ancient Synagogue*, 2nd ed. New Haven, CT: Yale University Press, 2005.

HISTORY OF THE JEWS IN LATE ANTIQUITY

Gedaliahu Alon, *The Jews in Their Land in the Talmudic Age*. Jerusalem: Magnes Press, 1980–1984; Michael Avi-Yonah, *The Jews under Roman and Byzantine Rule*. New York: Schocken, 1976.
These are two comprehensive surveys of the history of Palestine in late antiquity. Alon concentrates more on the rabbinic evidence than does Avi-Yonah.

Seth Schwartz, *Imperialism and Jewish Society, 200 BCE–640 CE*. Princeton, NJ: Princeton University Press, 2001.
A wide-ranging social history of the Jews in the ancient world.

EARLY RABBINIC JUDAISM

Shaye J. D. Cohen, *From the Maccabees to the Mishnah*, 2nd ed. Louisville, NY: Westminster John Knox Press, 2006.
A general survey of Jewish religion over the indicated time; not so much a study of early rabbinic Judaism as an introduction to the background out of which rabbinic Judaism emerged.

Lee I. Levine, *The Rabbinic Class of Roman Palestine in Late Antiquity*. New York: Jewish Theological Seminary of America, 1989.
A brief study of the early Palestinian rabbinate: its internal structure, its place in the larger community, and so on.

Jacob Neusner, *History of the Jews in Babylonia*. Leiden: Brill, 1964–1970.
A five-volume work by one of the most prolific scholars of the twentieth century. The book provides a combined view of political and religious developments among the masters who produced the Babylonian Talmud.

Ephraim E. Urbach, *The Sages*, 2nd English ed. Jerusalem: Magnes Press, 1979.
Not as historically rigorous as the Neusner work, this book provides a much more complete survey of intellectual developments in ancient rabbinic Judaism.

JEWISH WOMEN AND THE JEWISH FAMILY

Ross Kraemer, *Her Share of the Blessings.* New York: Oxford University Press, 1992.
A survey of women's religious lives in the Greco-Roman world. The chapters examine pagan, Jewish, and Christian examples.

Michael Satlow, *Jewish Marriage in Antiquity.* Princeton, NJ: Princeton University Press, 2001.
An examination of different Jewish attitudes toward the institution of marriage, the emotional and financial aspects of marriage as revealed in archeological discoveries, and finally, the development of the rabbinic rules of marriage. Many ancient Jews freely disregarded these rules, but they became normative in the Middle Ages.

ANCIENT JEWISH MYSTICISM

Erwin Goodenough, *Jewish Symbols in the Greco-Roman Period.* Princeton, NJ: Princeton University Press, 1953–1968.
In this thirteen-volume work, Goodenough developed the thesis that Diaspora Jews, under the influence of Hellenistic mystery religions, had developed a form of Jewish religion very different from the Palestinian varieties that flowed into rabbinic Judaism. This distinctly nonrabbinic Judaism saw Jewish rituals as gateways to direct mystical experience of the Divine.

Gershom Scholem, *Major Trends in Jewish Mysticism*, 3rd rev. ed. New York: Schocken, 1974.
A difficult but classic work. One chapter deals with merkava (chariot) mysticism among the Jews of late antiquity.

STUDIES OF PARTICULAR LOCALITIES (SELECTED)

Aryeh Kasher, *The Jews in Hellenistic and Roman Egypt.* Tübingen: J. C. B. Mohr (Paul Siebeck), 1985.

Lee I. Levine, *Caesarea under Roman Rule.* Leiden: Brill, 1975.

Leonard Rutgers, *The Jews in Late Ancient Rome.* Leiden: Brill, 1995.

Index